Online Resources & Audiobook

Included with your purchase are multiple online resources. This includes the practice tests in an interactive format and this book in audiobook format. There is also a convenient study timer to help you manage your time.

Instructions for accessing these resources can be found on the last page of this book.

Texas Real Estate License Exam Prep 2025 and 2026

3 Practice Tests and Preparation Guide Book
[Includes Detailed Answer Explanations]

Joshua Rueda

Copyright © 2025 by TPB Publishing

All rights reserved. No part of this publication may be reproduced, distributed, or transmitted in any form or by any means, including photocopying, recording, or other electronic or mechanical methods, without the prior written permission of the publisher, except in the case of brief quotations embodied in critical reviews and certain other noncommercial uses permitted by copyright law.

Written and edited by TPB Publishing.

TPB Publishing is not associated with or endorsed by any official testing organization. TPB Publishing is a publisher of unofficial educational products. All test and organization names are trademarks of their respective owners. Content in this book is included for utilitarian purposes only and does not constitute an endorsement by TPB Publishing of any particular point of view.

ISBN 13: 9781637752104

Table of Contents

Welcome ----- 1

Quick Overview ----- 2

Test-Taking Strategies ----- 3

Introduction ----- 7

Study Prep Plan ----- 8

Property Ownership ----- 11

   Practice Quiz ----- 19

   Answer Explanations ----- 20

Land Use Controls and Regulations ----- 21

   Practice Quiz ----- 26

   Answer Explanations ----- 27

Valuation and Market Analysis ----- 28

   Practice Quiz ----- 33

   Answer Explanations ----- 34

Financing ----- 35

   Practice Quiz ----- 43

   Answer Explanations ----- 44

General Principles of Agency ----- 45

   Practice Quiz ----- 51

   Answer Explanations ----- 52

Property Conditions and Disclosures ----- 53

   Practice Quiz ----- 59

   Answer Explanations ----- 60

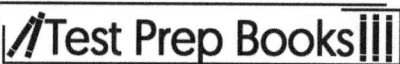

Table of Contents

Contracts —— 61
    Practice Quiz —— 68
    Answer Explanations —— 69
Transfer of Title —— 70
    Practice Quiz —— 76
    Answer Explanations —— 77
Practice of Real Estate —— 78
    Practice Quiz —— 87
    Answer Explanations —— 88
Real Estate Calculations —— 89
    Practice Quiz —— 98
    Answer Explanations —— 99
Specialty Areas —— 100
    Practice Quiz —— 102
    Answer Explanations —— 103
Texas Real Estate Commission —— 104
    Commission Duties and Powers —— 104
    Licensing —— 106
    Practice Quiz —— 109
    Answer Explanations —— 110
Special Topics in Texas State Real Estate —— 111
    Practice Quiz —— 114
    Answer Explanations —— 115
Practice Test #1 —— 116
Answer Explanations #1 —— 128

Table of Contents

Practice Test #2 ---------- *137*

Answer Explanations #2 ---------- *149*

Practice Test #3 ---------- *158*

Answer Explanations #3 ---------- *170*

Index ---------- *179*

Online Resources & Audiobook ---------- *185*

Welcome

Dear Reader,

Welcome to your new Test Prep Books study guide! We are pleased that you chose us to help you prepare for your exam. There are many study options to choose from, and we appreciate you choosing us. Studying can be a daunting task, but we have designed a smart, effective study guide to help prepare you for what lies ahead.

Whether you're a parent helping your child learn and grow, a high school student working hard to get into your dream college, or a nursing student studying for a complex exam, we want to help give you the tools you need to succeed. We hope this study guide gives you the skills and the confidence to thrive, and we can't thank you enough for allowing us to be part of your journey.

In an effort to continue to improve our products, we welcome feedback from our customers. We look forward to hearing from you. Suggestions, success stories, and criticisms can all be communicated by emailing us at support@testprepbooks.com.

Sincerely,

Test Prep Books Team

Quick Overview

As you draw closer to taking your exam, effective preparation becomes more and more important. Thankfully, you have this study guide to help you get ready. Use this guide to help keep your studying on track and refer to it often.

This study guide contains several key sections that will help you be successful on your exam. The guide contains tips for what you should do the night before and the day of the test. Also included are test-taking tips. Knowing the right information is not always enough. Many well-prepared test takers struggle with exams. These tips will help equip you to accurately read, assess, and answer test questions.

A large part of the guide is devoted to showing you what content to expect on the exam and to helping you better understand that content. In this guide are practice test questions so that you can see how well you have grasped the content. Then, answer explanations are provided so that you can understand why you missed certain questions.

Don't try to cram the night before you take your exam. This is not a wise strategy for a few reasons. First, your retention of the information will be low. Your time would be better used by reviewing information you already know rather than trying to learn a lot of new information. Second, you will likely become stressed as you try to gain a large amount of knowledge in a short amount of time. Third, you will be depriving yourself of sleep. So be sure to go to bed at a reasonable time the night before. Being well-rested helps you focus and remain calm.

Be sure to eat a substantial breakfast the morning of the exam. If you are taking the exam in the afternoon, be sure to have a good lunch as well. Being hungry is distracting and can make it difficult to focus. You have hopefully spent lots of time preparing for the exam. Don't let an empty stomach get in the way of success!

When travelling to the testing center, leave earlier than needed. That way, you have a buffer in case you experience any delays. This will help you remain calm and will keep you from missing your appointment time at the testing center.

Be sure to pace yourself during the exam. Don't try to rush through the exam. There is no need to risk performing poorly on the exam just so you can leave the testing center early. Allow yourself to use all of the allotted time if needed.

Remain positive while taking the exam even if you feel like you are performing poorly. Thinking about the content you should have mastered will not help you perform better on the exam.

Once the exam is complete, take some time to relax. Even if you feel that you need to take the exam again, you will be well served by some down time before you begin studying again. It's often easier to convince yourself to study if you know that it will come with a reward!

Test-Taking Strategies

1. Predicting the Answer

When you feel confident in your preparation for a multiple-choice test, try predicting the answer before reading the answer choices. This is especially useful on questions that test objective factual knowledge. By predicting the answer before reading the available choices, you eliminate the possibility that you will be distracted or led astray by an incorrect answer choice. You will feel more confident in your selection if you read the question, predict the answer, and then find your prediction among the answer choices. After using this strategy, be sure to still read all of the answer choices carefully and completely. If you feel unprepared, you should not attempt to predict the answers. This would be a waste of time and an opportunity for your mind to wander in the wrong direction.

2. Reading the Whole Question

Too often, test takers scan a multiple-choice question, recognize a few familiar words, and immediately jump to the answer choices. Test authors are aware of this common impatience, and they will sometimes prey upon it. For instance, a test author might subtly turn the question into a negative, or he or she might redirect the focus of the question right at the end. The only way to avoid falling into these traps is to read the entirety of the question carefully before reading the answer choices.

3. Looking for Wrong Answers

Long and complicated multiple-choice questions can be intimidating. One way to simplify a difficult multiple-choice question is to eliminate all of the answer choices that are clearly wrong. In most sets of answers, there will be at least one selection that can be dismissed right away. If the test is administered on paper, the test taker could draw a line through it to indicate that it may be ignored; otherwise, the test taker will have to perform this operation mentally or on scratch paper. In either case, once the obviously incorrect answers have been eliminated, the remaining choices may be considered. Sometimes identifying the clearly wrong answers will give the test taker some information about the correct answer. For instance, if one of the remaining answer choices is a direct opposite of one of the eliminated answer choices, it may well be the correct answer. The opposite of obviously wrong is obviously right! Of course, this is not always the case. Some answers are obviously incorrect simply because they are irrelevant to the question being asked. Still, identifying and eliminating some incorrect answer choices is a good way to simplify a multiple-choice question.

4. Don't Overanalyze

Anxious test takers often overanalyze questions. When you are nervous, your brain will often run wild, causing you to make associations and discover clues that don't actually exist. If you feel that this may be a problem for you, do whatever you can to slow down during the test. Try taking a deep breath or counting to ten. As you read and consider the question, restrict yourself to the particular words used by the author. Avoid thought tangents about what the author *really* meant, or what he or she was *trying* to say. The only things that matter on a multiple-choice test are the words that are actually in the question. You must avoid reading too much into a multiple-choice question, or supposing that the writer meant

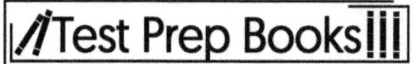

Test-Taking Strategies

something other than what he or she wrote.

5. No Need for Panic

It is wise to learn as many strategies as possible before taking a multiple-choice test, but it is likely that you will come across a few questions for which you simply don't know the answer. In this situation, avoid panicking. Because most multiple-choice tests include dozens of questions, the relative value of a single wrong answer is small. As much as possible, you should compartmentalize each question on a multiple-choice test. In other words, you should not allow your feelings about one question to affect your success on the others. When you find a question that you either don't understand or don't know how to answer, just take a deep breath and do your best. Read the entire question slowly and carefully. Try rephrasing the question a couple of different ways. Then, read all of the answer choices carefully. After eliminating obviously wrong answers, make a selection and move on to the next question.

6. Confusing Answer Choices

When working on a difficult multiple-choice question, there may be a tendency to focus on the answer choices that are the easiest to understand. Many people, whether consciously or not, gravitate to the answer choices that require the least concentration, knowledge, and memory. This is a mistake. When you come across an answer choice that is confusing, you should give it extra attention. A question might be confusing because you do not know the subject matter to which it refers. If this is the case, don't

eliminate the answer before you have affirmatively settled on another. When you come across an answer choice of this type, set it aside as you look at the remaining choices. If you can confidently assert that one of the other choices is correct, you can leave the confusing answer aside. Otherwise, you will need to take a moment to try to better understand the confusing answer choice. Rephrasing is one way to tease out the sense of a confusing answer choice.

7. Your First Instinct

Many people struggle with multiple-choice tests because they overthink the questions. If you have studied sufficiently for the test, you should be prepared to trust your first instinct once you have carefully and completely read the question and all of the answer choices. There is a great deal of research suggesting that the mind can come to the correct conclusion very quickly once it has obtained all of the relevant information. At times, it may seem to you as if your intuition is working faster even than your reasoning mind. This may in fact be true. The knowledge you obtain while studying may be retrieved from your subconscious before you have a chance to work out the associations that support it. Verify your instinct by working out the reasons that it should be trusted.

8. Key Words

Many test takers struggle with multiple-choice questions because they have poor reading comprehension skills. Quickly reading and understanding a multiple-choice question requires a mixture of skill and experience. To help with this, try jotting down a few key words and phrases on a piece of scrap paper. Doing this concentrates the process of reading and forces the mind to weigh the relative importance of the question's parts. In selecting words and phrases to write down, the test taker thinks about the question more deeply and carefully. This is especially true for multiple-choice questions that are preceded by a long prompt.

9. Subtle Negatives

One of the oldest tricks in the multiple-choice test writer's book is to subtly reverse the meaning of a question with a word like *not* or *except*. If you are not paying attention to each word in the question, you can easily be led astray by this trick. For instance, a common question format is, "Which of the following is…?" Obviously, if the question instead is, "Which of the following is not…?," then the answer will be quite different. Even worse, the test makers are aware of the potential for this mistake and will include one answer choice that would be correct if the question were not negated or reversed. A test taker who misses the reversal will find what he or she believes to be a correct answer and will be so confident that he or she will fail to reread the question and discover the original error. The only way to avoid this is to practice a wide variety of multiple-choice questions and to pay close attention to each and every word.

10. Reading Every Answer Choice

It may seem obvious, but you should always read every one of the answer choices! Too many test takers fall into the habit of scanning the question and assuming that they understand the question because they recognize a few key words. From there, they pick the first answer choice that answers the question they believe they have read. Test takers who read all of the answer choices might discover that one of the latter answer choices is actually *more* correct. Moreover, reading all of the answer choices can remind you of facts related to the question that can help you arrive at the correct answer. Sometimes, a misstatement or incorrect detail in one of the latter answer choices will trigger your memory of the subject and will enable you to find the right answer. Failing to read all of the answer choices is like not reading all of the items on a restaurant menu: you might miss out on the perfect choice.

11. Spot the Hedges

One of the keys to success on multiple-choice tests is paying close attention to every word. This is never truer than with words like *almost*, *most*, *some*, and *sometimes*. These words are called "hedges" because they indicate that a statement is not totally true or not true in every place and time. An absolute statement will contain no hedges, but in many subjects, the answers are not always straightforward or absolute. There are always exceptions to the rules in these subjects. For this reason,

you should favor those multiple-choice questions that contain hedging language. The presence of qualifying words indicates that the author is taking special care with his or her words, which is certainly important when composing the right answer. After all, there are many ways to be wrong, but there is only one way to be right! For this reason, it is wise to avoid answers that are absolute when taking a multiple-choice test. An absolute answer is one that says things are either all one way or all another. They often include words like *every*, *always*, *best*, and *never*. If you are taking a multiple-choice test in a subject that doesn't lend itself to absolute answers, be on your guard if you see any of these words.

12. Long Answers

In many subject areas, the answers are not simple. As already mentioned, the right answer often requires hedges. Another common feature of the answers to a complex or subjective question are qualifying clauses, which are groups of words that subtly modify the meaning of the sentence. If the question or answer choice describes a rule to which there are exceptions or the subject matter is complicated, ambiguous, or confusing, the correct answer will require many words in order to be expressed clearly and accurately. In essence, you should not be deterred by answer choices that seem excessively long. Oftentimes, the author of the text will not be able to write the correct answer without offering some qualifications and modifications. Your job is to read the answer choices thoroughly and completely and to select the one that most accurately and precisely answers the question.

13. Restating to Understand

Sometimes, a question on a multiple-choice test is difficult not because of what it asks but because of how it is written. If this is the case, restate the question or answer choice in different words. This process serves a couple of important purposes. First, it forces you to concentrate on the core of the question. In order to rephrase the question accurately, you have to understand it well. Rephrasing the question will concentrate your mind on the key words and ideas. Second, it will present the information to your mind in a fresh way. This process may trigger your memory and render some useful scrap of information picked up while studying.

14. True Statements

Sometimes an answer choice will be true in itself, but it does not answer the question. This is one of the main reasons why it is essential to read the question carefully and completely before proceeding to the answer choices. Too often, test takers skip ahead to the answer choices and look for true statements. Having found one of these, they are content to select it without reference to the question above. The savvy test taker will always read the entire question before turning to the answer choices. Then, having settled on a correct answer choice, he or she will refer to the original question and ensure that the selected answer is relevant. The mistake of choosing a correct-but-irrelevant answer choice is especially common on questions related to specific pieces of objective knowledge.

15. No Patterns

One of the more dangerous ideas that circulates about multiple-choice tests is that the correct answers tend to fall into patterns. These erroneous ideas range from a belief that B and C are the most common right answers, to the idea that an unprepared test-taker should answer "A-B-A-C-A-D-A-B-A." It cannot be emphasized enough that pattern-seeking of this type is exactly the WRONG way to approach a multiple-choice test. To begin with, it is highly unlikely that the test maker will plot the correct answers according to some predetermined pattern. The questions are scrambled and delivered in a random order. Furthermore, even if the test maker was following a pattern in the assignation of correct answers, there is no reason why the test taker would know which pattern he or she was using. Any attempt to discern a pattern in the answer choices is a waste of time and a distraction from the real work of taking the test. A test taker would be much better served by extra preparation before the test than by reliance on a pattern in the answers.

Introduction

Function of the Test

The Texas Real Estate Commission examination tests candidates on their knowledge and competency in the legal and practical matters of the real estate business. The Texas Real Estate Commission (TREC) requires successful completion of the exam before issuing a license to a candidate. Obtaining a license issued by the Texas Real Estate Commission is compulsory for a real estate broker, broker-salesperson, or salesperson before they can practice in Texas. Each test includes a Texas state section and a national section. To successfully complete the exam and obtain a license, a candidate must pass both sections.

Test Administration

Once a candidate has met all of the requirements of the Texas Real Estate Commission, the candidate may file an application to take the exam. The candidate has one year to successfully pass the exam; during this time, they may take the exam as many times as they wish. If the candidate passes only one section of the exam (state or national), they only need to retake the failed section, not both. If the candidate does not pass both sections within one year, they must reapply with TREC.

TREC contracts with PSI Services to conduct the exam. The PSI Real Estate test is administered at PSI testing sites across Texas, or out-of-state by special request. Registering for the exam can be done over the internet, telephone, fax, or by postal mail. When you arrive for testing, you must provide two forms of identification; all information must match with the information on your TREC eligibility letter. Be sure to check for up-to-date instructions and security procedures before you go to the testing site. Reasonable arrangements can be made for candidates under the Americans with Disabilities Act of 1990.

Scoring

The test is scored differently for Salesperson and Broker exams. For a salesperson license, the candidate must score a 56 on the national section and a 21 on the state portion. For a broker license, the candidate must score a 60 on the national section and a 30 on the state portion. When you take the test, your scores will be shown on screen immediately at the end of the exam. You will also receive an official, printed report after the exam.

Study Prep Plan

1 **Schedule** - Use one of our study schedules below or come up with one of your own.

2 **Relax** - Test anxiety can hurt even the best students. There are many ways to reduce stress. Find the one that works best for you.

3 **Execute** - Once you have a good plan in place, be sure to stick to it.

One Week Study Schedule

Day 1	Property Ownership
Day 2	Financing
Day 3	Contracts
Day 4	Real Estate Calculations
Day 5	Practice Tests #1 & #2
Day 6	Practice Test #3
Day 7	Take Your Exam!

Two Week Study Schedule

Day 1	Property Ownership	Day 8	Practice of Real Estate
Day 2	Land Use Controls and Regulations	Day 9	Real Estate Calculations
Day 3	Financing	Day 10	Texas Real Estate Commission
Day 4	General Principles of Agency	Day 11	Practice Test #1
Day 5	Property Conditions and Disclosures	Day 12	Practice Test #2
Day 6	Contracts	Day 13	Practice Test #3
Day 7	Transfer of Title	Day 14	Take Your Exam!

Study Prep Plan

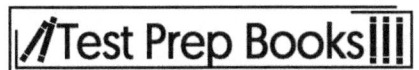

One Month Study Schedule

Day 1	Property Ownership	Day 11	Property Conditions and Disclosures	Day 21	Texas Real Estate Commission
Day 2	Practice Questions	Day 12	Practice Questions	Day 22	Practice Questions
Day 3	Land Use Controls and Regulations	Day 13	Contracts	Day 23	Special Topics in Texas State Real Estate
Day 4	Practice Questions	Day 14	Practice Questions	Day 24	Practice Test #1
Day 5	Valuation and Market Analysis	Day 15	Transfer of Title	Day 25	Answer Explanations #1
Day 6	Practice Questions	Day 16	Practice of Real Estate	Day 26	Practice Test #2
Day 7	Financing	Day 17	Practice Questions	Day 27	Answer Explanations #2
Day 8	Practice Questions	Day 18	Real Estate Calculations	Day 28	Practice Test #3
Day 9	General Principles of Agency	Day 19	Practice Questions	Day 29	Answer Explanations #3
Day 10	Practice Questions	Day 20	Specialty Areas	Day 30	Take Your Exam!

Build your own prep plan by visiting the Online Resources page.

Instructions and a QR code can be found on the last page of this guide.

Property Ownership

Classes of Property and Real Estate

Property is any item that may be owned by a person, or artificial person, such as a business entity or trust. Property may be divided into two major classifications: (1) real property and (2) personal property.

Real property is a parcel (piece) of land; everything else is considered personal property. **Personal property** is an item that may be owned by a person, or artificial person, and is not real property. Owning real property is not exclusive to the land itself. It includes natural and artificial property that is attached to the piece of land. Under the **doctrine of ad coelum**, a real property owner owns everything above and below the surface of the land. **Attached natural property** would include such things as trees or minerals embedded in the ground. **Attached artificial property** would include such things as buildings or sewer piping embedded in the ground.

Real property includes appurtenances. An **appurtenance** is property that is possessed by a larger entity and cannot be removed from the real property. For example, a drive way, garage, large trees or shrubs (if their removal would cause noticeable damage to the real property) are all considered appurtenances.

Owning land includes rights: (1) surface rights, (2) air rights, and (3) mineral rights. **Surface rights** are the rights of the landowner to occupy and use the surface of the land as desired. **Air rights** are the rights of the landowner to occupy and use the airspace above the surface of the land as desired. **Mineral rights** are the rights of the owner to use the minerals embedded within the land as desired. These rights also include the non-use of these rights. It is a landowner's choice unless applicable law states otherwise.

Real property includes improvements that have been added to the land. **Improvements** are items that have been affixed on the land with the intent that the improvement shall remain on the land indefinitely, such as buildings, sheds, garages, fences, and other similar items. A bare piece of land may be called a **lot** or **parcel**; this is land that has no improvements upon it. Improvements on the property are significant factors in determining the value of the land. Therefore, bare land is cheaper than similar land that has an improvement.

Personal property may become real property, this is known as a fixture. A **fixture** is personal property that has been attached to real property with the intent to leave the fixture attached indefinitely. Often it is ambiguous whether property that is affixed on the real property is considered a fixture. There is a test used to determine whether property qualifies as a fixture. If the personal property can be removed from the real property without causing damage to the real property, it is not considered a fixture. If the removal of the personal property would cause damage to the real property, then it is considered a fixture and cannot be removed (unless it is by the landowner's discretion). The terms improvement and fixture refer to the same concept, but the term fixture is used to describe smaller personal property items that are attached to real property, such as an installed curtain rod. The term **improvement** is used to describe items that are obviously real property and cannot easily be moved, such as a building.

When it is not obvious if an item is intended to be a fixture, you can consider the method of attachment (*i.e.*, screwed into the wall), adaptation of the real property around the fixture (or vice versa), and the purchase agreement to determine how the item should be treated.

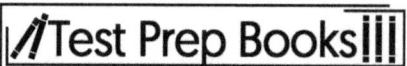

Fixtures are considered real property and will transfer ownership when the real property is subject to a purchase agreement, unless otherwise stated or agreed upon by the parties. If a seller removes a fixture that was not excluded under the purchase agreement, then the seller is in breach of the purchase agreement.

Emblements are cultivated crops and are generally owned by the planter of the seed. **Trade fixtures** are fixtures installed by a commercial property tenant for the use of the commercial business, such as a business sign or a commercial grade oven. Trade fixtures are not installed with the intent to remain indefinitely; these items are installed with the intent to remain until the business will no longer use the premises. When the commercial tenant leaves, so do the trade fixtures. Emblements and trade fixtures are personal property, not real property. These items would not be subject to a purchase agreement for the sale of real property.

Personal Property

Personal property is an item that may be owned by a person, or artificial person, and is not real property. Personal property may be tangible or intangible. **Tangible** personal property is a movable and existent item that can be used or consumed. Examples of tangible personal property include vehicles, groceries, clothing, appliances, equipment, and other similar items. Tangible personal property can also be referred to as **chattel**. **Intangible** personal property is an item of value that cannot be physically felt or touched, such as one's likeness, image, copyrights, trademarks, and patents.

Generally, a transaction for the sale of real estate from the seller to the buyer is limited to the land and the improvements and fixtures attached to it. However, there are times when a buyer may purchase personal property from a seller in addition to the real property covered under the purchase agreement. Desired personal property purchases generally include furniture or appliances (that are not attached to the property). The purchase agreement does not cover the sale of the personal property, only the real property.

To transfer ownership of personal property in conjunction with a sale of real property, it must be included in a bill of sale. A **bill of sale** is a document that identifies the personal property to be sold and is signed by the parties. A bill of sale is like the *purchase agreement,* but it conveys personal property, not real property. However, if a realty listing advertises real property and additional personal property for a stated price, the personal property does not need to be added in a bill of sale because it is part of the existing listing.

It can be confusing to determine if personal property would be considered an improvement or a fixture or be subject to a bill of sale requirement. The determining test is whether the item can be moved. For example, an installed curtain rod cannot be moved as easily as a free-standing fridge. The installed curtain rod would be considered real property, but the freestanding fridge would be considered personal property and may be subject to a bill of sale requirement.

Types of Ownership (Estates and Encumbrances)

To better comprehend the extent and complexity of ownership, it is best to think of ownership as a bundle of sticks. Each stick within the bundle represents a different right associated with ownership and each right is distinct from another. Additionally, each stick represents present and future interests, but not past interest (because that has already been owned by a preceding titleholder). More rights have been interpreted to be ancillary to an overarching right (or stick) within a bundle; think of these additional rights as slivers of a corresponding stick. The bundle of ownership rights can be enumerated in the following:

(1) right to possess (the real property);

(2) right to control/regulate (the real property);

(3) right to exclude (others);

(4) right to use and enjoy (the real property, as legally permitted);

(5) right to transfer (the real property to others); and

(6) right to destroy (the real property).

Finally, all or a portion of each of these rights can be transferred to another – this is how different forms of ownership and rights are formed. When a "stick" is conveyed, the owner cannot convey more than what the owner has or reconvey to another; if an owner gives one stick (or sliver) away, then the owner has one less stick (or sliver) to give away at a later time. The content below illustrates these interests and rights in function.

Present property interests can be broken down into two main categories: (1) freehold interests and (2) leasehold interests. Both interests are present possessory interests – an interest holder has a present right to possess and use the real property. **Freehold estates** are indefinite in duration of ownership. **Leasehold estates** are definite in duration and are not a form of ownership, only an interest in possession of the real property.

Freehold estates can be divided into three categories: (1) fee simple absolute; (2) defeasible fees; and (3) life estates.

Fee simple absolute is the highest form of ownership. It has the maximum amount of rights and is indefinite in duration. It is the most widely known form of ownership.

Defeasible fees are ownership interests that terminate present ownership if a specified event (stated in a conveyance) occurs. Additionally, when these interests are created, the future interest is vested in the grantor or a third person. Generally, the conveyance will have durational language such as "so long as." Example: "From Alan to Bianca so long as Bianca does not marry." Here, Bianca is the owner of the conveyed property so long as Bianca does not marry.

There are multiple future interest types, but two will be discussed to the extent that the interests affect the real estate subject matter presented in this material. Two relative future interests are: (1) reversion and (2) remainder. **Reversion** is a future interest that belongs to the owner of the property that was conveyed. This occurs when the owner reserves the future interest for the owner or when the owner does not convey a future interest. Once the present interest is terminated, it reverts to the grantor. Example: "From Alan to Bianca so long as Bianca does not marry and I, Alan, shall retain reversion" or "From Alan to Bianca so long as Bianca does not marry." Under both conveyances, Alan holds the reversion of property interest. The grantee is the owner until the stated event. After the stated event, the future interest will become active, and the future interest holder (here, the grantor) will then own the property in fee simple.

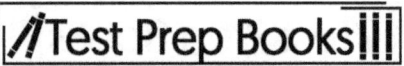

Remainder is the same concept as reversion, but the future interest belongs to a third person (not the grantor or grantee). Example: "From Alan to Bianca so long as Bianca does not marry and remainder to Carla." Carla holds the remainder of the property interest. The grantee is the owner until the stated event. After the event, the remainder holder will own the property in fee simple.

Life estate is similar to the defeasible fees, but the property interest termination is contingent on death. Additionally, a granting of a life estate can create a reversion or remainder. However, in the conveyancing it must state "for life" and not "so long as [X] lives." The distinct language creates different interests, and different laws apply to different interests. Examples: "From Alan to Bianca for life and I, Alan, shall retain the reversion;" "From Alan to Bianca for life;" "From Alan to Bianca for life and remainder to Carla."

Life estate pur autre vie is the same as life estate, but the measuring life is based on the life of the grantor or that of a third person, rather than the grantee's life. Example: "From Alan to Bianca for the life of Alan" or "To Bianca for the life of Carla." Here, the grantee is the owner until the death of Alan or Carla, respectively. Additionally, future interest language may be added to convey the future interest after the stated measuring life. Example: "From Alan to Bianca for the life of Carla, and I, Alan, shall retain the reversion" or "From Alan to Bianca for the life of Carla and remainder to Diego."

A **leasehold**, or nonfreehold estate, commonly called a **lease**, is a type of property interest. This property interest allows a tenant (or lessee) to occupy the landlord's (or lessor's) property, but the tenant does not own the property. The tenant gains the right to occupy, use, and enjoy the premises as desired for a definite duration. Lease tenancy duration can be categorized as the following types: (1) tenancy for years; (2) periodic tenancy; (3) tenancy at will; and (4) tenancy at sufferance.

- **Tenancy for years** is a lease that has a determined expiration date, such as September 30, 2008. This lease does not automatically renew after the expiration date. Additionally, it does not require notice of intent to terminate the lease – because it is stated in the expiration.

- Periodic tenancy is a lease that renews on a periodic basis – such as week to week or month to month. This lease type will renew automatically under the same terms of the previous lease and will renew upon lease payment until notice of intent to terminate is given.

- Tenancy at will is a lease that is indefinite in duration. Either party may choose to terminate the lease at will.

- Tenancy at sufferance occurs when a tenant is a holdover tenant. This means the tenant has stayed on the premises past the lease's expiration without the landlord's consent. However, if the landlord accepts a lease payment from the tenant, then this creates a periodic tenancy. Jurisdictions may differ on the periodic tenancy length. Example: Edward has a written 1-year residential lease with Frank, but it expires and Edward becomes a holdover tenant. Then Edward pays Frank. Under their specific jurisdiction, the new lease may only be for a maximum month duration because that is what their jurisdiction's law allows.

An **encumbrance** is a legal or equitable claim against property by a nonowner. Commonly referred to as *clouds on title*, it is a nonpossessory interest in the property. The following are types of encumbrances: (1) easements; (2) lien; (3) encroachment; (4) license; and (5) lis pendens.

Easement is the right to use someone else's land for a stated purpose. Generally, this interest must be in writing between the grantor and grantee. The land is subject to the easement until it is terminated by merger, release, or abandonment (by the easement holder). **Merger** occurs when the easement holder becomes the owner of the property and the easement interest is extinguished. In this case, the new owner now has all the metaphorical sticks, and the property owner cannot bring a lawsuit against himself/herself regarding the property. Types of easements are: (1) appurtenant easement; (2) easement in gross; and (3) easement by necessity.

Appurtenant easement is an easement of land (servient estate) that allows another's land (dominant estate) to use and benefit the other's land. **Easement in gross** is an easement held by a particular person to use the land for that person's benefit – the land is a servient estate, but there is no dominant estate. **Easement by necessity** is an implied easement that is held by a private person who owns landlocked land and does not have a way to access the land. The easement by necessity allows the landowner to use a reasonable route across the land so they may access the land locked parcel.

Lien is a claim that is attached to the land to secure payment on an underlying obligation. Lien types include mortgages, mechanics liens, property tax liens, judgments, and other tax liens. Property taxes are not a lien on the property, they are an obligation associated with the property. Failure to pay outstanding property taxes in a timely manner may mature into a tax lien on the property.

Encroachment is an unpermitted intrusion onto a neighboring property from a physical structure that is extending above or below the surface – including plants. These matters are not covered under title insurance or an attorney's title opinion because it requires visual inspection of the property. However, encroachments may be shown on an improvement location certificate (ILC) or land survey.

License is permission given by a land owner to enter and use the land. Permission may be oral or written, require payment, or be revocable by the landowner.

Lis pendens is legal notice (recorded) that there is a pending lawsuit regarding the real property's title.

Forms of Ownership

An attorney determines the ownership (title) of the property, and real estate licensees should not advise on legality matters of title or advise how property should be taken.

Sole propriety is ownership that is held by one person, or artificial person. It may also be called **estate in severality**. Title held in a partnership is owned by different partners based on the partnership's organization. Under a general partnership, all partners own equal profits and liabilities of the property. However, under a limited partnership, the general partner(s) are liable for the investment of the property and limited partner(s) are liable for the amount of their contribution to the investment.

Concurrent ownership is ownership that is held by more than one person, or artificial person, at the same time. There are three types of concurrent ownership: (1) joint tenancy; (2) tenants in common; and (3) tenancy by entirety.

Joint tenancy creates **joint tenants** and the right of survivorship. This right means that when one of the joint tenants dies, the interest of that owner will immediately be acquired by the remaining joint tenant(s). The interest will not be able to be passed by the estate or will of the decedent because there is no interest to be conveyed. However, in some jurisdictions, joint tenancy must be created by the 4

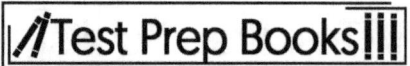

unities of title, PITT: possession, interest, time, and title. This requires that joint tenancy may only be created when a property's possession and interest are passed under the same time of title transfer.

Tenancy by entirety is a type of tenancy that applies in some jurisdictions, and exclusively applies to married couples. Here, property may not be transferred without the consent of both spouses.

Common interest ownership properties are properties that are owned by many persons, but also exclusively to some extent. Such properties include: (1) condominiums and townhomes; (2) cooperatives; and (3) time-shares.

Condominiums and **townhomes** are properties that have individual units within the property that are owned by individual owners, but share ownership (and use) of the common areas. Common areas include hallways, stairwells, laundry facilities, recreational facilities, parking lots, etc. A buyer of this type of property finances for the individual unit, but is generally financially liable for a portion of the common areas with the other relevant property owners after the purchase. Tax amounts for these types of properties are based on the individual unit ownership and common areas portion ownership.

Cooperatives are buildings that are owned by a corporation, but the units within are leased to the corporation's shareholders. Buyers purchase the corporation's stock, and receive bylaws and a proprietary lease for their individual unit and common areas. A deed is not used to transfer interest because the ownership remains the same (the corporation). Additionally, stock ownership represents a portion of ownership of a company. Buyers buy a portion of the corporation through stock and the corporation leases the unit to its owner, the shareholder. The portion (percentage) of corporation ownership is determined by how many shares are owned and how many shares there are in total.

Time-shares are properties that have multiple owners in property, but for certain durations within a year. These types of properties are generally used in vacation locations.

Land Characteristics

Characteristics of land may be divided into two categories: (1) physical and (2) economic.

Physical characteristics of land are the characteristics regarding land's physical state. Land is coveted because it is: (1) immobile; (2) indestructible; and (3) unique. Immobile means that land is unable to be picked up and moved to a different location. Indestructible means that the land cannot be destroyed, although the improvements and fixtures upon it may be destroyed. A land's location makes a parcel of land unique, because there is no other parcel of land with that land's location and features. For this reason, uniqueness is a substantial factor when determining a parcel of land's value.

Economic characteristics of land are the characteristics regarding land's value in the marketplace. Land is coveted because of: (1) scarcity; (2) improvements; (3) permanence of investment; and (4) location/area preference. Scarcity means that land has limited surface and natural resources. Natural resources may include oil, coal, natural gas, metals, minerals, and other nonrenewable substances. Improvements, such as buildings, also help to determine a parcel of land's value. Permanence of investment means that there is a long term and stable probability that the land will retain its value and earn additional value in the future; value may even come from buildings or utility lines built on or within the land. Location/area preference means that land is valuable based on its location and proximity to certain desirable features or places.

Legal Description

Legal description of land is a description of a parcel of land's features that is sufficient for legal purposes. The description contains the land's location, measurements, and boundaries for the purposes of ownership. This description will show how much land in the area the owner legally owns and where the adjacent landowner's property begins. A proper legal description is necessary to resolve future real estate disputes or transactions. There are three methods of land description: (1) metes and bounds; (2) rectangular survey; and (3) recorded plat.

Metes and bounds are legal descriptions that use directions and compass degrees to measure a parcel of land. The measurement describes the land in a clockwise motion from a referenced monument. Example: *Commencing at the street sign of Walker Avenue and 34th Street, go 200 feet south and then go 250 feet west.*

Rectangular description, also called the **government survey system,** is a legal description that uses meridians, townships, ranges, tiers, and sections to describe parcels. **Township** is a division of a parcel of land that has been subject to a land survey. It contains 36 sections (36 square miles).

A **section** is a piece of land one square mile in area that forms one of the 36 subdivisions of a township – 1 mile x 1 mile: 640 acres. An **acre** is a measurement of land that is equal to 43,560 square feet.

Township Map

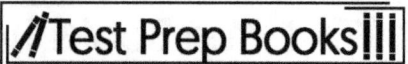

Survey, or *land survey*, is physical measurement of the property boundaries (lines) and may show improvements, encroachments, and zoning violations. A survey creates or verifies a legal description. Monuments, or markers, are used in a survey to assist in determining property boundaries.

Recorded plat is a legal description that uses a plat map recorded by the property owner to describe a parcel of land. Generally, plat maps are recorded in residential areas and each parcel within is referred to as a lot. Within these maps, the description will designate a plat name and lot numbers. This is completed prior to obtaining building permits for the properties within the plat. Example: Lot 3 of Woodland Hills Plat in the City of Abilene in Taylor County in the state of Texas.

Practice Quiz

1. What are the two main classes of property?
    a. Real property and personal property
    b. Tangible property and intangible property
    c. Commercial property and residential property
    d. Improvement property and fixture property

2. Owning land does NOT include which rights?
    a. Surface rights
    b. Air rights
    c. Past ownership rights
    d. Mineral rights

3. Which of the following is real property?
    a. Emblements
    b. Appurtenances
    c. Cars
    d. Trade fixtures

4. Gabriel has a freestanding refrigerator in Gabriel's house, what is the classification of this fridge?
    a. Fixture
    b. Trade fixture
    c. Personal property
    d. Improvement

5. Helena has entered a purchase agreement for the sale of a home and farmland. Which of the following is NOT covered under the purchase agreement?
    a. Installed shelf
    b. Planted crops
    c. Installed fridge
    d. Planted trees

See answers on the next page.

Answer Explanations

1. A: Choice A is correct because property is either categorized as real property or personal property. Choice B is incorrect because these are forms of real property and personal property. Choices C and D are incorrect because these are types of real property.

2. C: Choice C is correct because ownership does not include past ownership rights. Choices A, B, and D are incorrect because they are present and future rights included in land ownership.

3. B: Choice B is correct because appurtenances are properties that are ancillary to real property and are considered real property. Choice A is incorrect because emblements are cultivated crops that are generally owned by the planter of the seed. Choice C is incorrect because cars are movable objects that are not connected to real property. Choice D is incorrect because trade fixtures are personal property installed on real property by commercial tenants, but are not installed with the intent to remain indefinitely.

4. C: Choice C is correct because the fridge is not attached to their real property. Choices A and D are incorrect because a fixture and an improvement must be installed upon the real property. Choice B is incorrect because a trade fixture, although considered personal property, is attached to commercial properties. Here, Gabriel has the fridge in Gabriel's residential property.

5. B: Choice B is correct because planted crops are emblements, and emblements are personal property that are not subject to a purchase agreement (unless there was a bill of sale or the crops were part of the listing). Choices A and C are incorrect because they are fixtures. Choice D is incorrect because planted trees are natural improvements.

Land Use Controls and Regulations

Government Rights (PETE)

A person may own their property, but it is subject to the limitations of government powers that may be used against the property: (1) police power; (2) eminent domain; (3) taxation; and (4) escheat. An acronym that can be used to remember these four powers is PETE. **Police power** gives the state the ability to control property, protect citizens, enforce laws, and provide overall care for the community. **Eminent domain** gives the government the right to buy a citizen's property, even if the individual does not wish to sell it, if the acquisition of the property is necessary for the good of the city, state, etc. **Taxation** allows the state to charge a property tax against a property owner; the tax is then used to pay for governmental services. **Escheat** allows the state to take the land when there is no longer an owner of or heir to the land.

Police power is not a power that allows the state to take property away from an owner. It is an authority that regulates how the property should be used, and which standards apply to the type of property. Police powers that regulate real estate are building codes and zoning. These are rules that are created by the government, or its entity, and apply to property owners.

Eminent domain allows a state to take a person's property, but this power has limitations. Such seizure of property may occur only when the land will clearly benefit the greater good of the community, such as building a hospital or for the use of a utility company. However, before a state may take the land, the United States Constitution requires that the property owner be paid reasonable compensation for the land. Generally, this amount is the fair market value of the property as it is (not what the value will be). Compensation is paid through condemnation, a procedure that the state must go through to exercise its eminent domain power and take the property. The alternative to a condemnation is an "inverse condemnation." Inverse condemnation is the process that allows a person to force the government to purchase land that is so regulated by the government it has resulted in a loss in value by the property owner and the owner is unable to use it as the owner enjoys; such land is so regulated it might as well be physically taken from the owner and paid for.

Taxation imposes a property tax on property owners. The property tax is a fee that is paid by the owner to the state, and the amount is subsequently used to provide for government services. When a property owner does not pay property taxes, it can result in a tax lien on the property. A lien is an interest in land by the lienholder (here, the state) and the lien may not be discharged until an obligation is satisfied. This lien may sometimes result in a tax sale that allows another person to purchase interest in the property; if a person does not pay property taxes, then that person could lose ownership in the property. The state may also levy a **special assessment tax** on property owners within a designated area to pay for a local project (such as road or sewer maintenance).

Escheat occurs when a property owner is deceased and has no heirs to take the property (because of lack of heirs or because the heirs do not want the property). The property then "escheats" to the state, and the land is owned by the state.

Zoning, Building Codes, and Environmental Impact Reports

Zoning (or zoning power) is an exercise of a state government's police power, but it is limited by sections of the United States Constitution. Counties, cities, and townships may exercise zoning on behalf

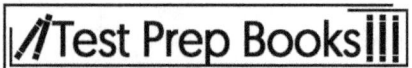

of the state, but only if authorized by state enabling acts (statutes). Zoning allows a state to divide its jurisdiction into zones in which certain uses or developments of land are permitted or prohibited. The purpose of zoning statutes is to reasonably control the use of land for the protection of the health, safety, morals, and welfare of the citizens within the jurisdiction. For example, a zoning statute that states that a residential property may not be built within x number of miles from an airport. Zoning exercises that do not conform are "ultra vires" (exceeding permitted authority) and void.

A **Master Plan** is a non-binding guide for future land use, often over the course of several decades. It can serve as a basis for zoning, but it is not itself a legal document.

There are two types of zoning exercises: (1) cumulative ordinances and (2) noncumulative ordinances. **Cumulative ordinances** create a tier system of land use. For example, from highest to lowest, a land tier may be set to (1) residential, (2) commercial, (3) industrial, and (4) agricultural. Under a cumulative zoning ordinance, land may be zoned for a specific purpose or higher. For example, property zoned for industrial land could also be used as residential or commercial land, but it could not be used as agricultural land.

Under a **noncumulative zoning ordinance**, the land may be used only for a specific zoning purpose. For example, property zoned as industrial land could only be used as industrial land, and not as residential, commercial, or agricultural land.

A **nonconforming use** occurs when property already had a use that existed at the time a zoning ordinance was implemented, and this pre-existing use does not conform to the ordinance's regulation. Generally, a nonconforming use may continue indefinitely, but a change in the use must comply with the zoning ordinance's regulation. For example, a change would be tearing down an older building and replacing it within a new building; the new building must conform to *new* use regulation.

A **variance** is a granted official exception to a zoning ordinance. It may be granted to a property owner who shows the ordinance imposes a unique hardship on them. Additionally, they must show that the variance would not be contrary to public welfare.

A **special use permit** is sometimes required for a use even though the zoning ordinances would allow that type of use. This can be the case with hospitals and funeral homes in a commercial zone; these commercial establishments have an additional requirement in order to operate.

Building codes are regulations that provide standards to which a building must conform. Generally, these codes are designed for a building's structural integrity or safety. Codes may determine the types and quality of construction materials used and how the materials may be used. Additionally, codes are used to provide standards for plumbing, electrical, heating, cooling, etc. Before a building may be occupied, it must receive a certificate of occupancy. This certificate is issued by a state agency or building department and certifies under its inspection and applicable building codes that the building is fit for occupancy. The purpose of this certification process is for the general welfare because otherwise people might occupy properties that could be a harm to them or others.

An **environmental impact report** (EIR) may be required before construction or land development is undertaken. An EIR identifies the action that is being proposed and details the impacts it will likely have on the environment. It also presents viable alternatives to the proposal, including the projected impact of doing nothing at all.

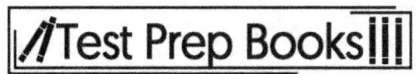

Environmental Issues

Environmental issues can affect properties and property value. In the United States, environmental issues are regulated on the federal level by the Environmental Protection Agency (EPA). If an environmental issue affects a property, it must be disclosed by the seller and the seller's agent because it is a material matter; such properties may also face additional restrictions on their sale or development.

There are several special land types regulated by the EPA. These include floodplains, coastal zones, and wetlands. **Floodplain** regulations aim to reduce the risk of flood loss. Traditionally, the minimum area of a floodplain plans for a **base flood** (or 100-year-flood); this is a level of flooding which has a 1% chance of occurring in any given year. Building within a floodplain is normally banned, both for the safety of people and property that would be within the floodplain, and to preserve a floodplain by avoiding undue modification. When construction or development impacts floodplains, this can result in damage to areas previously outside of the floodplains as water and runoff are redirected in unforeseen ways. **Coastal plains** are regulated similarly, as they are also at risk for flooding, but they are additionally regulated to protect coastlines from erosion and protect the ecosystem. **Wetlands**, areas of surface water which support vegetative or aquatic life, are regulated both as floodplain areas, and as areas essential for the growth and reproduction of flora and fauna. Development of wetlands is highly regulated to preserve and restore their natural functions and maintain the ecosystem.

Environmental hazards

There are five typical environmental hazards that may affect a property: (1) asbestos; (2) lead-based paint; (3) radon; (4) carbon monoxide; and (5) mold.

- Asbestos is a mineral used in buildings, even though it may cause respiratory disease. It is harmful for a person to inhale its fibers from any exposed source. "Asbestos abatement" is the removal process of asbestos from a building and should be completed by a licensed professional before a demolition or renovation. However, if an open source of asbestos is discovered in other circumstances, it is often the better choice to seal the source (encapsulate it) than attempt to remove it.

- Lead-based paint requires additional disclosure requirements. The seller must give a copy of an EPA pamphlet to buyers if the home was built prior to January 1, 1978. Buyers of these properties have a ten-day opportunity to have the home inspected for lead-based paint, but they may waive this opportunity. A seller is not required to conduct a lead inspection or remove the paint for the buyer. Commonly, lead is found in soil, pipes, and paint rather than in the walls. Brokers have a duty to ensure all parties comply with these regulations and procedures.

- Radon is a naturally occurring odorless radioactive gas. It enters a building through cracks in the basement and may cause lung cancer. This harm may be mitigated by adding a ventilation system to move the gas outside of the building. Detection and mitigation of radon are relatively inexpensive.

- Carbon monoxide (CO) is another odorless gas that may cause harm. It is a byproduct of combustion and may come from things like appliances, furnaces, and wood stoves. However, if there is proper ventilation within a building, then CO is not a threat.

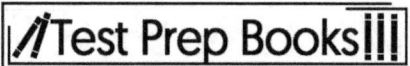

Land Use Controls and Regulations

- Mold (or toxic mold) is created by excess moisture in an area and requires moisture to grow. Possible indications of mold in a building include a musty smell, water damage, high humidity, and water leaks. However, not all mold is hazardous. If mold is found in a building, it can be toxic and require "remediation." Remediation in this context refers to the process of mold removal; it should be competed under applicable EPA and state regulations and procedures. Federal law does not require a mold disclosure, but state disclosure laws vary.

Private Controls on Land Use

Private controls on land use are restrictions that have been placed on land by a titleholder or preceding titleholder. Once a restriction is created, it is binding on subsequent interest holders of the land. A restriction is effective until it is rescinded or invalidated. Generally, and broadly, titleholders place restrictions on land to preserve its value and protect its interest holders. Such restrictions may be in limiting the type of improvements on the land or what the land may be used for, such as "only condos or single-story homes may be built here" or "this land may be used only for residential purposes." This type of restriction is broad and at the discretion of the restricting titleholder. The requirement for a restriction is that it be legal, and, in the case of residential land, it may not violate fair housing laws.

There are multiple ways that a restriction may be placed on the land or its interest, but the best-known ways are (1) a deed restriction or (2) the placing of a covenant or restriction in public record. A deed restriction is a restriction that is placed in a deed that it is conveying land to a grantee. Ordinarily, a grantee would receive all the rights that the grantor had in the land, but in this instance the grantor would preclude the new titleholder from one or more of those rights. For example, if a deed restriction states that the front door cannot be painted white, then the new owner is legally precluded from painting the door white. Recording a covenant or restriction is a similar concept, but the restriction is made into public knowledge and runs with the land. This means that no matter who owns that land, it is subject to those restrictions. In the alternative, the deed restriction is placed on a private party-grantee and is binding on the grantee and subsequent titleholders under the chain of title.

A **homeowner's association** (HOA) is an organization that makes and enforces private controls over properties within a subdivision, condominium building, or planned community. Purchasing property within HOA jurisdiction automatically enrolls the purchaser as a HOA member, meaning that they must pay dues and abide by the HOA's regulations. HOAs typically list their rules in a **declaration of covenants, conditions, and restrictions** (CC&Rs), enumerating rights, restrictions, and penalties for violation. Many HOAs provide services such as snow removal or trash pickup, and some also provide landscaping or community spaces for residents.

Water Rights

Different jurisdictions use different legal principals to determine who has rights in a body of water. Additionally, it depends on the type of water. In the context of rights, there are three types of water: (1) watercourses; (2) groundwater; and (3) surface water. Watercourses are waters that run in a course, such as streams, lakes, and rivers—this applies to both above-ground and below-ground watercourses. Groundwater, or percolating water, is generally water that comes from a well. Surface water is water that follows no course but accumulates on the surface of the land, such as from rain and melted snow.

Generally, watercourse rights are the most debated because it is a traveling source that affects different land and landowners. There are two popular doctrines used throughout the United States to determine who has rights in a watercourse: (1) riparian doctrine and (2) prior appropriation doctrine.

Under the riparian doctrine, the landowner whose land borders a body of water has rights in the watercourse. Riparian owners may make reasonable uses of the water, but not to the extent that it interferes with other riparian owners of that watercourse, such as someone downstream.

Under the prior appropriation doctrine, water rights are determined by the first person that uses the water for a beneficial purpose. For example, a farmer that may travel to the watercourse to appropriate it to water cattle so that they may eventually be sold for meat production.

Practice Quiz

1. Which of the following falls within the regulatory authority of the state?
    a. Escheat
    b. Eminent domain
    c. Zoning
    d. Condemnation

2. Which type of zoning specifies the category of use that is permitted for a specific area?
    a. Cumulative ordinance
    b. Noncumulative ordinance
    c. Inclusive ordinance
    d. Private ordinance

3. Rosa recently purchased a great investment property in a commercially zoned neighborhood. The building has potential and could be used for many purposes. Under a cumulative ordinance, may Rosa residentially rent the property to Shen?
    a. Yes
    b. No
    c. Only if Rosa seeks a variance
    d. Only if Rosa seeks a special use permit

4. Tim recently purchased a great investment property in a commercially zoned neighborhood. The building has potential and could be used for many purposes. Under a noncumulative ordinance, may Tim residentially rent the property to Umar?
    a. Yes
    b. No
    c. Only if Tim seeks a variance
    d. Only if Tim seeks a special use permit

5. Victoria owns a shoe store that that has an upstairs studio attached; they have been living in the studio for the past ten years. Recently, the city passed an ordinance that classifies the area that the building sits as a commercial area. What is the status of the upstairs studio?
    a. It is a special use.
    b. It is a nonconforming use.
    c. It is a variance.
    d. It is a violation of law.

See answers on the next page.

Answer Explanations

1. C: Choice C is correct because it depicts the exercise of the state's regulatory power to determine how land may be used. Choice A is incorrect because escheat is the process of the state acquiring land after someone is deceased. Choice B is incorrect because eminent domain allows the state to take a person's property, *not* regulate how it should be used. Choice D is incorrect because condemnation is the process that is accomplished to exercise eminent domain.

2. B: Choice B is correct because under a noncumulative ordinance, the property cannot be used for any other purpose other than the specific zoning. Choice A is incorrect because under a cumulative ordinance, a property may be used for a zoning's classification, or a higher tiered use allowed within the jurisdiction. Choices C and D are incorrect because these are not zoning types.

3. A: Choice A is correct because under cumulative zoning, a property may be used for a zone's particular classification or for a higher classification—generally a residential classification is on a higher tier than a commercial classification. Choice B is incorrect because of the reasons stated for Choice A. Choice C is incorrect because the property may be used as residential without seeking a variance. Choice D is incorrect because special use permits are obtained for particular businesses to operate, such as hospitals.

4. B: Choice B is the correct answer because under a noncumulative ordinance, the property may only be used for commercial purposes. Choice A is incorrect for the reason stated for Choice B. Choice C is incorrect because, under the facts provided, Tim is not experiencing a hardship due to the ordinance and a variance would likely not be granted. Choice D is incorrect because a special use permit is obtained for a particular business to operate, such as a hospital.

5. B: Choice B is correct because Victoria was using the studio as a residence before the ordinance was effective. Choice A is incorrect because a special use permit is obtained for a particular business to operate, such as a hospital. Choice C is incorrect because a variance is granted by the government to a property; there is no mention of or need for governmental consent here. Choice D is incorrect; the use does not conform to the ordinance but is permitted because it precedes the ordinance.

Valuation and Market Analysis

Market Value

The **market value** is the most probable price that a property would sell for in a competitive and open market. This should not be confused with cost; the correlation between the dollars spent to build a property on a parcel of land and the dollars needed to purchase the final product is not a direct one. Spending $50,000 on a lot and $150,000 on materials and labor does not ensure a sales price of $200,000 or more.

There are several forces that can have an impact on value:

- **Social forces** influence value as populations in an area change.

- **Economic forces** influence value by means through supply and demand for goods, services, and real estate and the anticipated ability of consumers to pay for those demanded goods, services, and real estate.

- **Political forces** influence value through the legal climate and the political actions of national and local government.

- **Physical forces** influence the value of a property or neighborhood based on the migration pattern of its population, meaning where people have moved from or where they are moving to. Additionally, new roads, other construction, or environmental changes influence value.

Market Price

The **market price** is what a willing and able buyer will pay for a property, assuming the seller will accept it. Once a completed transaction has occurred, this sale will become part of the basis for establishing the market price of future real estate transactions in the same area. Prices rise and fall based on supply and demand, the condition of the property, and the interest rates available to buyers at any given point.

Market price should not be confused with market value. Sometimes it seems as though a property should be able to be sold for one amount, based upon current market trends, but in the eyes of the buyer it is not worth that. What may seem valuable to a seller may be less valuable to a buyer. For instance, the $20,000 pool the seller installed may seem important to the seller, but a buyer may not feel it warrants an additional $20,000 in price, especially if the buyer is more concerned about the extra work involved in maintaining the pool. Or perhaps a buyer sees that a large house is certainly well-built and nicely decorated but is sitting on a very small lot with little room to park; the overall value of the property will decrease for that buyer, and so will the price the buyer is willing to offer.

DUST

To determine if a property has value, use the acronym **DUST**: demand, utility, supply, and transferability.

- **Demand**: the potential consumer base for a product or property. When marketing a product, the current market must be examined and potential customers identified so that the product will meet the future needs of the buyers and the ability of the buyers to purchase it.

Valuation and Market Analysis

- **Utility**: the benefits of a product to a consumer. Do the research with a new product and ensure that it fills the predicted needs and has the permission to meet those needs based on local standards. In the case of property, ensure that it meets all local standards and ordinances.

- **Supply**: the available inventory of similar products or properties. Who are the competitors? How many similar offerings are nearby?

- **Transferability**: the ability of the seller to transfer the title to a buyer. If there are too many barriers or restrictions on transfer of title or future use of the product, the product is of little to no value to a new buyer.

Principles of Value

- **Supply and demand**: Value will increase if increased demand for a particular product results in scarcity of supply.

- **Highest and best use** is the most profitable use of a property, meaning one that will yield the highest net return on investment.

- **Substitution** means basing the value of the subject property to that of an equally desirable property. This reflects the tendency of people to pay no more for one property than they would pay to have a substitute property with equivalent usefulness.

- **Contribution** is the calculation of the effect that the cost of a component of a property will have upon the value of the whole. There is not a dollar-for-dollar return on home improvements; for example, adding marble floors to a starter home will not add as much value as the cost incurred.

- **Change** is the representation of the normal evolution in neighborhood/property conditions. The stages of change are growth/development, stability, decline/disintegration, and revitalization. Change is reflected through appreciation (rising) or depreciation (decreasing) of property value.

- **Conformity** is the condition of value being created, strengthened, or sustained when similarity exists. This general similarity might be encouraged or enforced through vehicles such as zoning laws in a town or architectural restrictions in a neighborhood. Two basic principles are at play in conformity:

    - **Progression**: Smaller or under-improved properties increase in value by having larger, more-improved properties nearby.

    - **Regression**: Larger or over-improved properties decrease in value when smaller or less-improved properties are in the area.

- **Anticipation of value** is the prediction in today's dollars of what the future value of the property will be.

- **Competition** is the potential for profit that attracts new buyers and sellers to a market. If there is an excess of buyers, the value of buyers will decrease and give more value to the sellers (seller's market). If too many houses are for sale, the value of the sellers decreases and will give more value to the buyers (buyer's market).

- **Plottage** means combining one or more adjacent lots into one larger lot with the result being increased value or utility.

Appraisal

An appraisal is the unbiased, estimated value of a property by a licensed appraiser. Because there are different uses for appraisals, the appraiser should understand why it is being ordered. Banks and individuals alike can request an appraisal to establish the following: assessed value, rental value, scrap value, loan value, insurable value, and market value. Appraisals are required for all FHA, VA, and conventional loans.

Most appraisals consist of at least two of three potential approaches to arriving at the estimated value: the sales comparison approach, the income approach, and the cost approach. The appraiser then uses reconciliation to combine the results from each approach to determine the property's estimated value.

A more informal method of determining estimated value is the **comparative market analysis (CMA)**. Real estate agents generate this number by comparing recently listed and sold properties in the area to the subject property. This is for informational purposes and will never be used to finance a property. Another version of this is the **broker price opinion (BPO)**, which is a less expensive and less formal version of an appraisal that financial institutions can request to determine relative value of a property, typically one in foreclosure.

The CMA or BPO uses only the sales comparison approach to value, as opposed to the reconciliation of the three approaches that appraisers use.

Methods of Estimating Value

The **sales comparison approach** uses the comparison of recently listed and sold properties that are similar to the subject property but the price adjusted to account for differences between the comparables (comps) and the subject. When estimating value using the sales comparison approach, the agent or appraiser is looking for properties that would essentially be a reasonable substitute for the subject property. The following factors are considered:

- **Recent sales data**: Conventional wisdom encourages at least three to six comps that have sold within the last six months. Current listings should be considered, as well. Comps over six months old can be less reliable in determining current market value.

- Verification of data: Data is objective and not affected by personal involvement with comparable properties or the subject property.

- Comparison with subject: Most comps will be similar to, but not exactly like, the subject property. Adjustments must be made to account for differences between the comp and the subject. The best comps will have the fewest adjustments needed. The factors considered when making adjustments include the following:

    o Time of sale: closing date of comparable property. The most reliable comps have sold within the last six months.

Valuation and Market Analysis

- Location: physical location of comparable property should be similar to the subject property: same zip code, same neighborhood or section of neighborhood, same high school zone, same zoning classification, cul-de-sac versus busy street corner, etc. The closer the comp can come in physical location to the subject property, the more accurate the estimated value will be.

- Physical characteristics: Adjustments are made to account for differences between comp and subject. Examples would include age, lot size, construction materials, number of bedrooms and bathrooms, etc. The price per square footage is an important marker for comparison.

- Sales concessions: Allowances are made for concessions made to the buyer by the seller, such as paid closing costs, which effectively reduce the amount the house actually sold for.

The **income approach** is a comparison approach that is applied only to income-producing properties. Comps selected for the income approach must be in a similar market; residential rentals should not be compared to commercial properties, for example. This approach has two methods for arriving at value, the capitalization approach and the cost approach:

- A **capitalization approach** is used to value commercial and investment properties. It uses the income stream to determine present value.

    - The NOI formula is net operating income (NOI) equals gross potential income (GPI) minus vacancy minus operating expenses. Gross income can include fees other than rent, like parking permits and laundry fees. Operating expenses do not include any loan payments of principal and interest on the property, but instead refer to repairs and maintenance, insurance, property taxes, management fees, utilities, etc. Example:

$$\$2{,}000 \text{ rent} \times 12 \text{ months} = \$24{,}000 \text{ (GPI)}$$

$$Vacancy \ of \ 2 \ months = \$4{,}000 \text{ (Vacancy)}$$

$$Total \ Operating \ Expenses = \$5{,}000 \text{ (Operating Expense)}$$

$$\$24{,}000 \text{ (GPI)} - \$4{,}000 \text{ (Vacancy)} - \$5{,}000 \text{ (Operating Expense)} = \$15{,}000 \ (NOI)$$

    - **Capitalization rate formula** is the general formula used to estimate the value of income-producing properties. The value of an income-producing is tied to the cap rate by using one of the two versions of this formula; the version of the formula that is used depends on the information available to the appraiser. The appraiser can use recent sales and financial data of similar properties to determine the market cap rate, and then use the cap rate to assign value to the subject property.

$$NOI \div Cap \ Rate = Value$$

or

$$NOI \div Value = Cap \ Rate$$

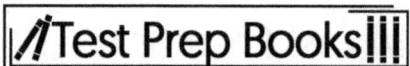

- The **gross rent multiplier (GRM)** is a ratio used to estimate the value of income-producing properties. The formula is simple, using only two pieces of information: sales price and total gross rent for a property.

$$GRM = Sales\ Price \div Monthly\ Potential\ Gross\ Income$$

Example: $Avg.Sales\ Price\ of\ a\ Property = \$100,000$

$Avg.Monthly\ Potential\ Gross\ Income = \$900$

$$GRM = Sales\ Price\ (\$100,000) \div Monthly\ Gross\ Income\ (\$900) = \$111$$

- Knowing the GRM, you can use comps to determine the estimated market value for a property based on the amount received each month from rent, which will then assist with deciding if a potential purchase is worth the investment.

$$Estimated\ Market\ Value = GRM \times Monthly\ Potential\ Gross\ Income$$

- In the **cost approach**, the replacement cost is estimated by figuring the land value and the depreciated value of the building after improvements. This is typically used with non-income-producing properties that have no good comps available. There are three steps in this approach:

  - **Estimate the value of the land**: This is separate from the structure since land does not depreciate.

  - Estimate the building's reproduction or replacement cost: Determine the cost to either create an exact replica or create a more modern building with the same utility.

  - Estimate the accrued depreciation: This concerns a loss in property value from one or more types of deterioration. Some deterioration is curable, meaning it can be easily corrected with cosmetic fixes or basic updates. Other deterioration is incurable and involves large, expensive structural issues. Depreciation occurs from the following:

    - **Physical** deterioration: anything from normal wear and tear to major structural damage.

    - Functional obsolescence: outdated design or utility (that is, several bedrooms with only one bathroom, or only a wood-burning stove for heat).

    - External obsolescence: an outside influence that affects the property (that is, an airport next door, or a new interstate built in recent years).

Practice Quiz

1. If a buyer wants to estimate the future profits from the purchase of an apartment building, which approach to value would an agent use to help this buyer?
    a. Profit approach
    b. Income approach
    c. Cost approach
    d. Investment approach

2. Which concept is NOT an element of value?
    a. Obsolescence
    b. Transferability
    c. Utility
    d. Scarcity

3. Which scenario describes external obsolescence?
    a. A tree in the front yard that has been hit by lightning
    b. Outdated fixtures in the kitchen and bathrooms
    c. Poorly maintained properties in the neighborhood
    d. Convenient access to schools

4. In which circumstance can a CMA be used?
    a. As proof for a homeowner to get a home equity loan
    b. As information for a buyer to use when selecting a home
    c. As legal proof of property value
    d. As a guarantee of a sales price

5. When an appraiser looks at results from multiple approaches to calculating value, which process are they using to determine the estimated value of a property?
    a. Stabilization
    b. Survey
    c. Application
    d. Reconciliation

See answers on the next page.

Answer Explanations

1. B: Choice B is correct because the income approach is applied to income-producing properties. An apartment complex has renters who pay rent to the landlord or property owner. Choices A and C are privately owned properties that are not assumed to be income-producing. Choice D has not specified any improvements that could produce income.

2. A: Choice A is correct because obsolescence is not part of the acronym DUST, which describes the ways to determine whether a property has value: demand, utility, supply, transferability. Choices B, C, and D are all included in DUST.

3. C: Choice C is correct because external obsolescence is an outside influence that affects the property, as poorly maintained nearby properties would do. Choice A is incorrect because it describes an easily corrected issue with landscaping. Choice B is incorrect because it is, at worst, functional obsolescence and easily changed. Choice D is incorrect because the location convenient to schools would be a positive factor in determining value.

4. B: Choice B is correct because a CMA is an estimate of value for comparable homes in that market at that time. Choice A is incorrect because a formal appraisal would be needed during a loan process. Choice C is incorrect because the CMA is not a formal tool to assess value, simply an estimate of approximate value. Choice D is incorrect because the sales price should never be guaranteed to a seller.

5. D: Choice D is correct. Reconciliation is the process that appraisers use to combine the results from each possible method to determine the closest approximate value of a property. Choices A, B, and C are incorrect because none of them is a method of calculating estimated value.

Financing

Lender Requirements, Qualifying Buyers, and Loan Application Procedures

Prior to granting a loan, lenders evaluate a potential client's integrity and reputation. Potential clients demonstrate propriety by maintaining good credit scores. Additionally, lenders assess the value of a potential client's liquid assets. Both factors indicate a potential client's ability to fulfill the conditions of their loan.

Lenders and real estate agents may act a bit like detectives when they evaluate the qualifications of a prospective client. Conversations between a prospective client and a real estate agent or lender usually begin with general questions about the client's goals, and these conversations become more specific as the two parties establish the terms of a final contract. Lenders and real estate agents may rely on social media to verify a potential client's claims. Some agents and lenders may feel that these tactics are a bit sneaky, but many agents and lenders actively research prospective clients to develop a more comprehensive profile.

When a lender has enough information about a prospective client, he or she may feel comfortable pre-approving a client for a loan. Likewise, when a real estate agent has enough information about a prospective client, he or she may feel comfortable engaging with this client as a potential buyer. Often, a prospective client will present a seller with a letter from a financial institution that verifies their status or standing with that financial institution. Financial institutions, such as banks, preapprove a potential client for a certain amount of money, based on a client's savings, income, assets, debt, and credit rating.

Types of Loans

There are many types of loans available to assist with the purchase of property:

- A straight term loan is an interest-only loan; it is used primarily for short-term purchases.

- A fully amortized loan is paid off in periodic payments of principal and interest over the life of the loan (fifteen, twenty, or thirty years). It is the most common type of loan. The reduction of a loan amount over time is called amortization.

- A partially amortized loan is as also known as balloon mortgage; it is paid off with a series of periodic payments for a set period of time followed by a single balloon payment to satisfy the loan. Periodic payments will be smaller, but the balloon payment is large. This is best for short-term or commercial purchases.

- With a negative amortization, the mortgage payment is smaller than the interest due, which causes the loan balance to increase instead of decrease.

- With an adjustable-rate mortgage (ARM), the interest rate for the loan is tied to an economic index, so the payments will be adjusted from time to time as interest rises and falls.

- A conventional loan is not government insured, and private mortgage insurance (PMI) is required for borrowers who borrow more than 80% of the purchase price. Once the borrower exceeds 20% equity in the property (meaning that they have paid off and hold ownership of at

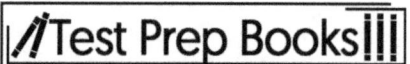

least 20% of the property), they can request for the PMI to be removed. Conventional loans typically have the highest down payment requirements.

- A reverse annuity mortgage (RAM) is a loan for home owners 62 and older that allows them to borrow against the value of their property so that they can receive either monthly payments, a lump sum, or credit. This type of loan is good until the borrow dies, moves, or sells their property.

- An open-end mortgage is also called a home equity loan. This is when someone takes the most money they qualify for a loan, and any unused amount of money after the home is paid for can be used for home improvements.

- A subprime loan is for the buyer who cannot qualify for prime financing due to a low credit score. Interest rates are higher and prepayment clauses are mandatory.

- A wrap-around mortgage is a loan that a buyer takes out that is paid directly to the seller. The buyer's loan is incorporated into the seller's loan. The seller takes on the full responsibility and risks associated with this type of loan and profits based on the difference in mortgage amounts and interest rate variation.

- A construction loan is a variable-rate loan in which loan amount is disbursed at agreed-upon stages of the construction process. Interest is charged only on money disbursed, not the full amount of loan.

- A sale and lease back is an arrangement where the seller of a property leases it back from the buyer immediately after the sale.

- Several forms of down payment assistance (DPA) are available to help cover the initial expense of purchasing a property. Some lenders offer second mortgages and deferred payment loans; the state may offer grants which do not require repayment to those who qualify.

Conventional and Insured Conventional Loans

Conventional loans are not government insured, but they offer flexibility in terms and interest options, compared to government-backed FHA or VA loans. The terms available vary anywhere from fifteen to thirty years in length; interest options include fixed-rate, adjustable-rate, and hybrid. Conventional loans typically require a higher down payment, but they require less paperwork since they do not need the approval of any government agencies.

Insured conventional loans are conventional loans with private mortgage insurance (PMI). A borrower must pay for PMI if they are borrowing more than 80% of the purchase price. Once the borrower exceeds 20% equity in the property, they can request for the PMI to be removed.

Government Programs

There are three types of government-secured loans:

- **FHA-insured loan**: A loan that is 100% insured by the FHA and provided by private lenders. Because they are 100% federally backed, lenders are more likely to approve these loans for first-time homebuyers, low-income buyers, or buyers with bad credit histories. These loans

Financing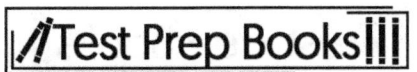

require a smaller down payment than conventional loans, which allows buyers with less cash on hand to still qualify for a loan. Instead of using the conventional loan structure of PMI, the mortgage insurance in an FHA loan is financed into the loan; unlike PMI, this mortgage insurance cannot be removed and remains for the life of the loan.

- **VA-guaranteed loan**: A loan available for veterans, military personnel, and military families for up to 100% of the purchase price, no down payment required. Borrowers must have suitable credit and income, as well as a certificate of eligibility (COE). Borrowers must also use the home as a primary residence. Benefits to a VA loan include a limit to the amount buyers can be charged for closing costs, no PMI is required, and the right to prepay the mortgage without penalty.

- **USDA loan**: A USDA home loan is a special loan that is given to people that meet certain qualifications. One of the main qualifications is that the home to be purchased must be in a rural, less developed area. These loans are beneficial since they do not require any down payment. The borrower must be a low-income U.S. citizen or permanent resident purchasing a primary residence in a rural area. This loan stipulates that the mortgage payment—which includes the principal, interest, taxes, and insurance (PITI)—must be under 30% of the borrower's monthly income. This loan boasts low interest rates, no down payment, and no prepayment penalty. Mortgage insurance is required.

Loan Money Sources

There are two types of lenders available to offer loans to prospective buyers: institutional and non-institutional.

Institutional Lenders

- **Savings and loans associations (S&Ls)** are often more local than many commercial banks and similar to credit unions. They are frequently a good place to find competitive interest rates since S&Ls are required to maintain 65% or more of their assets in residential mortgages.

- **Commercial banks** are local and national financial institutions that primarily make money by offering different types of loans to customers and then collecting the interest. They offer a full range of services in addition to loans, including savings and checking accounts and investment vehicles like CDs.

- **Life insurance companies** focus primarily on commercial real estate loans with longer terms (10-30 years). They typically require a loan amount to be capped at 65%, or up to 75% for borrowers with good credit.

- **Mortgage bankers** are similar to mortgage brokers (see below), but they originate and close loans in their own name (company or individual), using their own funds. Mortgage bankers frequently sell the servicing rights to the loan to another entity after closing; they earn their money through loan origination fees. Mortgage bankers represent one institution: a credit union, an S&L, a bank, or even themselves. Mortgage bankers also retain the right to approve or reject loan applications.

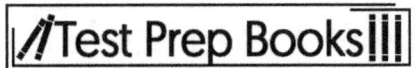

Non-Institutional Lenders

- **Mortgage brokers** are similar to mortgage bankers, but they originate and close loans with multiple institutions. They have the ability to shop for the best rate and terms for a given borrower. They are intermediaries in the process; they do not approve or reject loan applications.

- **Private money lenders** are not banks and are used primarily in real estate investment for properties that would not be approved for a traditional loan (distressed properties, in particular). They establish a set interest rate that is typically higher than any bank and a repayment term that will be much shorter. A private money lender has the right to foreclose in the event of non-payment. Loan decision is based more on property value and return-on-investment (ROI) potential than on the income or net worth of the borrower.

- **Credit unions** are cooperative organizations similar to banks but owned and controlled by their members. They typically offer lower rates and fees because savings are passed to the members. They tend to service the loans themselves more often, which provides more stable and personalized service, and they may have ways to help non-traditional borrowers get a loan when other cannot. Borrowers must be a member of the credit union to be approved for a loan.

- In **seller financing**, the seller agrees to finance all or part of the purchase price, as in a junior (subordinate) mortgage. There are four common methods of purchasing property with seller financing:

    - **Contract for deed (installment land contract):** The seller allows the buyer to move onto the property while making installment payments directly to the seller. The seller retains full legal title (ability to transfer/sell) until the buyer has fulfilled a predetermined percentage of the financed amount, at which point the seller records the deed and passes the title to the buyer. The installment land contract gives equitable title (financial interest) to the buyer until the full title is transferred. This method is similar to "rent-to-own;" the seller can evict the buyer for non-payment.

    - **Purchase money mortgage:** The seller essentially becomes the mortgage company. This type of financing usually is a short-term arrangement, up to five years or so. The buyer retains the title to the property, as with all other mortgage arrangements.

    - **Junior (subordinate) mortgage:** The seller agrees to carry a mortgage for the balance of the sales price when the primary lender will not cover it. The seller's mortgage is subordinated to the primary mortgage; if the buyer defaults, the primary mortgage will need to be satisfied before the seller can collect any payments.

    - **Assumable mortgage:** Allows the buyer to take the seller's place on an existing mortgage. Once the assumption process is completed, the buyer will pay off the mortgage according to its terms.

        - **Due-on-sale clause:** Not all mortgages are assumable; mortgages with a due-on-sale clause require repayment upon the property's sale or conveyance. A portion of the property's sale proceeds may be used to satisfy the original mortgage.

Primary and Secondary Markets

There are two main mortgage markets that manage mortgages. **Primary mortgage markets** directly service a buyer as the lender, setting up mortgage loans as part of their investment portfolio. The **secondary mortgage market** does not initiate loans, instead buying and managing existing mortgage loans to generate profit. Primary markets such as banks commonly sell mortgages to the secondary market to increase their available capital.

Mortgage Terms

Although the words "mortgage" and "loan" are frequently used interchangeably, they are two different things. A loan is the money that is lent to someone in exchange for the promise of future repayment. A mortgage is the lien on the property for which the loan was secured. This is, in effect, a claim to that property for the duration of the loan repayment period.

There are certain critical elements of a mortgage:

- It contains all the essential elements of a valid contract.

- It must be in writing to be enforceable.

- There are two parties: **mortgagor** (borrower) and **mortgagee** (lender).

- The buyer pledges the property as collateral (hypothecation) without giving up rights of ownership or possession, instead allowing the lender the right to sell the property if the buyer defaults.

- The buyer can transfer in writing the loan obligation to a third party (assignment).

- A mortgage is recorded with the local government. The first mortgage recorded against a property is given priority for debt repayment. A subordination clause is inserted to establish that other debts using the property as collateral are secondary to the primary mortgage.

- There may be a **prepayment penalty** established by the lender in the mortgage contract. This is an additional fee charged by the lender when some or all of the principal is paid early.

- The defeasance clause establishes that the lender will terminate its interest in the property once all payments are made. The lender acknowledges that fact in writing (satisfaction).

- The **acceleration clause** allows the lender to demand payment-in-full if the borrower defaults on payments or allows another party to assume the mortgage without having informed the lender.

- The lender holds the mortgagor to certain covenants. These include the following:

    o Payment of taxes

    o Maintenance of property insurance

    o Protection from loss of title

    o Maintenance of the physical property

- Permission for mortgagee (lender) to re-enter the property (foreclose) in case of mortgagor default or breach of contract

Title Theory and Lien Theory

When the buyer signs the mortgage, the title (deed) does not pass to the lender. In half of the states in the U.S. (lien theory states), the title is given to the buyer, who will retain possession and ownership rights but have a lien placed on the property until the loan has been satisfied.

In the other half of the United States (title theory states), the title is given to the buyer, who then immediately issues a deed of trust naming the lender as the beneficiary. The deed of trust will be held by a third-party trustee. The buyer will retain possession and ownership rights. Upon loan satisfaction, the lender will issue a deed of reconveyance to the buyer to indicate their possession of a clear title to that property.

Financing Instruments

Mortgage and **deed of trust** are two similar but distinct vehicles that give a lender the right to foreclose on a property that a borrower defaults on. Both are used in conjunction with a promissory note.

- **Mortgage**: Between two parties, lender and borrower. When a promissory note is signed for real estate, the lender attaches a mortgage to establish the recourse if the loan isn't paid. A mortgage is recorded in public records, and foreclosure proceedings are judicial and must go through the court system.

- **Deed of trust**: Agreement is between borrower, lender, and trustee. After closing on a property, the buyer deeds the title to the trustee to hold until the debt is repaid. Once the loan is paid in full, the trustee reconveys the title to the buyer. The deed of trust is recorded in public records, but foreclosure proceedings are non-judicial and not required to go through the court system.

Both the mortgage and deed of trust establish the following situations as triggers for foreclosure proceedings: non-payment of principal and interest; non-payment of taxes; inadequate or lacking insurance; and alienation. **Alienation** occurs when the borrower attempts to sell the property without paying off the loan.

When a mortgage note is paid, the lender give the borrower **satisfaction (defeasance)** and releases the lien. When a deed of trust is paid, the trustee gives a deed of reconveyance to the buyer and releases the lien.

Often confused with a mortgage, a **promissory note** is a promise to pay a sum of money that has been borrowed. It enumerates the parties to the agreement, the amount of the loan, the terms of repayment, the interest rate, and the collateral, if any, and the date and signature of the participants. It does not address the recourse to the lender if the borrower defaults. A secured promissory note includes an item of value (such as a house) being offered as collateral in exchange for the loan; an unsecured promissory note contains no collateral and rests solely on the borrower's ability to pay. Promissory notes are not recorded in public records.

Financing

Credit Laws and Financing Laws

The **National Consumer Protection Act (Truth in Lending)** was established by Congress in 1968 as part of the Consumer Protection Act. It protects consumers by requiring disclosure of all key terms and costs related to the lending arrangement. As of late 2015, this disclosure is required using two specific forms: the **loan estimate** and the **closing disclosure (CD)**.

- The **loan estimate** must be given to the buyer within three business days of applying for the loan. It clearly spells out the estimated interest rate, the monthly payment, the estimated taxes and insurance, any prepayment penalties, and the estimated closing costs. This form does not indicate approval of the loan application; it allows the buyer to clearly see the numbers involved and to decide if moving forward is appropriate.

- The closing disclosure must be provided to the buyer at least three days before closing; this three-day window between receipt of the closing disclosure and the closing allows the buyer to compare the numbers and ask any final questions before getting to the closing table.

Truth in Lending is also known as "**Regulation Z**." This regulation applies to any individual or business that offers credit, if four conditions are met:

- The credit is offered to consumers.
- The credit is not for a business, commercial, or car loan.
- The credit is subject to interest or must be paid in more than four installments.
- Credit is offered on a regular basis.

The **Real Estate Settlement Procedures Act (RESPA)** was created to combat the temptation of lenders, real estate agents, and title companies to provide undisclosed kickbacks to each other, which effectively inflated real estate transaction costs to the buyers and prevented true competition among service providers. At the time of a loan application, lenders must provide certain things to the prospective borrowers:

- A **mortgage servicing disclosure** explains the lender's possible intentions of selling the loan to another lender. This document also outlines the lender's history of selling loans versus servicing the loans themselves.

- A good faith estimate (loan estimate) is detailed accounting of the settlement costs associated with the loan being applied for. Most numbers at the time of application will be estimates; to this end, the borrower should provide to the lender as much requested information as possible to allow for the most accurate estimate.

- A special informational booklet contains information about settlement costs.

The **Equal Credit Opportunity Act (ECOA)** prohibits credit discrimination based on race, color religion, national origin, sex, marital status, age, receipt of public assistance, or good faith exercise of any rights under the Consumer Credit Protection Act (of which the ECOA is a part). Under ECOA, borrowers also have the right to know the specific reason why a creditor rejected their loan application.

Fraud and Lending Practices

Both lenders and clients may commit mortgage fraud, and lenders and clients may do so intentionally or unintentionally. Thus, lenders and clients must remain vigilant when applying for or approving mortgage loans.

Clients may commit mortgage fraud intentionally or unintentionally by inaccurately reporting their income. For many people, one's income may change from year to year or month to month. Clients should divulge any changes in expected income to lenders, as well as any factors that may cause their income to change or fluctuate. While unexpected changes in income occur, a client who fails to divulge known or expected changes in income may face allegations of mortgage fraud. Additionally, a client should do their best to accurately report the value of potentially lucrative assets, such as boats, vacation homes, and small businesses. Overestimating the value of such assets could constitute mortgage fraud. Examples of intentional mortgage fraud include if a client sends a proxy to apply for a loan on a client's behalf, and if a client receives money for the down payment of a loan, from the property seller, to qualify for a loan. The latter scenario may occur when a seller needs to get rid of an unwanted piece of real estate.

In addition to mortgage fraud, clients should also watch out for predatory lending practices. A common form of predatory lending occurs when a lender issues a loan that he or she knows a client cannot afford. The terms and conditions of a predatory loan might be concealed from the client. These loans may include high interest rates and fees, hidden or otherwise. Clients should carefully read all the conditions of any loan they accept.

Fortunately for borrowers, usury lending laws exist to protect them from many forms of predatory and exploitative lending. In essence, usury laws limit the maximum amount of interest that a client must pay on a loan. While this is helpful in theory, maximum interest rates vary by state because states are responsible for managing and enforcing usury laws. Furthermore, banks are allowed to charge clients the maximum interest rate in the state where they are incorporated, rather than the maximum interest rate in the state where the client lives. While usury laws do help protect customers from many forms of predatory and exploitative lending, clients must remain vigilant when reviewing the terms of their loans.

Other forms of predatory lending practices may not appear obvious to a client initially. Devious lenders use tactics such as "balloon payments" and "loan flipping" to extract more money from a client throughout the lifetime of a loan. Balloon payments allow lenders to present low fees to clients at the beginning of a loan's lifetime by saving a disproportionately large payment for the end of the loan term. This practice, like loan flipping, encourages clients to refinance their loan(s), which makes it difficult for clients to overcome debt.

Practice Quiz

1. What is the correct term for the practice of placing other debts claiming the subject property as collateral as secondary to the primary mortgage?
    a. Defeasance clause
    b. Subordination clause
    c. Acceleration clause
    d. Hypothecation

2. If a borrower (mortgagor) arranges for another party to assume the mortgage without informing the lender (mortgagee), the mortgagee is allowed to demand payment-in-full according to which legal agreement?
    a. Lien theory
    b. Hypothecation
    c. Acceleration clause
    d. Prepayment penalty

3. Which of the following will NOT trigger foreclosure proceedings?
    a. Non-payment of HOA fees
    b. Non-payment of taxes
    c. Non-payment of principal and interest
    d. Non-payment of insurance premium

4. In a contract for deed, where is the buyer getting the money for the purchase?
    a. Private money lender
    b. Credit union
    c. Seller
    d. Mortgage broker

5. Which loan option requires no down payment at closing?
    a. VA
    b. FHA
    c. Conventional
    d. Insured conventional

See answers on the next page.

Answer Explanations

1. B: Choice *B* is correct because the subordination clause stipulates that the primary mortgage will always be satisfied first. Choice *A* is incorrect because the defeasance clause says the lender will terminate interest in the property upon full payment of the loan. Choice *C* is incorrect because the acceleration clause allows the lender to demand payment-in-full. Choice *D* is incorrect because hypothecation is the act of pledging a property as collateral while retaining the right of ownership and possession.

2. C: Choice *C* is correct because the acceleration clause allows the lender to demand payment-in-full if specific contractual obligations are not fulfilled by the borrower. Choice *A* is incorrect because lien theory refers to the practice of allowing the borrower to hold title and ownership rights to a property but acknowledge a lien to be placed on the property by the lender until the loan is paid in full. Choice *B* is incorrect because hypothecation is the act of pledging a property as collateral while retaining the right of ownership and possession. Choice *D* is incorrect because the prepayment penalty refers to a common practice among lenders, namely, of penalizing borrowers for paying a loan off faster than originally contracted (thus avoiding paying some of the interest).

3. A: Choice *A* is correct because HOA payments are not a requirement for satisfying a mortgage. Non-payment of HOA dues will cause a lien to be placed on the property so that they will be collected before the borrower can complete a sale of the property. Choices *B*, *C*, and *D* are incorrect because neglecting any one of those items will trigger the foreclosure process to begin.

4. C: Choice *C* is correct because a contract for deed is a type of seller financing in which the seller allows the buyer to move onto the property and make installment payments directly to the seller. Choices *A*, *B*, and *D* are incorrect because they are all examples of other non-institutional lender options available to borrowers.

5. A: Choice *A* is correct because a VA loan is a loan for up to 100% of the purchase price with no down payment required. Choices *B*, *C*, and *D* are incorrect because they each require a percentage of the purchase price to be paid at time of closing.

General Principles of Agency

Common Laws in Agency

The word **agency** is used to describe the fiduciary (legal) and consensual relationship between an agent and a principal (client). An **agency relationship** is required for the agent to provide any professional services to the principal.

Express agency is established in writing through a **buyer representation agreement** or a listing agreement. **Implied agency** is created purely through the actions of the parties involved but should not be used in real estate transactions. All real estate contracts must be written, **express contracts**, meaning that their terms and conditions are stated plainly.

In the **fiduciary relationship** between the real estate agent and their client, the agent has six specific legal obligations that they must abide by in their dealings with the principal. These obligations relate to the trust that the principal has placed in the agent during the transaction. The acronym **OLD CAR** summarizes these six obligations: obedience, loyalty, disclosure, confidentiality, accounting, and reasonable care and skill.

Obedience to a principal means that the agent will obey all instructions from their principal for the duration of the agency relationship. The agent is free to express ideas contrary to the principal and provide professional guidance on how to proceed, but in the end the principal's wishes should be followed, so long as the actions are not illegal or immoral.

Loyalty requires the agent to put the interests of the principal ahead of the interests of all others in the transaction (including the agent).

Disclosure involves the obligation of the agent to reveal to the principal any material information related to the transaction. This could include facts related to the desirability of the property, the other party's bargaining position, and the identity of other potential purchasers. Disclosure should not be confused with the duty of a real estate broker to treat all persons honestly and to disclose all known material facts about a property and its value; the duty to treat all persons honestly is constant, *with or without* an agency relationship.

Confidentiality is paramount in the agency relationship; it also survives the expiration of the agency relationship, which means nothing can be disclosed to anyone else, with just a few exceptions:

- When the principal has given permission to the agent to disclose information;
- When it is required by law to divulge such information;
- When the agent is defending themselves in a legal setting against accusations of wrongdoing.

Accounting is required of the agent in two areas: money and paperwork. The agent obviously must account for any money (typically earnest money) that a principal contributes toward the completion of a transaction. Additionally, the agent must account for all paperwork related to the transaction and provide copies of all such documents to the principal. As with confidentiality, the duty of accounting never expires.

Reasonable care and skill refers to the pains the agent should take and expertise the agent should have. The agent should use this care and skill to negotiate the deal in the principal's best interest. An agent is not expected to display skill in areas outside of their expertise, nor should the agent try to do that.

Persons Involved in Agency Relationship

Principal: A person or entity (client) who enlists another party (agent) to represent them in a real estate transaction.

Agent: The party empowered to represent a principal (client) in a real estate transaction. The agent will not be the licensee directly working with the principal; the agent is the broker-in-charge (BIC) of the licensee's real estate brokerage. While "agent" is sometimes used more broadly, in this context it refers to the broker-in-charge.

Subagent: The licensee assigned to assist the principal (client) on behalf of the agent (BIC). As the agent, the BIC is responsible for the actions of the subagent.

Dual agent: An agent (BIC) who represents two clients (buyer and seller) in the same real estate transaction. This occurs only with the prior informed and written consent of both parties that is signed prior to a written offer from the buyer. Certain fiduciary duties (obedience, loyalty, and disclosure) are limited under a dual agent relationship because of the competing interests of the parties. Not all states allow dual agency.

Designated agent: The licensee (subagent) designated by the dual agent (BIC) to solely represent the interests of one client in a real estate transaction in which a dual agency relationship exists. This occurs only with the prior informed and written consent of both parties that is signed prior to a written offer from the buyer.

Transaction broker: A person who performs only ministerial acts in a transaction. This person does not represent either party in the transaction; instead, a transaction broker provides information on the property, shows the property, and acts as a scribe for completion and presentation of paperwork between the parties. A transaction broker does not offer advice, counsel, or expertise during the offer or negotiation phases of a deal because the transaction broker is working on behalf of neither party exclusively; the transaction broker is acting as a facilitator only. Not all states allow transaction brokers.

Third party: Anyone who is *not* a principal (represented by the agent through a written agency agreement) in a real estate transaction.

Customer: A specific third party who has chosen not to enter into an agency relationship but still requests assistance from an agent in a real estate transaction. An agent may not provide fiduciary services (obedience, loyalty, and disclosure) to a customer; the agent, however, shall still provide the customer honesty, fair dealing, accounting for money, and reasonable care. The agent may also provide pre-printed materials, such as contracts, and may act as a scribe for the customer, but the agent may not explain the documents or advise the customer on their use.

Attorney-in-fact: A person who has been given written authority to legally act on behalf of another. This written permission is called **power of attorney (POA)**.

The category of principal and the category of agent can each be broken down into three subsets. The difference between the types of principal is the amount of *liability* that falls on the agent: (1) disclosed principal, (2) partially disclosed principal, or (3) undisclosed principal.

Disclosed principal: The identity of the principal is known to all parties in the transaction. Most residential transactions involve a disclosed principal.

Partially disclosed principal: The identity of the principal is not known to any third parties in the transaction, although the existence of the principal has been established. This is a rarely used structure in residential real estate.

Undisclosed principal: The existence of a principal is not disclosed; instead, the agent acts as the principal and uses their own name on the contract, et al. This is risky for the agent because if the actual principal breaches the contract, the liability will remain with the agent named on the contract. This structure is more common in commercial real estate.

Similarly, the difference between the types of agent is the amount of *authority* the agent possesses: (1) universal agent, (2) general agent, or (3) special agent.

Universal agent: An agent who is given broad authority to conduct business on behalf of a large entity. An example would be an agent who works on behalf of chain of grocery stores and is tasked with finding and purchasing new locations for the stores.

General agent: An agent who is given authority to work on behalf of another agent. Subagents fall into this category; a subagent works with the principal as the representative for the agent hired by the principal.

Special agent: An agent who is hired by a principal. This will typically be the broker-in-charge of a firm, who will enter into the agency relationship and be given a specific level of authority to act on behalf of the principal.

Real Estate Agents Listing and Selling

The agent who represents a seller in a home sale transaction is called a **listing agent**. The agent who represents a buyer in a home sale transaction is called the **selling agent**.

The listing agent is responsible for collecting all the relevant information about a property that is being offered for sale. This agent solicits this information from the seller, as well as from other reputable sources, such as tax records, school district websites, and homeowner's associations, for example. The information presented in the MLS listing must be as accurate as possible; the listing agent has promised in the listing agreement to market the property in a truthful and ethical manner, without providing false and/or outdated information violates that agreement. Adding a disclaimer that indicates that the selling agent is responsible for verifying all the information does not remove the ethical responsibility of the listing agent to be as accurate and forthcoming as possible. The listing agent must also remember that the selling agent (also called the **cooperating agent** once a ratified contract is in effect) is their partner in any deal; nobody benefits if incorrect information causes a deal to fall apart. No one gets paid if the deal does not close.

The **selling agent** is responsible for guiding the clients throughout the homebuying process. Buying a home is one of the largest transactions most people will encounter in their lives, and clients place a lot of trust in a selling agent. The selling agent should use experience and expert knowledge about the local market to focus a client's efforts on properties that fit the budget and needs of the client, rather than visiting a large number of homes that may not satisfy the requirements. Buying a home can be emotionally charged and overwhelming, and a selling agent can keep things organized by explaining the process thoroughly and moving the client through it step by step in an objective manner. The selling agent assists the client with scheduling all inspections and submitting any repair requests. The selling agent should be communicating regularly with the listing agent and the lender, as well, to ensure that good relationships are built so that the transaction will proceed smoothly. This benefits everyone involved.

Types of Listing and Listing Agreement

An agency relationship with a seller is called a **listing agreement**. In the listing agreement, the agent and the seller obligate themselves to one another by virtue of the contract. The contract involves four essential elements: express agreement (written and signed by both parties), negotiable commission, enumerated price and terms, and a specified termination date.

There are several types of listing agreements that can be created, although not all of them are allowed in every state:

- **Open listing**: This allows the seller to hire as many agents as they want. The seller will only be obligated to pay commission to the agent who brings the successful contract. The seller also has the right to sell the property and pay no commission to any agent.

- **Exclusive listing**: The seller hires only one agent to represent them in the sale of the property. There are two different version of this: **exclusive agency**, which allows the seller to sell the property themselves and pay the agent no commission, and **exclusive right to sell**, which commits the seller to paying the agent a commission regardless of who brings the buyer.

- **Net listing**: The seller and the agent agree that the seller will receive a predetermined amount at closing. The agent will receive as commission the *difference* between the final sales price and that predetermined amount.

The agent agrees to the following in the listing agreement:

- To promote the seller's interests above all;

- To seek a contract with sales price and terms that are favorable and acceptable to the seller;

- To market the property in a truthful and ethical manner through the use of the seller property disclosure and general advertising methods;

- To present all offers and counteroffers as soon as reasonably possible, regardless of whether the property is under contract or not;

- To disclose to the seller all relevant information that is known (or should be known) by the agent;

- To advise the seller on matters of real estate, but to encourage the seller to seek outside expert advice for matters about which the agent has no expertise;

- To account for all money and documents entrusted to agent in the course of the transaction;
- To pay commission and referral fees only to other brokerage firms, not their licensees (and never to unlicensed people).

The seller agrees to the following:

- To compensate the agent for work done on behalf of the seller as stipulated by the terms of the listing agreement;
- To reimburse the agent, if stipulated to in the listing agreement, for costs incurred during the preparation and advertising of a property that does not sell and is subsequently removed from the market;
- To provide the opportunity for the agent to perform the duties stipulated in the listing agreement, which include keeping a clean and neat property available for photos and showings, responding quickly to showing requests, and providing reasonable access to property for buyer showings;
- To conduct themselves appropriately as suggested by agent during the course of the transaction (for example: to vacate the property during showings instead of hovering at the house, or to remove pets from the home during showings);
- To provide indemnity to the agent in the event of loss or damage in the course of the transaction;
- To show good faith in dealings with the agent and to act according to the terms and the spirit of the listing agreement.

Buyer Agency Agreement

An agency relationship with a buyer is called a **buyer representation agreement**. In the buyer representation agreement, the agent and the buyer obligate themselves in the same manner as sellers and agents do. Termination of the buyer representation agreement occurs in the same ways, as well.

Much like listing agreements, there are several types of buyer Representation Agreements:

- **Open buyer representation agreement.** This allows the buyer to hire as many agents as they want. The only agent to receive commission is the one who facilitates the successful purchase. The buyer also reserves the right to buy the property on their own and pay no commission to any agent.
- **Exclusive buyer agreement.** The buyer hires only one agent to represent them in the purchase of a property. There are two different version of this: *exclusive agency*, which allows the buyer to purchase the property themselves and owe the agent no commission, and *exclusive right to purchase*, which commits the buyer to paying the agent a commission regardless of who facilitates the purchase.

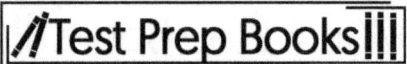

Managing Property

Real estate licensees are able to provide **property management services**, in addition to facilitating the sale and purchase of property. Agency and obligations related to provision of these services is similar to that of buyers and sellers:

- The property owner and broker-in-charge of the real estate brokerage will sign a property management agreement stipulating that the BIC will be property manager as a general agent of the property owner. Similar to a listing agreement, this agreement will specify the property description, the length and terms of the agreement, the compensation of the property manager, the authority of the property manager, and the responsibilities of each party to one another.

- The property manager or their designated licensee will market the property to attract well-qualified tenants.

- The property manager will negotiate leases and verify applicant qualifications.

- The property manager will collect rent and security deposits. Security deposits will be kept in a separate trust account, not to be commingled with any other funds.

- The property manager will prepare and deliver detailed financial reports.

- The property manager will distribute rent monies to the property owner according to the terms of the property management agreement.

Termination of agency

Agency can be terminated (with both buyers and sellers) in several ways:

- **Expiration**: All agency agreements must have a defined termination date.

- **Performance**: The transaction is closed successfully. Also known as **completion**.

- **Loss of authority**: This refers to the death or incapacitation of the agent or the principal.

- **Destruction:** The property is no longer viable due to comprehensive damage.

- **Loss of title**: The owner no longer has legal right to the property.

- **Bankruptcy:** Either the agent or principal is bankrupt.

- **Force majeure:** Broadly, termination due to circumstances which could not have been anticipated.

- **Mutual agreement**: The parties agree to terminate their relationship.

- **Renunciation**: The agent fires the principal.

- **Revocation**: The principal fires the agent.

Practice Quiz

1. After already agreeing to represent the interests of one potential buyer, a real estate agent secretly chose to represent another without disclosing this information to either. What law has the agent defied?
    a. Antitrust Law
    b. Law of Agency
    c. Fair Housing Law
    d. Real Estate Law

2. What is an agreement called where the listing agent will be paid a commission regardless of who finds the buyer?
    a. Open Listing
    b. Exclusive right to sell
    c. Exclusive agency listing
    d. Net listing

3. Which of the following details is an agent NOT required to tell a potential buyer?
    a. Previous water damage
    b. Recent repairs to the property
    c. Previous owner's occupation
    d. Potential hazards

4. A broker named Kristin is showing property listed for sale through her company to buyer Bob. After having agency relationships explained to him, Bob refuses to sign a buyer representation agreement. What is Bob's relationship to Kristin?
    a. Client
    b. Principal
    c. Fiduciary
    d. Customer

5. A seller, Manuel, signed a 90-day listing agreement with a broker, Bill. Then Manuel died before the listing expired. What happens now?
    a. The listing is terminated automatically because Manuel died.
    b. The listing is still in effect because Manuel clearly stipulated to it and signed the agreement.
    c. The listing is binding if any offers come to the broker before the 90 days expire.
    d. The listing is binding on Manuel's spouse for the duration of the 90 days.

See answers on the next page.

Answer Explanations

1. B: Choice B is correct because, under the Law of Agency, an agent is allowed to represent more than one client, but only if they have the consent of the first. If they do so secretly without informing either, then they are in violation of this law. Choice A is incorrect because Antitrust laws were made to limit the marketing power of firms, which in turn combats monopolies. Choice C is incorrect because Fair Housing laws prevent buyers from being discriminated against based on their race, religion, nationality, or sex. Choice D is incorrect because Real Estate Law refers to the controlling or ownership of land.

2. B: Choice B is correct because in an exclusive right to sell agreement, the seller agrees to pay the listing agent regardless of who brings the buyer. Choice A is incorrect because in an open listing, the seller has listing agents compete to bring the buyer. Choice C is incorrect because in an exclusive agency listing, the seller can bring the buyer and avoid paying the listing agent altogether. Choice D is incorrect because in a net listing the agent receives a commission if the house sells above a previously-negotiated price.

3. C: Choice C is correct. Buyers have no need of knowing unnecessary personal information about a previous owner, therefore an agent does not need to disclose this information. Previous water damage to a home could cause mold growth and structural damages, so an agent must give the potential buyer this information. Therefore, Choice A is incorrect. Potential buyers must be aware of any recent repairs to the home or property in order to relay this information to future home inspectors. Knowing of any recent plumbing, roofing, or foundational updates can help the potential buyer know what problems to pay attention to in the future. Therefore, Choice B is incorrect. Hazards such as potential flooding, nearby toxic waste, or asbestos are all important information that a buyer must know in order to make a decision on the property. Hazards can affect the health and safety of the buyer, so this is vital information, therefore, Choice D is incorrect.

4. D: Choice D is correct because anyone who does not enter into an agency relationship is considered a customer. Choices A and B are incorrect because they both describe a buyer who has established an agency relationship with an agent. Choice C is incorrect because it describes the role of the agent in the agency relationship with a principal.

5. A: Choice A is correct because the death of one of the parties to the agency agreement is one valid reason to terminate the agreement. Choices B and C are incorrect because the intent of the principal does not survive death, regardless of how much time was left in the agreement. In order for the broker to receive commission for bringing a buyer for that property, the heir to the property would need to enter into a new agency agreement. Choice D is incorrect because we have no indication that the spouse (if any exists) had signed the agency agreement, too.

Property Conditions and Disclosures

Seller's Property Disclosure

Property disclosures are disclosures made by the seller concerning the condition of the property that is being sold. Generally, jurisdictions have minimum requirements as to what kind of disclosures must be made to buyers. The disclosures may consist of a completed, preprinted form or a written list; they cover matters that may impact the buyer's choice to purchase the property. These matters are called **material defects** or **material facts** because the defects may materially affect whether the buyer chooses to proceed to closing on the property. The seller must complete the property disclosures, not the seller's agent. Additionally, the property disclosure must be completed with the current actual knowledge of the condition of property known by the seller.

Material defects may be visible or latent. **Visible defects** are defects that are openly visible and do not require special training to see that there is a defect, such as a hole in the wall. **Latent defects** are ones that are hidden and may result in a future harm. Latent defects may include such conditions as poor foundation of the property or house, leaks in the roof, plumbing issues, presence of a toxic substance (lead, mold, or asbestos), or faulty electrical wiring. Any known structural issues, visible or latent, must be disclosed; this includes issues such as damage to the roof, downspouts and gutters, windows, doors, or the foundation itself.

The seller must disclose an accurate representation of the lot size, as well as any encroachments or easements (such as utility boxes or electrical utility poles) relevant to the use of the property. Likewise, any relevant alterations or additions to the property should be clearly delineated.

Although the seller must complete the property disclosures, the duty to disclose all material facts of the property is imposed on both the seller and the broker. These facts must be revealed to the seller's broker/salesperson, the buyer's broker/salesperson, and the other party of the transaction. A broker/salesperson does not have a duty to discover latent defects in the property that were not disclosed by the seller. Regardless of whether the seller/buyer instructs their broker/salesperson to make a false statement or not make a statement at all concerning a material fact, the broker/salesperson must disclose all known material facts. If the broker/salesperson hides material facts or makes a statement about them that they know to be false, the broker/salesperson may be found liable for misrepresentation or fraud. Depending on the matter, it may render the contract voidable.

The listing broker must follow the seller's directions to prevent harm to others, especially when conducting showings of the property. For example, if the seller discloses a defect on the porch stairs and that no one should step on them until they are repaired, then the broker is responsible for people not stepping on them during a showing.

Other Broker/Salesperson Disclosures

A listing broker/salesperson has the duty to present all offers made on the property to the seller. However, the seller may provide a writing to the broker/salesperson that specifies which type of offers need to be presented. For example, the seller may provide a stated minimum price requirement. When multiple offers are received, the broker/salesperson must present the multiple offers simultaneously to the seller.

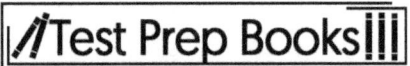

Property Conditions and Disclosures

The buyer's broker/salesperson has the duty to disclose whether the buyer can obtain financing for a purchase. This is considered a material fact because it materially affects whether the seller can receive the purchase price that was agreed on between the parties when the contract was made. If the buyer is unable to secure financing, then the parties cannot proceed to closing because the purchase price cannot be paid.

Brokers/salespersons owe a duty to parties that they do not represent. This is a duty of honesty, fair dealing, and care.

However, broker/salesperson may not inflate the price in the hope of securing a listing and then subsequently lower the price later. This is considered unethical behavior.

All environmental issues within the bounds of the property are considered material facts. However, environmental issues may extend outside the property boundary, and these would also be considered material facts that must be disclosed because these matters affect the value of the property and whether the parties proceed to closing.

Through their statutes, jurisdictions vary on which disclosures must be made concerning stigmatized or psychologically impacted property, such as the disclosure of whether a murder occurred on the property. Additionally, broker/salespersons must disclose to buyers any issues arising from **Megan's Law**, a series of federal and state laws regarding sex offender registration and notification.

New Home Construction Warranties

With new home construction, special warranties are provided to the first buyer of a new construction. A warranty may be a promise to repair property within a specific amount of time or impose a legal obligation incident to contracting parties—such as a seller and buyer or builder and first-buyer. Generally, a "warranty of fitness" or "warranty of quality" (or both) applies to property that is a new residential construction built by a professional builder. The purpose behind these warranties is that home buyers should get added protections because they are purchasing a new home from a professional who has heightened skills and qualities and is in the primary business of providing homes to the public.

Additionally, these home buyers do not always get the opportunity to inspect the property because it is being constructed or will be constructed. These warranties do not need to be put into the sales contract; these are implied warranties that are attached to the newly built property. The warranties make the seller/builder liable for defects of a property that a seller would not otherwise be liable for, because the matter was disclosed or an inspection turned up a defect that ordinarily would not have been noticed. However, sale contract terms may shift liability otherwise because it is the agreement of the seller and buyer.

Under some jurisdictions, the implied warranties may be passed on to a subsequent buyer of the property; however, some jurisdictions do not extend this right because the subsequent buyer is not the party that originally purchased the property from the builder. If a jurisdiction allows recognition of this extension, the recent buyer/owner must pursue the warranty claim against the builder because they are liable. The recent buyer/owner could pursue a claim of liability against the recent seller or previous owner on an alternate theory of liability, but that could not be on a claim based on one of these warranties.

Property Conditions and Disclosures

Home Warranty Programs

A **home warranty** is a service contract that is negotiated between parties and covers major housing systems and appliances of a property. Such systems and appliances could include plumbing, electrical wiring, heating and cooling systems, or a stove, refrigerator, or other appliances under the coverage of the contract. Coverage would last for a duration stated in the contract, beginning from the date the property is sold to the contract's expiration date. However, coverage may be eligible for renewal between the contracting parties.

Home warranties are negotiable and may be customizable to fit the needs of the covered homeowner. Home warranties are similar in function to home insurance, but they cover different events, damages, or losses. Home warranties protect heating and cooling systems, appliances, and similar items of a property from damages or losses that occur from ordinary wear and tear. Homeowners insurance is similar, but it covers damages or losses caused by unexpected events. Such events generally include fire or severe weather. Generally, a home warranty will cover most systems and appliances, but certain limitations may apply based on the home warranty's coverage criteria. When evaluating a home warranty, it is important to review: (1) what is covered, (2) what is not covered or coverage limitations; and (3) any deductibles or fees that may apply.

There is a variety of home warranty programs that may be offered by a provider and may be desired by different persons. For example, within the category of home warranty, there are distinctive options such as a seller's home warranty and a homebuyer's warranty. Under a seller's home warranty, there would be coverage extended to the applicable systems and appliances until the closing of the transaction. Closing on a property is costly for the seller and buyer, and the added coverage allows for protections to help reduce the stress and cost of broken systems or appliances during the escrow period. In the alternative, a homebuyer's warranty would cover systems and appliances that were affixed on a property that was recently purchased and a buyer would likely be unfamiliar with the condition of that system or appliance before the new ownership.

Need for Property Inspection and Obtaining and Verifying Information

The property inspection represents one of the last major tasks in the home-buying process. Complications at this stage may delay the sale of a home, so diligent real estate agents often take an active interest in the property inspection. Rather than present themselves as leading figures in the process, real estate agents are advised to serve as an advocate and resource for their client.

Property inspectors complete property inspections. Certified to evaluate the integrity of a home, property inspectors examine the important structural elements of the house, including the roof and foundation. Property inspectors check the roof for holes, missing shingles, and signs of weather or climate damage, including mold. Property inspectors check the foundation for cracks and signs of sinking. They also check the doors to ensure that they align with the foundation.

Property inspectors also evaluate non-structural elements of a home, including the septic system, electrical system, and life-saving appliances, such as smoke detectors. Property inspectors may take a closer look at a home's septic system if toilets fail to drain or fill properly when flushed. They may take a closer look at an electrical system if lights fail to turn on or if they observe obvious defects, such as ringing, buzzing, or flickering lights. Since smoke detectors and carbon monoxide detectors defend homeowners from accidents, property inspectors evaluate their function before approving a house for sale.

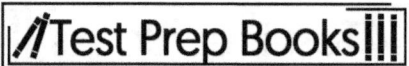

Property Conditions and Disclosures

Property inspectors complete property inspections on a buyer's behalf. As a representative of the buyer, real estate agents have a responsibility to inquire about any issue, structural or otherwise, that would compromise the safety of the home or affect the value of the property. Real estate agents do not possess the authority to complete a property inspection or uphold its findings, however. They should fulfill their role as mediator and advocate for their client without assuming legal responsibility for the property inspection.

Should the findings of a property inspection compel the seller to fix some part of the house, a buyer must present documents to account for this need. In some cases, the sale of a home may be delayed until a fix is made. In other cases, the findings of a property inspection may necessitate a reevaluation of the final cost of the house.

Material Facts Related to Property Condition or Location

Several significant material factors may impact the assessment and final cost of a piece of property. These factors may impact the structural integrity of buildings on the property, as well as the quality of life within homes.

Land and Soil Conditions

Land and soil conditions impact the stability of building structures. Additionally, land and soil conditions influence the utility of the property itself.

Land and soil that floods and overflows easily is undesirable for homeowners. The land around a home should expel water from rain, as well as water from melted ice and snow. Homeowners prefer land and soil that drains, without flooding. Land and soil that does not drain is a hazard to homeowners. Excess water build-up may compromise the foundation of a home. It may cause the land to shift over time and cause damage to a home's foundation. Land and soil with high saturation thresholds often causes the value of a home to decline.

Along with the threat it presents to the foundation of a home, land and soil with a high saturation threshold may also adversely affect a property's utility. Some property buyers, especially farmers, buy plots of land to grow crops and vegetables. Plants have a difficult time growing in oversaturated soil. Their roots may slip in the mud and break. They may also drown. Threats to vegetation caused by oversaturated soil is also a concern for homeowners who want to landscape or keep gardens.

Interior Environmental Hazards

Pests, such as insects, present one of the most common threats to a building's interior. The most destructive forms of pest infestation involve organisms that threaten the structural integrity of a building. Termites and carpenter ants chew away at wooden beams that are used to support the weight of a building. If these pests are not discovered in short course, they may cause permanent damage to the structure of a building. If discovered, sellers must eradicate these infestations before completing the sale of a house.

Mold, often caused by water damage, is another common interior environmental hazard. In addition to smelling bad and being an eyesore, mold is toxic. Humans should not live or reside in homes with a mold problem because it is unhealthy to breathe air that is infested by mold.

Mold removal is expensive. Often, it costs a few hundred dollars to hire a professional to evaluate a building for mold. The cost to remove a large infestation of mold may exceed $10,000.

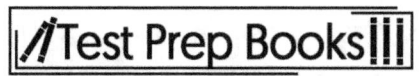

Property Conditions and Disclosures

Infrastructural Systems

The plumbing and electrical systems represent two important infrastructural systems that maintain a building's proper function. Degradation of these systems is a serious concern. Often, the cost of fixing these systems is high because problems with these systems may not be immediately noticed or determined.

Like a building's electrical system, a building's plumbing system runs below and behind walls and floorboards. Building owners may ascertain severe problems with a building's plumbing system by detecting leaks or low water pressure throughout the building, among other warning signs. Likewise, building owners may determine severe problems with a building's electrical system by observing the electrical system indirectly. Flickering or dim lights and stains around outlets are two signs of a faulty electrical system.

Contrary to problems with a building's plumbing and electrical system, problems with a building's HVAC system may be easier to determine by direct observation. HVAC systems provide filtered, conditioned air to a home or building. Thus, like any filtration system, ducts and vents may suffer a build-up of dust and debris. Building owners should frequently change filters, especially when buildup is apparent.

Potentially Uninsurable Property

Proper evaluation of the material factors that may impact the assessment and final cost of a piece of property represent significant concerns for both the buyer and seller of a property. Sellers who were unable to maintain the integrity of a building may lose their initial investment when they go to sell their property. Property buyers should maintain caution when purchasing a home with any form of significant structural damage, as such damage could make the building uninsurable. Property sellers should highlight mold and water damage as two factors worthy of concern. Insurance companies may not insure buildings with significant mold or water damage.

Material Facts Related to Public Controls and Statutes of Public Utilities

While real estate agents have a responsibility to divulge information related to property condition and location, they also must disclose information related to zoning and planning. Every municipality has its own zoning and planning conditions. Buyers may come across stricter zoning and planning regulations in one place than they find in another. In some cases, strict zoning and planning regulations may benefit a potential home buyer. In other cases, strict zoning and planning regulations may disrupt the plans of a potential home buyer.

Some home buyers plan to expand, via renovation, the square footage of their homes. Real estate agents must make these types of home buyers aware of any zoning or planning regulations that may limit expansion. Many home buyers think of their homes as an investment. They may plan to make a home more valuable over time. Zoning and planning regulations may limit the homeowner's ability to do so.

Conversely, other home buyers purchase a home because they like its size and place in the neighborhood. Real estate agents must divulge information about known plans to renovate or expand other homes in the neighborhood, along with information related to the ease or difficulty of building horizontally or vertically. Additionally, municipalities set land plans years in advance, so real estate agents must tell potential home buyers about plans to build commercial buildings, including restaurants and doctor's offices, in the area. These factors affect both the economic and aesthetic value of a home,

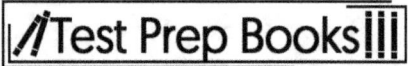

so real estate agents must tell potential home buyers about zoning and planning regulations in the area where a potential home buyer is looking for a home.

Other factors related to local laws and regulations that can affect the value of a home include school districts, flight paths, and taxes. There is a direct – though perhaps meandering – correlation between the quality of the schools and the property value of homes in an area. School districts, especially in more populous areas, are often divided along very fine lines. Two homes may stand within a few blocks of each other, but their costs might vary radically if they sit within separate school districts. Homeowners in good school districts often pay higher taxes.

Flight paths should impact the value of a home, and they may indicate a point of contention between a real estate agent and a home buyer. A neighborhood may sit miles away from an airport, yet air traffic may represent a consistent irritant to homeowners in the area. Real estate agents must present this as a factor to potential home buyers.

Practice Quiz

1. Who must complete the written documents of the property disclosure?
    a. The seller
    b. The seller's agent
    c. The seller's inspector
    d. The buyer's inspector

2. The seller completes the written disclosure of their property, but the buyer's inspector discovers a previously unknown defect in the basement of the property. Who is responsible for the nondisclosure of the defect?
    a. The seller
    b. The seller's broker
    c. The seller's inspector
    d. No one

3. Which of the following is a latent defect?
    a. A hole in the wall
    b. Visibly cracked porch step
    c. Contaminated soil
    d. Broken front doorknob

4. While touring a property in escrow, the seller's broker discovers a leak in the property. What must they do?
    a. Complete a written disclosure of the leak
    b. Disclose the leak
    c. Have the leak fixed before closing
    d. Nothing

5. Who has the duty to disclose a material defect of a property?
    a. A broker
    b. A salesperson
    c. Broker and salesperson
    d. Neither

See answers on the next page.

Answer Explanations

1. A: Choice A is correct because it is the seller's duty to complete the written disclosures about the property. Choices B, C, and D are incorrect because it is the seller's duty to complete the written disclosures.

2. D: Choice D is correct because the fact pattern said the defect was unknown. The seller is required to disclose known defects; this does not exclude that an additional defect may be discovered during escrow. Choice A is incorrect because the seller did not know of the defect. Choice B is incorrect because the seller, not the seller's broker, is responsible for completing the written disclosure. Choice C is incorrect because generally it is the buyer that inspects the property, not the seller. Additionally, the facts do not say that the seller used an inspector.

3. C: Choice C is correct because all other choices are examples of visible defects and would not require special training to recognize them. Therefore, Choices A, B, and D are incorrect because latent defects are not easily discovered.

4. B: Choice B is correct; the broker has a duty to disclose known defects. Choice A is incorrect because it is the seller's duty to complete the written disclosure of a defect, not the broker. Choice C is incorrect; the seller does not have an automatic duty to fix a defect, but parties may agree otherwise under the purchase agreement terms. Choice D is incorrect because, as Choice B states, the broker has a duty to disclose.

5. C: Choice C is correct because a broker and a salesperson have a duty to disclose a material defect of the property, and the duty is not imposed on one licensee classification. Therefore, Choices A, B, and D are incorrect.

Contracts

Basics of Contracts

A contract is a legal relationship between two or more people to do something or not to do something. This relationship and its agreement are legally binding and enforceable by a court of law. Contracts can be expressed or implied. **Expressed contracts** are created by expressed spoken words or writings. **Implied contracts** are created by implied circumstances, such as the sale of goods. A good is tangible, moveable property, such as a grocery item. A grocery store's primary business is to sell goods to consumers. Consumers go into the store, pick out goods, and take the goods to the cashier for purchase.

Generally, a consumer does not express that they intend to purchase the goods. It is implied by the circumstances that the consumer intends to buy the goods from the cashier: (1) the grocery store's primary business is to sell goods; (2) the consumer has selected goods to purchase; (3) the consumer has brought the goods to the cashier; (4) the cashier's purpose, in that position, is to sell the goods for the store and collect payment; (5) the consumer brought a form of payment into the store to purchase goods; and (6) it is common custom that people buy goods without expressing that they intend to form a contract for the sale of the goods.

However, some contracts cannot be implied because of the **statute of frauds (SOF)**. This statute requires that some contracts be in a written form and signed by the parties involved for there to be an enforceable agreement. The purpose of this statute is to prevent fraud and harm to parties involved. One common contract that is subject to the SOF is the sale or transfer of land from a grantor to a grantee. The **grantor** is the person transferring interest in the land, and the **grantee** is the person receiving it.

Within a contract, the rights and obligations of the involved parties under the agreement are defined in **contract clauses**. Clauses are the specific provisions that make up any contract.

Necessary Elements of a Valid Contract

There are five elements of a valid contract: (1) competent parties or contractual capacity; (2) mutual agreement or offer and acceptance; (3) lawful objective or legal purpose; (4) consideration or value; and (5) a signed writing (depending on the type of contract formed).

A person entering a contract must have contractual capacity. Contractual capacity requires that a person must be 18 years old (the age of majority) to enter a contract. A person under the age of majority may still enter a contract, but the contract is voidable by the minor's choice; the distinction in age determines the contract's validity. In instances where an individual has been determined to be mentally incompetent by a court of law, a contract becomes void. Only a court-appointed guardian may enter a contract to act on behalf of the incompetent.

Contract formation requires a "meeting of the minds." Generally, this is expressed by a party presenting an offer to another and the other party unequivocally accepting that specific offer. The acceptance of an offer must be expressed before an offeror revokes the offer. Prior to acceptance, an offer may be revoked, but when an offer is accepted, it cannot be revoked. Acceptance must be identical to the specific offer; a counteroffer or qualified acceptance terminates the original offer. A **counteroffer** is like the original offer but has a variation. A   is a statement that a party would accept the original offer, but

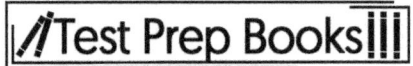

only if an additional desired term is added to the offer. For example, an offeree may say, "Yes, I will accept your offer to buy my car for $5,000 but only if you pay cash." This qualified statement created a new offer in which the buyer purchases the car for $5,000 with cash funds.

A contract must be made for a legally allowed purpose to be valid or have a lawful objective. A contract is void if it was created for an illegal purpose or requires an illegal performance by a party. Additionally, statutes may state that certain contracts may not be made.

Consideration is the value of the agreement, bargained for by the parties. It is received by the promisee from the promisor. In a bilateral contract, both parties receive a benefit. Referring to the house painting agreement example, both the seller and buyer are receiving a promise under this agreement. The consideration must be bargained for by the parties; an additional or alternate value conferred is not the contract consideration. In a land purchase transaction, the purchase price is the bargained for consideration. Earnest money is not the consideration of the purchase. Although it may be a portion of the consideration (the purchase price), it is not the consideration.

Under the statute of frauds, a sale or a transfer of land interest must be in a signed writing by the parties. Otherwise, there is not a legally binding or enforceable agreement for the purchase or transfer that can be compelled by a court of law. However, there are some instances, such as a short-term lease, where a transfer of land interest is not regulated by the statute of frauds.

Performance and Discharge of Obligations

Performance is the conduct that a party in a contract must do or not do because it was negotiated under the terms of the contract. Performance is conduct that is legally enforceable by a court of law. The person who must perform is called the **obligor** (because that person has the obligation to perform). Alternatively, the person who must receive the performance is called the **obligee** (because that person has the obligation to receive the performance).

There are two types of contracts regarding the duty of performance by a party: (1) unilateral contract and (2) bilateral contract. A **unilateral contract** is a contract based on a promise to perform that is exchanged (or bargained) for another performance. For example, an offeror says, "I will paint your house if you pay me $3,000." The promise to perform the painting the house is enforced only by the performance of a $3,000 payment. A **bilateral contract** is a contract based on a promise to perform that is exchanged (or bargained) for another promise to perform. For example, an offeror says, "I will paint your house," and the offeree says, "I will pay you $3,000."

Both contracts seem similar, but different contract formation rules apply to unilateral and bilateral contracts. In the first example, there was no finalized contract, only an offer. The offeror saying that the offeree would pay the $3,000 does not make a contract, and neither the offeror nor offeree could enforce the other's performance (because there is no contract formed yet). The offeree could only accept the offer by paying $3,000. Purchasing items in a store is an example of a unilateral contract; the store offers to sell a product for a price and the purchaser agrees to the contract by paying the price to purchase the product.

In the second example, offeree accepted the offer by promising to pay $3,000. Here, with mutual agreement, there was contract formation, and if the offeror refused subsequently to paint the home for $3,000, the offeree could legally enforce the offeror's performance to paint the home (because there is a contract).

When it is determined that there is a contract, it must be determined whether performance is required or excused. Under a contract there is a duty that the obligor fulfill the performance of the contract. Generally, once the performance is rendered to the obligee, the obligor is discharged from the duty of performance (because it has been completed). However, there are some defenses when a performance is discharged before performance is rendered.

There are some legal defenses to a contractual duty for performance: (1) illegality, (2) impossibility, or (3) death or incapacity. Illegality means that the purpose or the performance of the contract is illegal and performance cannot be enforced because a contract must be for a legal purpose or performance. Impossibility means that performance is impossible to complete due to an objective circumstance. For example, if there is a contract for the sale of land and the specific house that is affixed on that property, and subsequently a fire burns that house down. It is impossible to convey that specific house because it was burned down and no longer exists; it is impossible to sell that affixed house. The seller is discharged from the duty to sell the house (but not the land), and the buyer is discharged from paying for the house (but not the land). When a necessary person (the obligor or obligee) dies or becomes incapacitated, the duty to perform is discharged because the necessary person no longer exists or can no longer fulfill performance—however, in practicality, a person's estate may still be compelled to purchase property under a prior existing contract.

Two specific types of agreements relating to the transfer of contracted rights and obligations are assignment and novation. **Assignment** constitutes the transfer of the rights under a contract from one party to another party, from assignor to assignee; obligations remain with the assignor. **Novation**, while similar, constitutes the transfer of both rights and obligations/liabilities under a contract from assignor to assignee; novation fundamentally terminates the original contract and creates a new one.

Remedies for Breach of Contract/Default

A **breach of contract** is an intentional or unintentional violation of the contract's agreement. Contractual breaches may be repudiation of a promise (refusal to accept), failure to perform a promise, or interference with another party's performance under the contract.

Damages, or money, is the most common type of legal remedy for a breach of contract claim. However, other remedies may be awarded as well. One variation is a mutual rescission. A mutual rescission is the mutual agreement of all the parties under a contract to cancel the performance of the party involved. The intention is to return all parties into the positions that they were in before entering into the contract. Generally, parties enter a rescission where there are reasonable circumstances why a land purchase contract should be rescinded. Such as, the property is destroyed during the escrow process or inspections findings reveal too many or costly defects. However, it would not be acceptable in instances where it would be to the benefit of one party; for example, a buyer decides to buy a different property or has a subsequent change of mind and now no longer desires the property.

Default is an event that occurs when a borrow breaches a loan agreement. Default does not consist of missing a single timely payment. Default is a term with a designated meaning under the terms of the loan agreement or promissory note. For example, a borrower may go into default when there are three missed payments. When default occurs, the lender may be awarded a remedy for the resulting breach. The lender may have options of a remedy under the terms of the note: (1) specific performance; (2) liquidated damages; and (3) actual damages. Specific performance requires that the buyer do something, such as sell the property to satisfy the note amount. Liquidated damages are compensation (to the lender) that the lender and borrower have agreed to under the terms of the note agreement. For example, a note may require that a borrower pay a penalty fee for not making a timely mortgage payment. Actual damages are monetary compensation that the lender may seek for the injury of not receiving the timely payments. Remedies may be court compelled, but the lender is limited to one form of remedy.

Eviction (Constructive and Actual)

Eviction is the process of excluding a tenant from a leased premises so that a landlord may regain possession of the leased property. Generally, eviction is the result of a failure to perform under the lease agreement, such as not paying rent or failure to vacate the premises after a lease's expiration. There are two main types of eviction: (1) actual eviction and (2) constructive eviction.

Actual eviction occurs when a landowner of a leased property actually (physically) excludes the tenant from the entire property and the tenant is unable to use or access the property. When actual eviction occurs, it terminates the tenant's obligation to pay rent on the property because the tenant is no longer using the property.

Under **constructive eviction**, a landlord does not physically exclude a tenant from the premises. Rather, the landlord's conduct interrupts the tenant's right to enjoy and use the property as the tenant chooses. This is not a slight interference; it breaches the tenant's right to occupy and use the premises as stated in the terms of the lease. Within lease agreements, there is often an implied covenant (promise) of quiet enjoyment. This insures a tenant against a disturbance of their right to possess or use property.

Constructive eviction can be caused by a landlord's violation of the implied covenant of quiet enjoyment. The landlord's conduct, or failure to solve a problem, must interfere with the tenant's use and enjoyment of the lease premises. However, this form of eviction requires the tenant to provide sufficient notice to the landlord and for the landlord to fail to respond or correct the issue. Finally, the tenant must vacate the premises in a reasonable time after the landlord declines to respond or act.

Purchase Contract Stages

There are different variations on the stages to a purchase of land, but generally it occurs in six stages: (1) the execution of the contract for the sale of land; (2) the inspections of the property and examination of the property's title by the buyer; (3) the obtaining of financing from a lender by the buyer, if needed; (4) the closing of the transaction; (5) the recording of documents that transferred an interest or security in the land; and (6) the granting of title insurance.

The execution of the sales contract (also known as a purchase agreement) occurs when the seller and buyer sign it. At this point, generally parties with real estate licenses are acting on their behalf, presuming the seller and buyer are not representing themselves in the transaction. The parties then enter escrow and must meet certain conditions before they can close the transaction. Conditions are generally determined by the seller, buyer, and the buyer's lender that is financing the purchase.

Inspections may be done on the property. Common inspections include a general home inspection and a wood and termite inspection, and sometimes more specialized inspections are required. Additionally, the property's title will be examined. The title determines who holds a legal or equitable interest in the property subject to the transaction. The purpose of this examination is to verify the identity of all titleholders and ensure there are no outstanding interests or claims on the property.

Generally, a buyer will need to obtain a lender to finance the purchase of land. The lending agreement between the buyer and lender may add additional requirements to the buyer or the property to secure financing for the purchase. Some requirements may include a minimum down payment, a certain credit score, a certain debt-to-income ratio, and other considerations based on the buyer's finances.

Closing occurs when the seller and the buyer have satisfied all the conditions of the purchase agreement and the lender's ancillary requirements. At closing, escrow concludes, and the seller is paid sale proceeds in exchange for the buyer's receiving physical possession of and keys to the property.

After closing, the transfer documents are recorded. The most common recorded documents are the deed and the mortgage. A deed is a legal document that transfers the grantor's property interest and ownership to the grantee. A mortgage grants a property interest, but not ownership, to the lender to secure the promissory note that financed the property purchase. When the buyer has completed the repayment terms under the terms of the note, then the lender will release their interest in the property.

A title policy is granted to the buyer/new titleholder; this title policy is an assurance by an insurer that the titleholder owns the property. Additionally, if there are any defects in the title or it is not in the condition it was described as being in, then the insurer will attempt to cure any title defects or indemnify the insured titleholder for a resulting loss.

Types of Real Estate Contracts

There are three types of real estate contracts: (1) a purchase agreement or contract of sale; (2) a lease purchase contract; and (3) an option contract.

A **purchase agreement** and **contract of sale** are different terms that refer to the same type of transaction: a grantor/seller and grantee/buyer have entered a bilateral contract for the sale of land from the grantor to the grantee. A bilateral contract means that the parties in the contract have exchanged promises under the terms of the contract: (a) the grantor promises to sell the land and (b) the grantee promises to buy the land. This exchange of promises serves as consideration for a contract and makes the agreement legally binding when there is an acceptance of the contract terms. In a bilateral contract, both parties are the obligor who must perform an obligation to the obligee.

Various additional terms and duties may be in the written contract; these may obligate the buyer and seller to perform additional obligations to fulfill the broad performance of selling and buying the land. Some contracts contain a **contingency clause**. This clause allows a buyer to terminate the contract under certain conditions or events; there is a term in the contract that requires a specific event or action to occur for there to be a valid contract. Under this type of clause, a buyer may receive their earnest money back. Such as, there may be a contingency clause that the buyer must be able to secure financing to purchase the property. If the buyer is unable to secure financing, then the contract is terminated, the seller's and buyer's obligations are discharged, and the earnest money may be returned to the buyer (if stated within a contingency clause).

A **lease purchase** is a transaction that creates a lease that allows the buyer to buy the land at the end the end of a lease. The transaction contains two contracts: (a) a lease and (b) a purchase contract. Depending on the parties' agreement, a portion of funds paid to the lease may be applied to the sales price of the land.

An **option contract** is a promise by the seller to the buyer to allow the buyer to purchase the land at a set price for a stated time duration. For this option contract, there is an option fee that must be paid by the buyer. Whether the buyer decides to buy the land at the set price does not affect whether the seller may retain the option fee—the seller retains the fee because the seller is paid in consideration of keeping the option open to the buyer.

A specific kind of option is the right of first refusal. **Right of first refusal** is a contractual right that allows the rightsholder to consider a specific proposal before it is offered to any other party. The holder of the right may enter into the transaction but is not obligated to do so. Should the rightsholder decline to exercise their right of first refusal, the proposal may be presented to other prospective interested parties.

Lease Types

A leasehold, commonly called a **lease**, is a type of property interest. This property interest allows a tenant (or lessee) to occupy the landlord's (or lessor's) property, but the tenant does not own the property. The terms of the lease are generally defined within a written agreement between the tenant and the landlord. If a lease does not contain a term regarding a specific matter within the lease agreement, then statutes may govern the matter. Generally, residential leases are provided more statutory protections because the property is being used as a person's dwelling. However, commercial leases are more flexible on terms and may be less regulated by statues.

There are 5 lease types: (1) gross lease; (2) net lease; (3) percentage lease; (4) index lease; and (5) sale-leaseback. The distinctions between the types of leases concern how the tenant pays the landlord for the lease of the property, or how the monthly rental rate is calculated and who pays which expenses.

Under a **gross lease**, also called a **fixed lease**, a tenant agrees to pay a flat fee (rental rate) for the exclusive occupancy of the property. Additionally, the landlord covers all expenses associated with the property, such as utilities, property taxes, and special assessments.

Under a **net lease**, a tenant agrees to pay a flat fee for the exclusive occupancy of the property and all expenses associated with the property, such as utilities, property taxes, and special assessments. The net lease is commonly used for commercial leases.

Under a **percentage lease**, a tenant agrees to pay a flat fee for the exclusive occupancy of the property as well as a percentage of revenue generated on the leased premises. Revenue is income generated from a business's ordinary operations, such as the sale of products or services.

Under an **index lease**, a tenant agrees to pay a fee for the exclusive occupancy of the property, but the amount of the fee does not remain the same; it fluctuates. The fee is comprised of a flat amount and an amount that is influenced by an index. This is to ensure that payments remain current with inflation.

Under a **sale-leaseback**, one landowner sells property to another, and then the former-landowner leases the property back from the new-landowner under a long-term lease agreement. Generally, a landowner will engage in this type of lease when they need to raise capital but intend to remain on the property.

Statute of Frauds and Limitations

The **statute of frauds** is a statute that requires that certain contracts must be in a written form (such as paper documents) and signed by the parties for it to be legally binding and enforceable by a court of law. The purpose of this statute is to prevent fraud and harm to parties subject to the contract. Additionally, it prevents problems with oral real estate contracts and is beneficial to society due to the value and worth of real estate. Generally, this statute governs that sale or transfer of land interest be in a writing signed by parties. However, some transfers of land interest are not subject to the statute of frauds requirement. For example, a lease that is 12 months or less in duration is not subject to the statute. In these instances, spoken words are sufficient to create a contract for a lease.

A **statute of limitations** is a law that requires that an aggrieved party must bring a lawsuit claim within a certain amount of time in order to recover some type of award for the legally recognized harm. The statute concerns the duration during which a party is allowed to file a claim or lawsuit and can gain a recovery from the harm. The duration of time varies depending on the jurisdiction and the type of claim that a party wishes to pursue. The duration begins on the date the harm occurred. After a statute of limitations has expired, the claim is generally barred from being heard by a court of law. However, there are some instances in which an aggrieved party may still recover for their harm, depending on the facts that occurred and a jurisdiction's applicable law for the type of offense and type of claim. Statutes of limitations apply to both civil claims and criminal charges.

Practice Quiz

1. Which of the following best describes a contract?
    a. A written agreement between two or more people
    b. A legal agreement between two or more people
    c. An agreement for the sale of a property
    d. A right to a performance under an agreement

2. Maya verbally says to Nathan, "I will buy your real property for $100,000.00." Nathan replies, "I accept your offer!" What kind of contract have the parties made?
    a. An implied contract
    b. An expressed contract
    c. A sales contract
    d. There is no contract

3. Oliver goes grocery shopping. After Oliver picks out all their desired items, they take their groceries to the store cashier's counter. The cashier counts and totals the cost of all the grocery items. Is Oliver legally obligated to pay the cost of the groceries?
    a. No, they can unilaterally decide not to pay and leave.
    b. No, they are not obligated to pay the cost.
    c. Yes, there is a contract between the parties.
    d. Yes, because they picked out the items they wanted to buy.

4. A grantor/seller and a grantee/buyer have entered a contract for the sale of land from the grantor to the grantee. In this contract, the grantee takes all the grantor's interest in the land. Which type of transaction is this?
    a. Purchase contract
    b. Lease purchase
    c. Option contract
    d. Lease

5. Patrick pays Quincy a fee for the option to buy Quincy's property for $100,000, but Patrick must decide by Friday. On Thursday, Patrick decides not to buy Quincy's property. Under these facts, can Patrick get the fee back since the decision was to not purchase the property?
    a. Yes, because Patrick does not intend to buy the property.
    b. Yes, because it would be unfair to let Quincy keep the fee and be able to sell the house to someone else.
    c. No, Patrick cannot get the fee back.
    d. No, Quincy can keep the fee specifically because Patrick decided not to buy the property.

See answers on the next page.

Answer Explanations

1. B: Choice B is correct because it is the general definition of a contract. Choice A is incorrect because a contract is a legal agreement to do or not do something and it does not need to be written. Choice C is incorrect because the sale of property is a type of contract, but it is not the only type of contract. Choice D is incorrect because it does not define a contract; it focuses on what a contract gives a party.

2. D: Choice D is correct because the sale of land must be in a writing, as required by the statue of frauds; the parties in the question, Maya and Nathan, orally agreed to the sale of land. Choice A is incorrect because there were verbal exchanges between Maya and Nathan. Choice B is incorrect because the statute of frauds requires that the sale of land must be in a writing, an oral agreement is insufficient to create a sales contract for real property. Choice C is incorrect for the same reasons as Choice B.

3. C: Choice C is correct because there was an implied contract formed between Oliver and the cashier. Choice A is incorrect because Oliver does not have the authority to make a unilateral decision because regarding payment because the parties entered a traditional implied contract for the sale of goods. Choice B is incorrect because Oliver is obligated to pay. Choice D is incorrect because it does not answer the question whether Oliver has a legal obligation to pay.

4. A: Choice A is correct because the fact pattern describes a purchase contract. Choice B is incorrect because the facts do not provide that the grantee will take all the grantor's interest after a completed lease. Choice C is incorrect because there is a formed contract and not an option contract for an offer for sale to remain open. Choice D is incorrect because the grantee is taking all the grantor's interest in the land, not a limited portion that excludes ownership interest.

5. C: Choice C is correct because the parties entered an option contract and did not stipulate that Patrick could get the fee back after making a decision—the fee was paid to keep the option of buying Quincy's property for $100,000 until Friday. Choice A is incorrect because even if Patrick decided to purchase Quincy's property, Quincy would be under no obligation to return it or apply it to the sale under the agreement made in these facts. Choice B is incorrect because fairness has nothing to do with whether Quincy may keep the fee paid for the option contract. Choice D is incorrect because Patrick's determination, whether to purchase or not to purchase, has no bearing on whether Quincy may keep the fee.

Transfer of Title

Title Insurance

An **abstract**, or abstract of title, is a document that shows the history of a property. It shows the current and previous titleholders of the property and any other recordings that may affect the property. Some of the recordings include mortgages, easements, covenants, and more. The abstract is generally prepared by an abstractor, but possession is held by the current owner or the owner's agent. A title examiner uses the abstract to follow the chain of title for the conveyance history of the property. An attorney reviews the abstract and drafts a title opinion so that it may be used to obtain title insurance.

Title insurance is insurance that covers title defects or clouds of title. Before closing, a preliminary title commitment is produced. A title commitment shows current clouds of title and may state what must be done to discharge some matters, such as taxes and liens. The commitment serves as an agreement to the insured to cover title issues that may arise after closing.

Once closing has occurred and all necessary documents have been produced and filed, a title policy will be issued. The purpose of the title policy is to show that there is marketable title on the property covered under the policy.

The most common types of policies issued are owner's policies and lender's policies, which are granted to their respective parties during the transfer of ownership. The owner's policy protects those that have an interest in the property, and both policies are generally paid by the buyer before or at the time of closing. The final policies are generally issued to the policy holders after closing and the time depends on factors of the transaction.

If a dispute arises regarding the ownership of property, a quiet title action (lawsuit) may be filed. This suit determines ownership of the relevant real property. A party that has an ownership interest may file this suit against another, but it can also serve as a litigation for all others that have a potential claim to the land. If a party prevails under the suit, then others may not challenge the validity of title against that property and the determined owner (prevailing party).

Deeds

A **deed** is a legal document that transfers title of real estate from one person, or artificial person, to another. Title is the ownership of property and it determines who holds a legal or equitable interest to a property. The person that transfers title is known as the grantor, and the person that receives the title is known as the grantee. Under the statute of frauds, conveyance of land must be by a written document. A deed contains a reasonable description of the land, identification of the grantor and grantee, words of conveyance, and the signature of the grantor.

Description of the land is made by the legal description of the property and may include the commonly known address. The deed must also describe, or identify, the grantor conveying the property and the grantee that is receiving the property. The grantor executing a deed must be competent for a valid conveyance, which requires that they be at least 18 years old and mentally sound. The deed must also include words of conveyance, sufficient to show that the grantor intends to pass title of the property to the grantee; this is also called a granting clause. Finally, it must show the signature of the grantor because the statute of frauds requires it. This evidences that the grantor was aware of the deed and consented to the conveyance by signing the deed.

There are different types of deeds: (1) warranty deed; (2) specialty deed; and (3) quitclaim deed. Each deed transfers property with different covenants (promises that run with the land). These covenants can be thought of as warranties associated with the title of the land.

A **warranty deed** (or general warranty deed) contains the following covenants: (1) covenant of seisin; (2) covenant of right to convey; (3) covenant against encumbrances; (4) covenant for quiet enjoyment; (5) covenant of warranty; and (6) covenant of further assurances. These covenants do not need to be expressed in the deed. The covenants are implied by the deed type. Covenant of seisin is the promise that the grantor owns the land that is intended to be conveyed. Covenant of right to convey is the promise that the grantor has the legal authority to convey the property.

Covenant against encumbrances is the promise that there are no encumbrances (legal and equitable claims of nonowners) against the interest of the land being conveyed. Covenant for quiet enjoyment is the promise that the grantee will not be bothered by a claim of nonowners claiming to have an interest in the land. Covenant of warranty is the promise that the grantor will defend the grantee against any valid claims of interest in the land by others. Covenant of further assurances is the promise that the grantor will reasonably cure any defects of title in the land, such as completing necessary legal documents to transfer marketable title. Marketable title is title that is free from reasonable threat of an external legal claim.

While warranty deeds are most common, some circumstances dictate different deeds. A **special warranty deed** promises that the grantor did not create any title defects but does not promise anything that occurred prior to the current ownership. A **quitclaim deed** does not make any promises and only conveys what interest the grantor holds in the land.

Escrow/Closing

Escrow and closing are two events that occur during a real estate transaction. **Escrow** occurs from the moment of an executed purchase agreement to the closing of the transaction. **Closing** is the culmination of the real estate transaction. The terms and obligations of escrow and closing are stated in the purchase agreement, and applicable supplements or amendments.

In escrow, parties must perform certain conditions before they are able to close the transaction. Conditions are generally determined by the seller, the buyer, and the buyer's lender that is financing the purchase. Escrow may be conducted by a broker, escrow company, or other qualified agent. An **escrow agent** holds property in trust as a neutral third party until contractual conditions are fulfilled; the escrow agent bears fiduciary responsibility to both involved parties.

Closing occurs when the seller and the buyer have satisfied all the conditions of the purchase agreement, as well as the lender's ancillary requirements. A **closing statement** is completed to show the transference of money between the parties. The statement shows the money in the form of debit and credits of value to the parties. A credit is anything that shows an increase in value to a party, and a debit is anything that shows a decrease in value to a party. A credit or debit to the buyer would fluctuate the final amount the buyer must produce at closing.

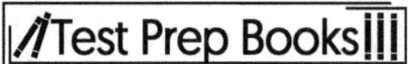

The buyer pays **closing costs,** unless other arrangements have been made (such as by concession from the seller). Closing costs include title insurance, origination fees, inspection fees, recording fee, flood certification, and other one-time costs. While it is difficult to estimate closing costs, they normally range between two and five percent of the property value. While a seller must also pay costs at closing, their payments (agent commissions, transfer taxes, etc.) are deducted from the proceeds of the sale.

Depending on the jurisdiction and the parties involved, taxes may be prepaid or paid in arrears. Prepayments (payments for something that will be used, such as rent) are prorated. Security deposits may be transferred in the name of the owner, but the amount is not prorated. Certain matters within the closing statement must show a proration in amount to accommodate the transfer of ownership and obligations of the parties and to ensure that each party is properly paying their portion of the obligations.

At closing, escrow concludes and the seller is paid sale proceeds in exchange for the buyer receiving physical possession and, often, the keys to the property.

Recording refers to the process of placing documents into public record. The purpose of recording is to give legal notice and protect interests within certain properties. Recording also may help establish priority. Priority determines who has superior claim to a certain property. Priority issues generally arise when a property was conveyed by a deed but the deed wasn't recorded and the same property was subsequently sold to another individual, or in security and foreclosure matters.

State laws regulate recording specifics, but they generally require a document to include: (1) execution by grantors; (2) date of execution; and (3) signatures of appropriate parties, depending on the document. Most jurisdictions also require notarized signatures, to ensure that the appropriate competent party signed the document and was not subject to duress.

Tax Aspects

Owning real property may affect a person's taxes. For income purposes, **capital gain** is the gain that is realized from the sale of a capital asset. Gain is the amount in difference that is between the original purchase price and the increased sales price of the asset. Taxing occurs on capital gains when the asset is sold. The amount difference is referred to as a capital gain or capital loss depending on whether the asset was sold for more or less than its original purchase price; higher will create a gain, lower will create a loss.

Example: B buys 10 shares of XYZ-stock for $10/stock, then subsequently sells each share for $13. B's capital gain is $30.

Special statutes may state that an owner does not have to be taxed on a gain realized, however it is best to speak with the proper professional to verify qualification. An example stipulation may be that within a five-year duration, the owner must have lived on the property as the primary residence for at least two years (regardless of whether it was consecutive).

An investment property may enter a tax deferral transaction known as a **§1031 exchange**. This is not a tax avoidance transaction, but a transaction that allows taxes to be paid at a later time rather than upon the sale of an investment property. It allows the property owner to sell the investment property, buy another, and put what would have been capital gains into the other property. The owner does not sell the property to realize the income, but to relocate the capital built within the first investment property.

The §1031 exchange can be very complicated and is subject to various regulations that determine how the transaction must be completed.

Some payments towards real property can be deductible. For legal purposes, a deductible is an expense that may be subtracted from a person's tax liability to reduce the amount owed. Deductibles may include property taxes, mortgage interest, and qualifying loan fees. Non-deductibles include principal payment, insurance premiums, and homeowners' association fees. The taxpayer/owner must utilize a tax return to qualify for a deduction.

Depreciation in an investment property's value allows for a deduction. However, tax depreciation can be a disadvantage when a property is sold and income is realized. For tax purposes, depreciation is treated like an expense and can only be applied to the building not the land itself. Depreciation may be calculated under a method called straight line depreciation. The depreciation amount is determined by dividing the difference between an asset's cost and its expected residual value by the number of years of the asset's expected life. Under straight line depreciation, residential income property must be depreciated over a 27.5. year period. However, commercial income property must be depreciated over a 39-year period. This depreciation method requires that property be depreciated by equal amounts over the period of its economic life.

$$Depreciation\ amount\ =\ Value\ \div\ Years\ being\ depreciated\ x\ Years\ used$$

Example question: A building that is valued at $420,000 is being depreciated over 39 years. After 12 years, how much will the building have depreciated?

Step 1: Determine value per year: $420,000 ÷ 39 years = $10,769.23

Step 2: Determine depreciation amount at desired time: $10,769.23 × 12 years = $129,230.77

Special Processes

A property may be conveyed to another after an owner's death, depending on whether the deceased died testate or intestate. Probate is a judicial process that is organized to compile all of the deceased's assets, funds, and liabilities and to pay out liabilities that the deceased was subject to. An administrator or executor is appointed on behalf of the deceased and completes these matters. If the owner died **testate** (with a will), the will must be presented within the probate proceeding and personal and real property shall be distributed. As stated previously, joint tenants do not go through this process because the deceased no longer has an interest in the property, and the probate is an accumulation of all the owner's interest. Under the right of survivorship, once the deceased passes, the interest was received by the other joint tenant(s).

There are different methods of transferring interest in a deceased's property: (1) devise and (2) bequest. **Devise** is the term used for when real property is conveyed under the terms of a will. Example: "In my grandparent's will, they devise the property to my parents." **Bequest** is the term used for when personal property is transferred under the terms of a will and may be shown under a bill of sale depending on whether it was a gift or of a sale of property.

If the owner died **intestate** (without a will), intestate laws of the jurisdiction will apply in determining proper heir(s) and which heir shall receive the personal and real property. These vary among jurisdictions.

Property interests may be acquired by nonowners by **involuntary alienation** (unconsented transfer) due to (1) adverse possession and (2) prescriptive easement (easement by prescription). **Adverse possession** is ownership acquired by a nonowner for the open, continuous, actual, notorious (hostile), and exclusive possession of the owner's property for the required statutory period (state law determines the duration). **Prescriptive easement** is an easement acquired by a nonowner due to open, continuous, actual, and notorious (hostile) use of the owner's land for the required statutory period; this does not require exclusive possession. Basically, if the nonowner obviously uses the land as if it belonged to them and the owner does nothing about it for years, then the court may grant interest in the property to the nonowner.

Foreclosure

When a borrower defaults on a mortgage, the lender has two options: collect the debt as promised by the borrower or foreclose on the mortgage. Once a borrower has missed a payment, the pre-foreclosure period begins. After 120 days of non-payment, the foreclosure process can begin; this involves several steps:

- **Redemption**: the opportunity for the borrower to redeem the property back from the lender.
    - **Equity of redemption** (prior to foreclosure sale): The borrower pays off the mortgage loan in full, plus interest and expenses that have accrued as a result of failing to pay within the established time frame and terms of the contract. This is the last chance for the borrower to retain the property.
    - **Right of redemption** (after foreclosure sale), which is not available in all states, allows the borrower a window of time to pay the lender the balance of the loan plus interest and expenses.
- **Title taken by lender**: In judicial foreclosure states, the lender will file a lawsuit asking the court for the right to sell the home and apply the proceeds to the debt. In non-judicial foreclosure states, the lender does not have to go through the court system to foreclose on the home, so it may go through the process more quickly. The borrower will get a notice of default that establishes a specified time frame to catch up on the loan before sale proceedings begin. If the borrower does not catch up on payments, the lender will sell the home at auction. In either case, the borrower will need to vacate the property once it is sold, or eviction proceedings will begin.
- **Deficiency judgment**: In some states, the lender is allowed to ask the court for a deficiency judgment, which would make the borrower responsible for any outstanding balance still remaining on the loan after the foreclosure sale.

In a **short sale**, a property owner sells their property for a lower price than the amount due on the property's mortgage. The mortgage lender must approve the decision to pursue a short sale, and all proceeds from a short sale go to the lender, not the seller. A primary motivation for a seller to pursue a short sale is that the long-term financial consequences are not as harmful as foreclosure; the seller's credit score is negatively impacted, but not to the extent of a foreclosure. The remaining balance to the lender not covered by the short sale may be forgiven, but the lender may still require repayment of the outstanding balance.

Real estate owned (REO) is a property owned by a lender or the government after the property failed to sell at a foreclosure auction. The lender will retain ownership until the property can be sold at a price that meets the lender's satisfaction.

Practice Quiz

1. Which legal document transfers title of real state from one person to another?
    a. Deed
    b. Promissory note
    c. Reversion
    d. Plat

2. Which of the following may NOT be required in a deed?
    a. Legal description
    b. Words of conveyance
    c. Common address
    d. Identification of the grantor and grantee

3. Which deed contains six covenants regarding prior and current title?
    a. Quitclaim deed
    b. Warranty deed
    c. Specialty deed
    d. Legal deed

4. Richard gives Samar a warranty deed. This deed contains covenants regarding title. Which of the following is not an applicable covenant?
    a. Covenant seisin
    b. Covenant of right to convey
    c. Covenant of intentions
    d. Covenants of further assurances

5. Tiffany gives Ursula title that is free of reasonable doubts or a threat of litigation. What is this called?
    a. Easement
    b. Concurrent tenancy
    c. Remainder
    d. Marketable title

See answers on the next page.

Answer Explanations

1. A: Choice *A* is correct because a deed is a legal document that transfers title of property. Choice *B* is incorrect because a promissory note is a legal document between the lender and the buyer regarding the financing of a purchase. Choice *C* is incorrect because a reversion is a property interest, not a document. Choice *D* is incorrect because a plat is a document used for legal descriptions.

2. C: Choice *C* is correct because a common address is not required to be in a deed because it states where the property is approximately located. Choice *A* is incorrect because a legal description will state a property's location and the extent of its boundaries. Choice *B* is incorrect because words of conveyance are necessary to show the intent of the grantor to convey the property. Choice *D* is incorrect because identification of the grantor and grantee are necessary to show who holds interests in the property.

3. B: Choice *B* is correct because a warranty deed contains the six covenants to title. Choice *A* is incorrect because a quitclaim deed does not make promises regarding title. Choice *C* is incorrect because a specialty deed does not cover title prior to the current owner's ownership. Choice *D* is incorrect because this is not a deed type.

4. C: Choice *C* is correct because it is a not a title covenant. Choices *A, B, D* are incorrect because these are covenants of title within a warranty deed.

5. D: Choice *D* is correct because marketable title is title that is free of reasonable doubts or a threat of litigation. Choice *A* is incorrect because an easement is a right to use another's land. Choice *B* is incorrect because concurrent tenancy is ownership granted to two or more people at the same time. Choice *C* is incorrect because remainder is a future interest in property.

Practice of Real Estate

Trust/Escrow Accounts

Often associated with monetary wealth, trust funds and accounts may also contain property, businesses, and stock. Trusts established between friends and family members work a bit like time capsules. The person who establishes the trust allocates specific assets to it. This person – the maker of the trust – determines when the trust matures and under what conditions the recipient will receive the assets held in the trust. Personal or familial trusts present opportunities to pass wealth and assets between friends and family members.

Real estate agencies, law firms, and other companies also utilize trust accounts to facilitate the process of buying and selling property. Potential buyers often pass earnest money to a real estate agency or other company, and real estate agencies or other companies often store earnest money in trust accounts. Essentially, earnest money acts as a deposit on a home or other piece of property. While an earnest payment may not compel a potential buyer to ultimately purchase the property, it does compel the real estate agency, or seller, to remove the property from public property listing channels.

There are plenty of reasons why a potential buyer would not complete the purchase of a home or piece of property after he or she transferred an earnest transfer payment to the trust account of a real estate agency or company. Most of these reasons have to do with the results of a property inspection or appraisal. When home inspections or appraisals produce different estimates than expected, buyers may back out of purchases and recoup the amount from their earnest payment.

Essentially, earnest payments jump-start the process of buying or selling a piece of property. Earnest payments correspond to a percentage of the cost of purchasing a piece of property. In other words, the cost of the property determines an appropriate amount for an earnest payment. Typically, an earnest payment comes out to less than 10 percent of the total cost of the property. Potential buyers should never make these payments to the seller directly. Both the buyer and the seller should work with a third-party institution that is adept at handling earnest payments.

Third-party institutions help protect buyers and sellers from illegal practices related to commingling and conversion. Essentially, commingling occurs when money holders mix funds together. Commingling constitutes a legal practice when several investors pool their money to invest in a property that none of them could afford on their own. To do this, multiple investors typically use specific types of trusts, often known as Real Estate Investment Trusts (REIT). Commingling constitutes an illegal practice when, say, a seller of a piece of property deposits money intended for an escrow account into their own personal checking account. In this scenario, conversion would occur if that same seller took the money that was intended as an earnest money payment and used it to pay for renovations, fixes, or any purpose other than for what the money was intended.

Federal Housing Laws

Under the Civil Rights Act of 1968, the protections of civil rights were expanded in the housing market. The Civil Rights Act of 1968 prohibited discrimination of **protected classes** of race, religion, national origin, and sex. Titles VIII and IX of this act is often referred to as the Fair Housing Act of 1968. The act applies protections to persons that are renting or buying a housing property, obtaining financing or

Practice of Real Estate

mortgage, pursuing housing assistance (such as broker services), and other housing related activities. The act applies to most housing but has limited exceptions.

There are four exceptions when the act does not apply to a housing property: (1) a building has no more than four units and the owner occupies one of the units; (2) an owner of a single-family house is selling or renting their property, without the use of a real estate licensee; (3) a religious organization operates housing occupancy for its members; and (4) a club provides housing occupancy for its members.

According to the U.S. Department of Housing and Urban Development, the following practices may not be conducted when the basis for the conduct is discrimination against the protected classes:

- Refuse to rent or sell housing
- Refuse to negotiate for housing
- Make housing unavailable
- Set different terms, conditions, or privileges for sale or rental of a dwelling (place of residence)
- Provide different housing services or facilities, or limit services or facilities
- Falsely deny that housing is available for inspection, sale, or rental
- Make, print, or publish any notice, statement, or advertisement with respect to the sale or rental of a dwelling that indicates any preference, limitation, or discrimination
- Impose different sales price or rental charge for the sale or rental of a dwelling
- Use different qualification criteria or applications, or sale or rental standards or procedures, such as income standards, application requirements, application fees, credit analyses, sale or rental approval procedures, or other requirements
- Evict a tenant or a tenant's guest
- Harass a person
- Fail or delay performance of maintenance or repairs on the property
- Discourage the purchase or rental of a dwelling
- Assign a person to a particular building or neighborhood (or area)
- For profit, persuade, or try to persuade, homeowners to sell their homes by suggesting that people of a particular protected class are about to move into the neighborhood (blockbusting)

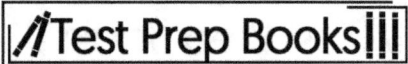

- Refuse to provide or discriminate in the terms or conditions of homeowners insurance to the owner and/or occupants of a dwelling

- Deny access to or membership in any multiple listing service or real estate brokers' organization

U.S. Dept. of Housing and Urban Development.
https://www.hud.gov/program_offices/fair_housing_equal_opp/fair_housing_act_overview

Fair lending laws also provide protections for the protected classes when attempting to secure mortgage financing for a property. The U.S. Department of Housing and Urban Development provides the following prohibited (and illegal) practices:

- Refuse to make a mortgage loan or provide other financial assistance for a dwelling;

- Refuse to provide information regarding loans;

- Impose different terms or conditions on a loan, such as different interest rates, points, or fees;

- Discriminate in appraising a dwelling;

- Condition the availability of a loan on a person's response to harassment; and

- Refuse to purchase a loan.

- The act also protects the classes from harassment based on their classification, and additionally it forbids sexual harassment. Other practices prohibited under this act include:

- Threaten, coerce, intimidate, or interfere with anyone exercising a fair housing right or assisting others who exercise the right; or

- Retaliate against a person who has filed a fair housing complaint or assisted in a fair housing investigation.

Amendment to Fair Housing

In 1988, the **Fair Housing Amendments Act (FHAA)** expanded the protections previously listed by its predecessor, the Fair Housing Act of 1968. The expansion included two new protected classes under fair housing laws to prohibit the discrimination based on handicap (disability) and familial status. The purpose of the expansion was to increase housing opportunities for people with disabilities and families with children under 18 years of age. Someone with a handicap condition was defined as any person who actually has a physical or mental impairment, has a record of having such an impairment, or is regarded as having such an impairment that substantially limits one or more major life activities such as hearing, seeing, speaking, breathing, performing manual tasks, walking, caring for oneself, learning, or working.

Under the FHAA, reasonable accommodations are required to make existing housing more accessible to persons with disabilities. A **reasonable accommodation** is an accommodation that is requested by a qualified protected person that seeks a property modification for their known physical or mental limitation. However, for the accommodation to be reasonable, it cannot impose an undue hardship on the housing provider. An undue hardship would be one that would require the housing provider to take on a substantial cost or obligation to meet the requested accommodation.

Reasonable structural modifications must be permitted if the modification is necessary for a person with a disability to be able to live in and use the property. The qualified person has the obligation for covering the cost of the modification. Modifications may be made to the interior of unit or property or common areas within a building. Common areas include such things as lobbies, hallways, recreational rooms, laundry rooms, etc.

In a lease situation, the landlord may place limitations on the accommodations that the landlord will provide. Such limitations include the renter restoring interior unit to the condition it was in before the accommodation (excluding normal wear and tear), providing a description of the proposed arrangements, and a guarantee that they be completed well and have all the necessary building permits.

In addition to structural modifications, the housing provider must make reasonable modifications in rules, policies, practices, or services necessary to allow a qualified person equal opportunity to use and enjoy the dwelling. For example, if a matter is regulated by a homeowner's association or landlord and the qualified person is unable to fulfill the obligations set under its regulation, they must be permitted a reasonable accommodation. Other examples include:

- Allowing a blind tenant to have a guide dog in a building that does not allow pets;

- Reserving a parking space for a mobility impaired tenant, and one that is closer to building entrance; or

- Allowing an aide access to common areas that would ordinarily require that they be accompanied by a tenant, such as a laundry room.

Familial Status

The fair housing laws prohibit housing discrimination against families that have children under the age of 18. The laws prohibit denial of housing to these families and prevent any special requirements or conditions being imposed on tenants that have custody of children. According to the U.S. Department of Justice, some prohibited practices include, but are not limited to:

- Locate families with children in a particular area a building or property;

- Place an unreasonable restriction on the number of persons that may reside in a dwelling; or

- Limit access to recreational services that are available to other tenants.

U.S. Dept. of Justice. https://www.justice.gov/crt/fair-housing-act-1

Generally, fair housing laws prohibit a housing provider from refusing to lease or sell to families that have children. However, the protections have limitations and cannot be applied to all properties. Some housing facilities are special designations that allow discrimination based on familial status, such as housing designated for persons 55 years old or older. These properties may operate as "senior housing." Housing properties like this meet standards set out under other applicable laws that govern the housing for persons that meet the age requirement. The Department of Housing and Urban Development has published regulations and guidelines regarding senior housing classification.

Segregating Families

Fair housing laws do not permit segregation of persons based on familial status (or based on other protected classes). The practice of **steering** occurs when a housing provider influences a potential home buyer or residential renter to purchase or rent certain property by limiting the potential buyer or renter's choice. Fair housing laws prohibit steering of families with children under the age of 18. Additionally, housing providers may not segregate residents (or potential residents) based on familial status. It has been concluded that Congress intended the fair housing laws to prohibit housing providers not only from totally excluding families with children, but also from: (1) steering families with children to housing outside a complex or only to certain dwellings in a complex and (2) taking into consideration the presence of minor children under or over a certain age in the family in determining which unit to offer such a subclass of families with children when more than one unit is available, or steering or excluding such families from the complex.

Steering is not an exclusive practice regarding familial status but is applicable to steering potential home buyers or residential renters based on any of the protected classes under fair housing laws.

Advertising, Fraud, and Technology Issues

Puffing
Puffing is a term used for making a statement that presents something as more marketable or appealing than it actually is but cannot be objectively determined; it is not a factual statement about the property. For example, a broker can puff by saying "This is the best house on the market." Although puffing may be misleading at times, it does not concern factual statements and does not constitute a statement of misrepresentation.

Truth in Advertising
Real estate agents receive a license to practice. As with any licensed professional, the privilege to practice real estate is contingent upon a real estate agent's ability to perform their duties ethically according to best business practices. False advertising is a surefire way to have a real estate license revoked.

False advertising typically falls within two broad categories: uninformed misrepresentation and deliberate misrepresentation. To avoid uninformed misrepresentation of advertised property, real estate agents should never make any verbal or written claims about a property that they cannot substantiate. Incompetence or ignorance is not a hall pass for dodging real estate fraud. Like all professionals, the law holds real estate agents to certain standards. The law may still hold real estate agents accountable for inaccurate statements, even if lack of experience or ignorance caused a real estate agent to make a false claim. Likewise, the law holds real estate agents accountable for withholding information, even if a real estate agent left information out of an advertisement because he or she didn't know the information was important.

Fair Housing Issues in Advertising
Issues unrelated to fraud may also compromise a real estate agent's status and position. Fair Housing laws prohibit real estate agents from focusing on or appealing to one group or demographic in advertisements. For example, real estate agents should avoid language that specifically calls on "young singles" to apply for pre-approval rates. Regardless of intention, this is a form of discrimination that implicitly excludes any individual who does not identify with the terms used in the advertisement.

Practice of Real Estate

In recent years, technology has introduced new issues around Fair Housing laws. When advertising online, real estate agents should ensure that they do not use filters that exclude individuals from specific demographics or locations. Real estate agents should strive to make their online advertisements readily accessible to everyone.

Broker Responsibilities

The term "broker" is often used interchangeably with "agent" and "realtor," as well as "broker-in-charge." Technically, the definition for each is slightly different. A **real estate agent** has the required qualifications (age, citizenship, background check, education, and testing) established by the state to facilitate the sale and purchase of property on behalf of others. A **real estate broker** has gone further with the education process and has earned a broker license; brokers can also work for themselves, as opposed to hanging their licenses under larger brokerage firms. Some states mandate that all agents become brokers before practicing real estate at all, and other states establish a waiting period of several years before real estate agents are allowed to apply for a broker license. A **realtor** is an agent or broker who has joined the National Association of Realtors (NAR). All realtors must subscribe to the NAR's strict code of ethics.

A **broker-in-charge (BIC)** is a broker who has legally established a brokerage firm and has real estate agents working on their behalf in that brokerage. Real estate agents can work for only one BIC at any given time within a state. There is only one BIC per office, but there may be associate brokers who handle various aspects of the brokerage business. The same person can be BIC at several office locations for a single brokerage firm. The BIC alone is legally responsible for the actions of the licensees in the brokerage office and for the management of all the brokerage trust accounts. More specifically, the BIC must do the following:

- Adequately supervise the real estate licensees in the brokerage. This includes providing regular guidance and training, as well as providing the tools and technology promised to the licensee at the time of recruitment and hire. The BIC must be readily available, or have a designated broker available, to answer questions within a reasonable time frame. Adequate supervision also includes ensuring that all licensees maintain active real estate licenses.

- Review all contract and disclosure forms in use by the brokerage and approve or edit as needed.

- Make themselves available to the public during regular business hours to support the efforts of their licensees. The BIC should be prepared to discuss details of transactions with clients and to resolve complaints or disputes that may arise during a transaction that involves an affiliated licensee.

- Create and maintain a written office policy that is readily available to every licensee, both at the time of joining the brokerage and after.

- Oversee the brokerage trust account, if needed. Not all brokerages accept responsibility for earnest money anymore, instead entrusting that responsibility to local attorneys.

Compensation of Real Estate Agents

Real estate licensees negotiate compensation with clients by using the agency agreements. In most cases, the commission is established and paid from the seller side, and the listing agent shares the commission with the selling agent. There is no standard compensation or fee schedule. Any compensation earned by the licensee is paid to the licensee's brokerage, which then passes on the adjusted compensation to the licensee. No licensee should be paid directly by a principal.

Additionally, if a licensee receives compensation from more than one source (that is, commission from sale plus a bonus), this should be communicated to the client and consented to in writing at the time the contract is signed. Only licensed agents should be compensated for a real estate transaction; no unlicensed individual should ever be compensated by a real estate brokerage.

Procuring cause refers to an agent's right to a commission as the primary actor whose actions resulted in the sale. In some cases, disputes can arise as to which agent is owed commission; procuring cause disputes are often resolved through arbitration but can be decided in court.

A **protection clause** guarantees the broker or agent a commission even if the property listing expires or is canceled. This ensures that the broker is still compensated for their diligence even if a buyer or seller attempts to buy or sell without them; this protects the agent from fraud and collusion.

There are several compensation options available to licensees:

- **Brokerage fee**. This is the most common practice, and the most straightforward. The licensee is paid the negotiated commission through the proceeds of the closed transaction. The seller, in practice, contributes the entire commission out of their earnings from the sale, which is divided between the agents representing the principals in the transaction. The division of the commission is established in the listing agreement, and the monies are sent by the closing attorney/title company to the respective brokerages for disbursement to the individual licensees. It is possible for the commission to be negotiated in such a way for the seller to provide only part of the commission; this would require the remainder to be paid by the buyer if such a structure were agreed to in the signed buyer's agency agreement.

- **Retainer fee**. This is a fee paid by the buyer to the brokerage upon signing the agency agreement. This fee is non-refundable, and it may (or may not) be put toward the brokerage fee in the event of a closed sale.

- **Service fee**. This is a fee paid by the buyer to the brokerage upon signing the agency agreement. This fee could be applied in several ways. The licensee could negotiate for this to be the *only* fee due from the buyer in the transaction; the licensee could request this fee on top of any brokerage fee they might receive from a closed sale; or the licensee could stipulate that it would be non-refundable but applied toward the brokerage fee in a closed sale.

- **Referral fee**. This is a fee that is earned by referring a client to another agent (the receiving agent) to service during a particular transaction. The agent who receives the referral fee should not participate in the transaction once it has been referred. Upon completion of the transaction, the receiving agent's brokerage will compensate the referring agent's brokerage with the agreed-upon fee (flat fee or percentage of earned commission), which will then be distributed to the referral agent according to the terms that the brokerage has established for its agents. (Note: Some agents have placed their licenses in referral status and hold them in a referral brokerage. This means that they have active licenses and are able to be paid from a real estate transaction, but they may not provide any client services or have access to the MLS. This means that they should not be offering real estate advice, showing properties, or writing offers, among other things.)

General Ethics

Real estate brokers may represent themselves as individual entities separate from other institutions, or they may form an agency. Real estate agencies typically include at least one broker, and several real estate agents work with the broker to represent clients. Brokers and agents have specific areas of expertise and competency within real estate, and they may face disciplinary action if they diverge from their specific areas of competency.

Since real estate agents and brokers work on commission, the temptation to take on more than one can chew is profound. In the long run, agents and brokers save more time and money by only handling accounts for properties that they understand and that they are licensed to facilitate. Real estate commissions, the governing and supervising bodies that license brokers and agents to operate in a particular state, determine when disciplinary action is taken against a broker or agent.

Policies and procedures vary from state to state since every state has its own real estate commission, but real estate agents across the country can rely on several general guidelines. How an agent or broker handles an account outside of their area of competency matters. As a rule, brokers and agents are advised to decline engagement for accounts outside of their areas of competency. That said, agents are not compelled to decline engagement on such accounts, and their engagement does not necessarily leave them vulnerable to disciplinary action. An agent who operates outside of their area of competency may avoid disciplinary action by gaining competency in the area that he or she has decided to engage, or by seeking guidance or partnership with a supervising or qualified broker or agent.

It should also be noted that agents and brokers must remain vigilant to avoid unauthorized practice of law. Giving legal advice outside of their authorized role may be tempting, as agents and brokers amass a mass of pertinent knowledge throughout their careers, but acting outside of their licensed practice can have severe ramifications. Agents and brokers must advise clients to consult a lawyer for matters outside of their specific practice of real estate.

Antitrust Laws

Antitrust laws attempt to encourage competition in the marketplace by regulating the power of businesses. In addition to general provisions against monopolies, antitrust laws also prevent agreements between separate organizations where such collusion would illegally concentrate power and resources and stifle freedom of choice. The **Sherman Antitrust Act** was passed by Congress in 1890 in an effort to ensure "healthy and free market competition." The law prohibits four practices:

- **Price fixing**: This occurs when there is collusion among brokerages related to commissions or fees. There can be no "standard" commission rate. Agents are prohibited from even casually discussing fees with agents from competing brokerages; the simple act of comparing notes is considered illegal under this law.

- **Group boycotting**: This occurs when two or more brokerages agree not to support a third party.

- **Market allocation**: This is the practice of dividing customers using an established metric (by zip code, street boundaries, and so on). This practice removes the ability of customers to have true freedom of choice when selecting an agent or property manager.

- **Tie-in**: This is the practice of conditioning one transaction on the fulfillment of another. For instance, if a brokerage has a parcel of land for sale and a builder wants to buy it, the brokerage will not be able to condition that sale on the builder's guarantee to list their future new homes with that same brokerage.

Practice Quiz

1. Under fair housing laws, which of the following is NOT a protected class?
   a. Race
   b. Religion
   c. Occupation
   d. Familial status

2. Which statute expanded civil rights into the housing market?
   a. Civil Rights Act of 1968
   b. Protected Persons Act of 1963
   c. Civil Rights Act of 1958
   d. Fair Housing Act of 1966

3. Who must abide by fair housing laws?
   a. A lender
   b. A broker
   c. A property leasing agent
   d. All of the above

4. A local church provides housing for its members. Who may the church decline to rent housing to?
   a. A person from a foreign nation
   b. A married couple with three children
   c. A single man with two children
   d. All of the above

5. Which of the following is a prohibited act under the Civil Rights Act of 1968?
   a. Puffing
   b. Zoning
   c. Harassment
   d. Escheat

See answers on the next page.

Answer Explanations

1. C: Choice C is correct because fair housing laws do not prohibit discrimination based on a person's occupation. Choices A, B, and D are protected classes under fair housing laws and may not be discriminated against.

2. A: Choice A is correct because the Civil Rights Act of 1968 expanded civil rights into the housing market. Choices B, C, and D are incorrect because these are not real statutes.

3. D: Choice D is correct because all the listed persons, as providers of housing services, must abide by fair housing laws. Choices A, B, and C are incorrect because all listed persons must abide by fair housing laws.

4. D: Choice D is correct because a church that is providing housing for its members may discriminate under fair housing laws. Choices A, B, and C are incorrect because the church may discriminate when providing housing for its own members, even if a person would generally be considered a member of a protected class under fair housing laws.

5. C: Choice C is correct because harassment is not permitted under the Civil Rights Act of 1968. Choice A is incorrect because this is not listed under the act. Chase B is incorrect because this is a police power that is permitted and is not related to the act. Choice D is incorrect because escheat is the process of the state acquiring the real property of a deceased.

Real Estate Calculations

Decimal and Fractions

A **fraction** is a numerical expression, such as 2/3 or 0.666. Each number represents a part of a whole. A decimal fraction is an expression that allows for real estate calculations to be determined, like .64 or 0.64. To convert a fraction into a decimal fraction, the numerator (top number) is divided by the denominator (bottom number). Fractions are converted into decimal fractions because computers and calculators generally recognize common fractions. Some fractions may also be further simplified, if need be.

As an example, 3/8 can be converted into a decimal by taking $3 \div 8 = 0.375$. On a calculator/computer, this number is shown either as .375 or 0.375.

Decimals are especially relevant when determining prorations (discussed above under Transfer of Title) or when calculating a value for a specific time.

Additionally, it is common for decimals to be rounded to the nearest hundredth for calculations. Different exams (and jurisdictions) may use different principles of calculations. It is possible that rounding numbers may create a calculating error and affect the final answer. However, for the purposes of an exam, guidance may be given for how calculation problems should be approached. The best practice is to pick the answer option that is closest to the calculated answer. Generally, a testing site will supply the necessary tools for calculation.

Percentages

Percentage is a portion of a whole number expressed in hundredths. A decimal may be converted into a percentage, and vice versa. If a number is in percentage form, removing the percent sign (%) and dividing by 100 converts the percentage into a decimal form. However, a decimal may be converted into a percentage by multiplying the number by 100 and adding a percent sign.

$$32.7\% \rightarrow \frac{32.7}{100} = 0.327$$

$$345\% \rightarrow \frac{345}{100} = 3.45$$

$$0.327 \times 100 = 32.7\%$$

$$3.45 \times 100 = 345\%$$

However, this may also be completed by removing (or adding) the percent sign and moving the decimal two spaces. To convert a percentage to a decimal, move the decimal two spaces to the left. To convert a decimal to a percentage, move the decimal two spaces to the right.

For PSI Real Estate testing centers that provide a calculator (or similar computer feature), some may have a % button that may be used. Be mindful that using the % button does not function the same way on all calculators. It is best to make conversions with the above information to reduce the likelihood of calculating errors in the final answer. This may be an issue when a problem requires multiple steps and the % button is being used repeatedly. In this case, each calculation compounds previous errors and strays farther from the correct answer. This may lead to picking the wrong answer choice.

Area Calculation (Lots, Buildings)

In real estate, it is common to calculate lot and building areas. However, lot and building area calculations may be complicated. It is best to allow a professional land surveyor or appraiser to determine these calculations. For test purposes, most lots will be square or rectangle in shape.

Lots are generally measured in feet, with the symbol ', as in 3' = 3 feet. Therefore, lot area—the area inside the lot—will be in the form of square feet. A square foot is 1' in length and 1' in width. Length and width refer to sides of a square or rectangle and length is generally the longer side of the rectangle. **Frontage** may refer to a land parcel that lies adjacent to a body of water or a street. It can also refer to portion of land that is in front of a building, and sometimes refers to front of a building. Generally, frontage is the first measurement that is used in describing dimensions of a lot. If a lot is noted as 85'x170', it can usually be assumed that the frontage measures 85' and the length between the front and back property boundary is 170'.

Square and rectangle area calculations: $Width \times Length = Area$

Example: $3 \text{ ft} \times 5 \text{ ft} = 15 \text{ ft}^2$

Generally, the area within a building, or floor area, is determined by the measurements of the building's exterior. At times this can be complicated, because some buildings are curved on one side and not square or rectangular in shape. Different jurisdictions and markets have different industry customs on how to calculate building areas, such as a garage or basement. Learning these industry customs will come from actual job experience within a market. For testing purposes, property areas are generally square or rectangular. When there is a matter of multi-level building, add each area to get the total area amount for the building. For testing purposes, the area is likely the same as it was on the first level. However, additional calculations may be given.

Circle Formulas

In real estate calculations, there are generally three variables involved in a formula or calculation. If two of the variables are known, then it is possible to calculate for the missing variable that is being asked in a question. As shown below, every calculation can have an inverted calculation to solve for the other variables.

Calculation: $Length \times Width = \boldsymbol{Area}$

Inverted calculation: $\frac{Area}{Width} = \boldsymbol{Length}$ OR $\frac{Area}{Length} = \boldsymbol{Width}$

Example question: For a lot that has a frontage of 35 ft and an area of 2,450 ft², what is the length of the lot?

$$\frac{2,450 \text{ ft}^2 \ (area)}{35 \text{ ft} \ (width)} = 70 \text{ ft} \ (length)$$

Real Estate Calculations

Other Variable Calculations

- If $A + B = C$, then $C - A = B$ and $C - B = A$.
- If $A \div B = C$, then $C \times A = B$ and $C \times B = A$.

Price per Square Foot

Appraisers compare evaluated properties by price per square foot. Depending on the market, a buyer or a seller may be concerned with the price per square footage for a property.

Price for square footage calculation:

$$\frac{Selling\ price}{Area\ in\ square\ feet\ (of\ property)} = price\ per\ square\ foot$$

Example question: What is the price per square foot of a house that measures 40' x 45' that sold for $240,000?

Step 1: Determine Area:

$$40\ ft \times 45\ ft = 1{,}800\ ft^2$$

Step 2: Determine price per square footage:

$$\frac{\$240{,}000}{1{,}800\ ft^2} = \$133.33\ per\ ft^2$$

Additionally, the formula may be inverted to determine square footage or price of a property.

$$\frac{\$240{,}000}{\$133.33\ per\ ft^2} = 1{,}800\ ft^2$$

$$\$133.33\ per\ ft^2 \times 1{,}800\ ft^2 = \$239{,}994\ (or\ \$240{,}000)$$

Math portions on the exam are not stringent and are sometimes very simplified. If a calculation does not arrive at the same amount as an answer choice, it is best to double check your work. If the amount is not the same, then pick the amount that is closest to the calculated answer. Additionally, there can be a vast difference in amounts across answer choices, making it obvious which answer should be picked.

Lending and Mortgage Calculations

Lending and financing, much like real estate, have many terms to remember. Different words are used to describe different conditions on various loan types and matters.

Loan-to-value (LTV) ratio is a ratio (fraction) that relates the amount of the proposed loan to the property's value. This is generally in the form of a percentage. To determine loan to value ratio, a lender uses either the property's selling price or the property's appraised value. Between the two, they will use whichever value is lower. Loans with a loan to value ratio of 80% or less receive the best terms offered by the lender. If the loan makes up 80% of the property's value, then the down payment must make up the remaining 20%.

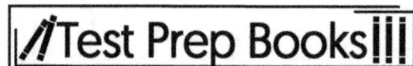

1) Calculation: $Loan \div Value \text{ (selling price or appraised value)} = $ **LTV ratio**

Inverted calculation: $LTV\ ratio \times Value\ \% = $ **Loan** $\%$ OR $LTV\ ratio \times Loan\ \% = $ **Value** $\%$

2) Calculation: $LTV\ ratio + Down\ payment\ \% = $ **100% Selling price** (*or appraised value*)

Inverted calculation: $100\% - Down\ payment\ \% = $ **LTV ratio** OR

$$100\% - LTV\ ratio = \textbf{Down Payment}\ \%$$

Equity is value that a person, or artificial person, holds in a property after the reduction of any liabilities that may be subject to the property, such as a lien. It shows how much liquidity an owner has in a property that is not subject to the mortgage obligation. A liability is an obligation that has yet to be discharged by full performance or satisfaction, such as a mortgage or a lien. A property that is 100% equity is a property that is clear of mortgages and liens and completely owned by the owner(s).

Calculation: $Value - Liabilities = $ **Equity**

Inverted calculation: $Value - Equity = $ **Liabilities** OR $Equity + Liabilities = $ **Value**

When originating (setting up) a loan, lenders may charge points to increase its income (yield). **Points** are determined by a loan amount, not a purchase price. Additionally, points maybe used to pre-pay a portion of the interest so that the interest rates may be reduced on the loan in the long term. However, this is done without reducing income expected to be derived from the loan. A point is equal to 1% of loan amount.

Calculation: $Loan\ amount \times 1\% = $ **Point**

Inverted calculation: $Point \div 1\% = $ **Loan amount** OR $Point \div Loan\ amount = $ **1%**

Loan factor charts are used to estimate loan payments for amortized loans among different loan terms and interest rates. A chart shows the dollar payment per $1000 for each combination of interest rates and loan terms. The payments represent an amount that is made up of principal and interest. These payments do not account for property taxes, insurance, HOA fees, or other durational property expenses.

Interest	15 years	20 years	25 years	30 years
6%	8.4386	7.1643	6.4430	5.9955
6.5%	8.7111	7.4557	6.7521	6.3207
7%	8.9883	7.7530	7.0678	6.6530
7.5%	9.2701	8.0559	7.3899	6.9921

Determine how many thousands of dollars ($loan\ amount \div 1,000$) make up the loan, then multiply it by the factor for the loan interest rate and loan term.

A **loan payment chart** is similar to a factors chart, but it is calculated for specific amounts at a range of interest rates and a loan's terms. The amounts in the chart are payments that are to be paid. Each chart only shows the specific loan amounts that are given in the chart title. The chart allows assistance to determine a proper loan qualification with the appropriate loan term and interest rate.

Real Estate Calculations

Loan interest calculations are formulated by an interest rate (generally an annual percentage), the principal (loan amount), and interest of the loan. Calculations for annual interest must be done with an annual rate to determine annual interest amount, but some calculations may use monthly interest and the monthly rate to determine a monthly payment. Generally, real estate loans are paid on a monthly basis. Therefore, **monthly installment** calculations for the entire loan are based on 1/12 of the year and 1/12 of the annual interest rate, not the days per a month. The lender computes the payments for 360 total payments for a 30-year loan and expects 12 payments per year. *Exam questions will generally require interest rates, so it is important to remember to divide the annual number by 12.*

Calculation: $Interest\ rate \times principal = $ **Annual interest amount**

$$\frac{Annual\ interest\ amount}{12} = Monthly\ installment$$

A real estate loan may have its initial payment include amounts to set aside to pay for things like property taxes and insurance. These may be referred to as PITI payments: principal, interest, taxes, and insurance. The lender collects the taxes and insurance payments in impound or escrow accounts and makes payments to the appropriate authorities or entities by the appropriate time.

When lenders decide whether to qualify a potential borrower for a loan, they often determine **buyer qualification ratios**. This percentage can be based on the applicant's debt-to-income ratio and housing expense ratio; the qualification ratios are an attempt to measure the likelihood that the borrower will be able to meet their repayment obligations. The **debt-to-income** ratio looks at a borrower's regular debt compared to their gross income. The **housing expense** ratio focuses more on the borrower's house-related expenses (such as mortgage principal and interest) compared to their gross income.

Property Tax

Property owners are liable for taxes that are levied to the property. An assessor, generally a county official, uses calculation methods to ascertain the value of a property within its county or jurisdiction. County officials and other entities determine their jurisdiction's budget based on the area's necessity for services and other expenses. The duty of the assessor is to distribute the tax burden among property owners. Taxing rates may be different depending on property type, whether it is residential, commercial, industrial, agriculture, or other.

After the assessor has determined the appraised value of a property, the appraised value is multiplied by the tax rate for the relevant property classification to determine the annual tax amount that will be levied against the property.

1) Calculation: $Appraised\ value \times assessment\ rate = $ **Assessed value**

Inverted calculation: $Assessed\ value \div Appraised\ value = $ **Assessment rate** OR

$$Assessed\ value \div Assessment\ rate = \textbf{Appraised value}$$

2) Calculation: $Assessed\ value \times Tax\ rate = $ **Annual tax amount**

Inverted calculation: $Annual\ tax\ amount \div Tax\ rate = $ **Assessed value** OR

$$Annual\ tax\ amount \div Assessed\ value = \textbf{Tax Rate}$$

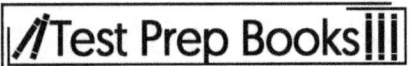

The tax rate is a fraction of the assessed value. It may be in the form of a percentage that is an amount charged for every $100 of the assessed value. Alternatively, it may be a **mill**, or an amount of tax per $1000 assessed value. If the tax rate is a whole number, such as 75 mill, it must be converted into a decimal expression for calculation by dividing by 1000 (because it is taxed per $1,000): 75 ÷ 1,000 = .075. If the tax rate is per $100 of the assessed value, then divide by 100 instead. Pay attention to decimal placing when dealing with hundredths and thousandths.

Tax calculations based on appraised (actual) value generally require two steps to reach the final answer: (1) determine assess value and (2) determine annual tax.

Example question: If an assessor has determined a property has an actual value of $250,000 and is subject to an assessment rate of 32% and the tax rate is 89 mills, what is the annual tax?

Step 1: $Actual\ value \times Assessment\ rate = $ **Assessed value**

$$\$250,000 \times 0.32 = \$80,000$$

Step 2: $Assessed\ value \times Mills = $ **Annual tax**

$$\$80,000 \times 0.089 = \$7,120\ \text{annual tax}$$

Proration

At closing, a settlement occurs between buyer and seller regarding expenses connected to the property. Such matters may include things like utility bills, HOA fees, and taxes. The purpose of the settlement is to allocate expenses to the current owner at the appropriate time. Example: a seller has prepaid HOA fees for the equivalent of a 3-month duration. However, 2 months into the 3-month expiration, the property is sold to a buyer. Under these conditions, the amount is prorated, the buyer will be debited one month, and the seller will be credited one month's portion of the prepaid fees.

When there is a debit or credit, there is a corresponding alternate credit or debit to the other party. The party that is responsible of the day of closing will generally be stated in effect and will need to pay that amount in full at closing.

Calculation: $Total\ amount \div Total\ time \times Time\ used = $ **Proration**

Example question: The seller has prepaid HOA fees in a 6-month duration. The prepayment amount was $1,000. At the end of the 5th month, the property was sold to the buyer. What is the prorated amount that will be debited to buyer?

Step 1: Determine the value per month.

$$\$1,000 \div 6\ \text{months} = \$166.67\ \text{per month}$$

Step 2: Determine the buyer's use.

$$\$166.67 \times 1 = \$166.67\ \text{proration}$$

Real Estate Calculations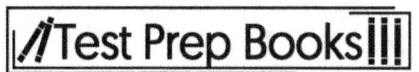

Commissions

Generally, the commission rate is a percentage of the selling price. It is common for the commission on the sale of a property to be 6%, paid by the seller: 3% will go to the listing agent (seller's agent) and 3% will go to the selling agent (buyer's agent).

There are industry customs regarding how much commission will be added to the sale of a property based on the value and selling price. However, commission rates are negotiable and can vary among different types of properties and different locations across the nation.

Calculation: *Selling price × Commission rate =* **Commission**

Inverted Calculation: *Commission ÷ selling price =* **Commission rate** OR

Commission ÷ Commission rate = **Sales price**

Example: $160,000 × 0.06 = $9,600 commission

Remember that total commission is split between listing agent and selling agent, 50/50. In this example, this means $4,800 per agent.

The net amount to the seller from the transaction may also be calculated from the same numbers.

Calculation: *Sales price × (100% − commission rate) =* **Net to seller**

Example: Using the same figures from the previous example

Step 1: Determine the net rate.

100% − 6% commission rate = 94% net rate

Step 2: Determine the net amount.

$160,000 sales price × 0.94% = $150,400

This could have also been determined by: *Sales price − Commission = Net amount*

Remember that total commission is split between listing agent and selling agent, 50/50. In this example, this means $4,800 per agent.

Commission Splits

Commission splits, or fee splits, refer to the allocation of a commission between a licensee and a sponsoring brokerage. These amounts are always negotiable between the company and the licensee. The two parties determine the total commission and agree on which party takes what amount. Commission splits vary among different brokerages. Some can be generous and allow the licensee to retain more of the commission. Other brokerages may require a greater amount than most, but these brokerages generally cover costs that the licensee would not have to incur, such as marketing, error and omissions insurance, continuing education, etc.

This fee split is a written agreement between the licensee and the sponsoring brokerage. Generally, it's common for a fee split to be 70/30% or 60/40%, with the greater amount going to the licensee.

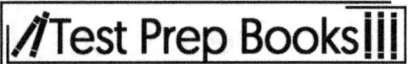

Another type of commission split that may occur is when two licensees under the same brokerage represent a party in a transaction and agree to split the fee, generally 50/50. However, this split does not occur until the brokerage has been paid its commission from the sale of the property.

Calculation: *Commission × Commission split rate = Licensee or brokerage commission*

Example: $4,800 × 0.7 commission split rate = $3,360 selling agent commission OR

$4,800 × 0.3 commission split rate = $1,440 brokerage commission

When there are two agents representing a party, the agent commission is further split after the brokerage is paid.

Calculation: *Commission split × Agent split rate = Agent commission*

Example: $3,360 × 0.5 agent split rate = $1,440 commission per agent

Appraisal and Valuation

Depreciation in an investment property's value allows for a deduction. However, depreciation can be a disadvantage when a property is sold and income is realized. For tax purposes, depreciation is treated like an expense and can only be applied to the building, not to the land itself. Straight line depreciation is a method of calculating depreciation. It is determined by calculating the asset's cost minus salvage value across the asset's economic life, or for the duration of time (generally years) that it may be used for its proper purpose. Depreciation refers to the income calculation and does not relate to the physical condition of the property, but the two may correlate. Additional information may be found in the Tax Aspects section in the chapter on Transfer of Title.

Comparative Market Analysis (CMA) may show the potential value of the property. It is determined by comparing the property to similar properties that have been recently sold in the area. However, retention of an appraisal is the best practice for determining the value of a property.

The CMA shows what a property is worth at a determined time. Due to fluctuations in the real estate market, prices continuously change. Property value may also change rapidly, therefore a CMA may only be valid for a few weeks.

Every property is going to be different. Because of the differences, a CMA will include any adjustments in the price of the property being evaluated (the subject property). The subject property will be evaluated against other similar properties. The adjustment allows for more accurate comparisons to determine a property's fair market value at a determined time. The accuracy of a CMA is contingent on the properties that are being compared to the subject property. *An exam may give you the value of certain features that may add or detract from your subject property to determine the approximate fair market value.*

When selecting comparable properties, it is best to pick properties that:

1. Were sold around the desired time frame of the CMA (and show the same or similar market conditions)

2. Are geographically close to the subject property (and show the same or similar market conditions)

Real Estate Calculations

3. Have the same or similar features of the subject property (such as the same number of beds, baths, or other features)

4. Have reasonable selling prices compared to similar properties (additional circumstances in a transaction may cause a substantially increased/decreased selling price)

Income approach to value is used for many income-producing properties because an owner or investor is interested in income derived from the property. **Capitalization** is the process of converting future net income into an estimate of value. Commercial property appraisers use this as a primary tool. The capitalization rate represents the income (yield) from an investment that an investor determines.

Example:

Potential Gross Income:	$70,000
−Debt (2.5%)	−$1,750
−Vacancy (4%)	−$2,800
Total/**Gross Income**:	$65,450
−Operating expenses	−28,600
Total/**Net Operating Income**:	$36,850

Once the net operating income is determined, subtracting the property's debt service (covering loan repayment) finds cash flow.

Calculation: $Net\ operating\ income - Debt\ service = \mathbf{Cash\ flow}$

The **gross rent multiplier (GRM)** is another tool for determining a property's potential value. Generally, it is used by investors seeking to purchase a rental property. However, this method does not include such matters as building expenses or vacancies. The GRM is like the CMA in that other similar properties are evaluated to determine the subject property's value. Comparable property values are determined like an appraisal. A GRM of 100 or more shows a monthly variable, but a rent may be expressed in an annual variable. For a GRM over 100 with an annual rent, divide the rent by 12 to get the monthly rent.

Calculation: $GRM \times Rent = Value$

Example question: A property is subject to a 150 GRM multiplier and the property has an annual rent income of $15,000, what is the property's value?

Step 1: Convert the annual rent to monthly rent.

$$\frac{\$15,000}{12\ months} = \$1,250$$

Step 2: Find the property value with the GRM multiplier.

$150 \times \$1,250 = \$187,500$ property value

Practice Quiz

1. Convert the following fraction into a decimal: ¾
    a. 0.75
    b. 0.66
    c. 0.88
    d. 1.00

2. Convert the following into a percentage: 0.5
    a. 50%
    b. 500%
    c. .005
    d. 5.0%

3. What is the area of a lot that is 25' x 30'?
    a. 55 square feet
    b. 120 square feet
    c. 500 square feet
    d. 750 square feet

4. What is the square footage of a lot that is 50' x 50'?
    a. 1 square foot
    b. 2,700 square feet
    c. 2,500 square feet
    d. 1,000 square feet

5. What is the price per square foot of a house that measures 25' x45' that sold for $260,000?
    a. $231.11
    b. $321.66
    c. $257.48
    d. $432.69

See answers on the next page.

Answer Explanations

1. A: Choice A is correct because $3 \div 4$ is 0.75. Choices B, C, and D are incorrect.

2. A: Choice A is correct because the decimal is moved two spaces to the right to convert a decimal into percentage. Choices B, C, and D are incorrect.

3. D: Choice D is correct because area is calculated by $width \times length$, here $25 \times 30 = 750$. Choices A, B, and C are incorrect.

4. C: Choice C is correct because square footage (area) is calculated by $width \times length$, here $50 \times 50 = 2,500$. Choices A, B, and D are incorrect.

5. A: Choice A is correct because 25 ft $\times$ 45 ft = 1,125 ft^2, then $260,000 $\div$ 1,125 square feet = $231.11 per square foot. Choices B, C, and D are incorrect.

Specialty Areas

Subdivisions and Development-Wide CC&Rs

Landowners and developers frequently purchase larger plots of land than they end up selling to individual homeowners. Subdivisions indicate the smaller plots of land that landowners or developers break up from larger plots of land. Originally, a county or municipality may have recognized one large piece of land as a single title. As subdivisions, smaller plots of land are recognized via a distinct, individual title.

Ostensibly, developers improve the quality of the land to make money by selling individual plots of land to homeowners, business owners, and so on. Certain conditions and criteria exist for improving and selling the land, and, ultimately, the municipality must recognize each plot of land within a subdivision before a developer can sell. Via land use regulations, municipalities determine and authorize the types of homes and buildings that a developer can build within a specified area. Likewise, Covenants, Conditions & Restrictions (CC&Rs) indicate the aesthetic conditions of buildings and homes in a specific area and limit the scope of individual choice for things like exterior paint color.

Commercial Property

Commercial Property is real estate that is used for income-producing purposes and is generally not used for residential purposes. For real estate to be used for commercial purposes, it must be zoned for commercial use or business purpose. However, properties may be zoned for both residential and commercial use. Examples of commercial properties include apartments, stores, healthcare facilities, office buildings, malls, restaurants, hotels or motels, and parking lots.

Generally, commercial real estate is more costly than residential real estate because of the value of the property's use. Commercial property is often leased to commercial tenants (businesses) for generating income.

Commercial property may be categorized into four classifications: (1) office space; (2) industrial use; (3) multi-family rental; and (4) retail. These classifications and specialties can be broken down further into subcategories. An **office space** is commercial property that may be used for an office to conduct its business. An **industrial use** property is a spacious commercial property that may be used to conduct industrial activities, such as manufacturing and production. A **multi-family rental** property is commercial property that is used to house multiple families into rental units, such as an apartment complex. A **retail property** is a commercial property that is used for businesses to sell goods to the public, such as a grocery store.

Business Opportunity Sales

A **business opportunity** refers to an existing business package being sold or leased to a buyer. The buyer is often provided with the goods and supplies needed to conduct a business and gets to use the existing business name and goodwill. **Goodwill** is the reputation or brand's notoriety that is specific to that business entity. In some areas of law, it has been determined that goodwill is an intangible asset of the company and has a corresponding monetary value. Simply, the more popular the company, the higher the value of its goodwill. For example, an international company's goodwill is going to have more monetary value than a small business that is only operating in a single town within the United States.

Specialty Areas

This is because the business is not known to the same extent as the international company and has a smaller consumer base.

Jurisdictions allow for the sale of a business, as well as its assets and goodwill. However, many of these jurisdictions require a broker's license if a person (who is not the owner) is selling the business and assets on behalf of another person, or artificial person, for compensation. For public policy purposes, these jurisdictions want to ensure that the persons engaging in and conducting financial matters on behalf of another are qualified in regards to the subject matter of the transaction. Additionally, these individuals are generally subject to additional ethical obligations to a client.

Practice Quiz

1. Real property used for income-producing purposes is what kind of property?
    a. Residential property
    b. Commercial property
    c. Personal property
    d. Business property

2. For property to be considered commercial property, what is required?
    a. The property must be zoned for commercial use
    b. The property must be valuable
    c. The property must have desirable location
    d. The property must not be zoned for residential use

3. A business owner seeks a location to rent for a modest-sized call center business. What type of property should they rent?
    a. Industrial space
    b. Retail space
    c. Office space
    d. Multifamily space

4. A business owner seeks a location for a car manufacturing business. What type of property should they rent?
    a. Industrial space
    b. Retail space
    c. Office space
    d. Multifamily space

5. A business that sells clothes and accessories to the public needs a modest-sized space for the company's headquarters and miscellaneous data processing. What type of property should they rent?
    a. Industrial space
    b. Retail space
    c. Office space
    d. Multifamily space

See answers on the next page.

Answer Explanations

1. B: Choice B is correct because commercial property is real property used for income producing purposes. Choice A is incorrect because residential property is used for residential occupation and habitation. Choice C is incorrect because personal property is distinct from real property. Choice D is incorrect because the correct name of the property classification is "commercial property," not business property.

2. A: Choice A is correct because property must be zoned for commercial use before it may be used as commercial property. Choice B is incorrect because property does not need to be valuable to be considered commercial property. Choice C is incorrect because a desirable location, although coveted, is not required for property to be considered commercial property. Choice D is incorrect because a property may be zoned for both commercial and residential use.

3. C: Choice C is correct because office space would be appropriate for a call center. Choice A is incorrect because industrial space is generally used for manufacturing and production use and would likely be too big for the modest-sized business. Choice B is incorrect because retail space is used for a business to sell goods to the public, but the business in question is a call center. Choice D is incorrect because multifamily space is used for renting to multiple families for residential purposes, not for business purposes.

4. A: Choice A is correct because industrial space is used for manufacturing and production uses. Choice B is incorrect because retail space is used to sell goods to the public, but the business owner is looking for a location to manufacture cars. Choice C is incorrect because office space would not be sufficient in size for car manufacturing. Choice D is incorrect because multifamily space would be used for residential purposes, but B needs a space for a commercial business.

5. C: Choice C is correct because the business needs office space to conduct miscellaneous data processing for their clothing business. Choice A is incorrect because industrial space would likely be too big for the business owner's purpose. Choice B is incorrect because the business needs space to conduct office activities, not space to sell the clothing to the public. Choice D is incorrect because the business owner is seeking space for office processing, not residential space.

Texas Real Estate Commission

Commission Duties and Powers

General Powers

Each of the nine members of the Texas Real Estate Commission (TREC) are appointed by the governor of Texas. Each member serves a six-year term. Six members of the commission are licensed real estate brokers. The other three members of the commission are non-broker members. These three non-broker members serve as representatives of the consumer public.

The commission is responsible for establishing the guidelines and procedures by which an individual becomes a licensed realtor. Although not a member of the commission, the executive director serves as a mediator between the commission, the state government, and other legal entities. The executive director ensures that the will of the commission is carried out in state and local government.

The TREC works in tandem with the Texas Appraisal Licensing and Certification Board (TALCB). The TALCB was created 40 years after the formation of the TREC, and today it operates as a distinct, yet incorporated entity. Together, both the TALCB and the TREC aim to ensure that realtors follow stipulated guidelines and procedures when they carry out real estate transactions in Texas.

Among its roles, responsibilities, and duties, the TREC licenses qualified individuals to operate as agents and brokers in the state of Texas. The TREC also retains the power to revoke licenses from agents and brokers who violate laws, regulations, or guidelines. Additionally, the TREC provides educational resources to individuals who are interested in becoming a real estate agent, broker, or inspector.

Ultimately, the TREC was established as an institutional means to defend consumers from predatory, harmful, unfair, or unregulated business practices. The TREC contains several divisions, many of which are responsible for educating realtors on fair business practices. Other divisions exist solely to receive and respond to consumer complaints.

Other divisions within the TREC focus on administrative upkeep. Some divisions focus entirely on financing, sales, and property management. Indeed, some positions within the TREC are designed to ensure that the commission maintains an operable budget. Other divisions maintain the social and technological infrastructure that ensures that realtors, applicants, and consumers can easily assess TREC resources.

The central function of the TREC is threefold. It acts as a mediating entity between consumers and realtors; between realtors and state laws and regulations; and between professional, practicing realtors and those who aspire to become realtors. The TREC maintains the administrative infrastructure to remain transparent about its functioning and accessible to the consumer public, as well as aspiring and established realtors.

Handling of Complaints

Handling complaints is one of the TREC's most important functions. The process of handling complaints allows TREC to engage in investigations, hearings, and disciplinary action, as warranted, on behalf of a consumer. This is how the TREC safeguards the consumer from unlawful, unfair, or unregulated business practices.

Consumers may file a complaint against a real estate broker or sales agent, an inspector, or an easement/Right-Of-Way agent. They may also file a complaint against an approved education provider. Additionally, consumers may file a complaint against unlicensed activity, as well as a timeshare plan.

Upon receiving a complaint, the TREC may launch an investigation of the accused party or parties. Some complaints require active investigation in the field, while investigators resolve other complaints by only reviewing pertinent documents. The TREC fulfills two types of investigations: headquarters investigations and field investigations.

TREC investigators complete headquarters investigations by reviewing case documents. Case documents include any documentation provided by the complainant, as well as responses from accused parties. At the onset of an investigation, TREC investigators request responses from the accused parties. Once a TREC investigator has compiled the required documents, the complaint is passed to an attorney.

TREC investigators complete field investigations by contacting witnesses and other third-party entities directly. Complaints that require a field investigation tend to be more complex. Investigators summon first-person testimonials. When they have accumulated all relevant information, they pass their information to an attorney.

Depending on the findings of an investigation, an attorney will prescribe either informal or formal disciplinary action. Informal disciplinary action, usually distributed in the form of an advisory letter, serves as a precedent for formal disciplinary action, should a consumer file a similar complaint against the accused party in the future. Formal disciplinary action may be administered in the form of a reprimand, or the suspension or revocation of a real estate license.

When administering formal discipline, attorneys communicate with the accused parties to determine whether they agree with the accusations or not. An attorney issues Agreed Orders to accused parties who acknowledge their wrongdoing, especially when accused parties make some effort to rectify the situation. An attorney issues a Notice of Alleged Violation when a complaint against an accused party is particularly severe or if an accused party has not responded to a complaint. If the accused party consents to the disciplinary action outlined in a Notice of Alleged Violation, then the complaint proceeds to a Final Order. Otherwise, the accused must attend a hearing to dispute the complaint.

TREC commissioners oversee hearings. If an accused party disagrees with the commissioners' decision, the accused party may request a rehearing. If the TREC denies the request for a rehearing, the accused party may appeal the Final Order. Appeals constitute an escalation to a higher court. These appeals appear in a district court.

Penalties for Violation

For the violation of the ethical or legal standards for operating as a licensed real estate professional in the state of Texas, penalties range from reprimands to the revocation of a professional license. The TREC outlines three tiers of possible violations, and the penalties associated with these violations correspond to the severity of the violation. Level One violations are considered the most severe category of violations, whereas Level Two and Level Three violations are considered less severe.

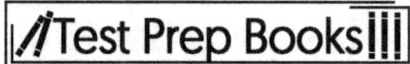

Level One violations include any activity, such as fraud and misrepresentation, that leads to a loss of funds exceeding $10,000. The TREC considers any form of mortgage fraud a Level One violation. Additionally, any activity that poses or presents a risk to personal safety, whether to the consumer, agent, or third party, constitutes a Level One violation. Finally, unlicensed activity constitutes a Level One violation. Unlicensed activity occurs when a real estate professional engages in activity that they are not licensed to administer, or when a real estate professional continues to operate while their license is suspended.

The TREC's authority for administering severe disciplinary action, including the suspension or revocation of a professional license, derives from its association with the state government, as well as its partnerships with attorneys. The Executive Director of the TREC is a licensed attorney who works closely with the state government to fulfill the commission's functions and uphold state law.

When a consumer suffers the loss of personal funds as a result of unethical or illegal actions taken by a licensed real estate professional, a consumer may apply for reimbursement of funds through the TREC's Real Estate Recovery Trust Account and Fund. This becomes necessary when a licensed real estate professional is unable to pay an aggrieved consumer out of their own pocket. The fund ensures that, one way or another, consumers receive the funds to which they are entitled.

Licensing

Activities Requiring Licensing

All real estate agents must have a real estate license to buy, sell, and rent property to consumers. In the state of Texas and elsewhere, real estate agents act as surrogates for real estate brokers. Real estate brokers collect commission by providing real estate services to consumers. Together, real estate agents and brokers may fall under the purview of a single entity known as a real estate agency or realtor group.

The state of Texas requires that real estate business entities, such as real estate agencies and realtor groups, maintain a license to operate. Several brokers and agents may comprise a single business entity. To be recognized and licensed by the state of Texas, the business entity must identify one licensed broker, in good standing, to act as a representative of it. This individual may be called an officer or manager, and they will possess the power to act on behalf of the business entity.

A distinction exists between real estate agencies or realtor groups, in a general sense, and Limited Function Referral Offices (LFRO) and real estate brokerage referral businesses. The distinction is that real estate agents consent to limit the scope of their practice when they act on behalf of LFROs and real estate brokerage referral businesses. Only licensed real estate brokers may operate LFROs and real estate brokerage referral businesses, and they may only contract with licensed real estate agents. Real estate agents who operate with these entities agree to limit their engagement to the referral of prospective clients.

Note that non-resident brokers, or brokers licensed in a state other than Texas, must submit all application paperwork as hard copies, along with relevant supporting documents and fees. To apply to become a licensed real estate broker in the state of Texas, out of state brokers may not complete their applications online.

Similar to the way real estate agents and brokers operate via a tiered relationship to each other, inspectors pass through a hierarchy from apprenticeship to professional. In the state of Texas, three tiers exist for real estate inspectors: apprentice inspector, real estate inspector, and professional real estate inspector. Throughout their training, apprentice inspectors operate under the direct supervision of professional real estate inspectors. Once apprentice inspectors become real estate inspectors, they develop greater autonomy and complete the functions of their assignment under the purview of a professional real estate inspector. Professional real estate inspectors possess the highest degree of qualifications and knowledge.

Licensing Process

Real estate agents receive a real estate license from the state where they live or plan to practice real estate. While requirements vary from state to state, all states require that real estate agents fulfill certain age and citizenship requirements. In general, applicants must be at least 18 or 19 years old, and they must have and maintain citizenship status in the United States. Across the country, states require prospective real estate agents to complete education requirements and pass the real estate licensing exam.

The state of Texas requires real estate agents to be at least 18 years old, and it requires that all applicants maintain citizenship in the United States or possess a green card or Permanent Resident card. The state of Texas does not allow applicants with Deferred Action for Childhood Arrivals (DACA) status to become licensed real estate agents. As with other states, pre-licensing education is also required to become a licensed real estate agent. In the state of Texas, an additional requirement exists: the Texas Real Estate Commission (TREC) requires that applicants live up to its code of conduct. The TREC recommends that applicants complete a Fitness Determination evaluation during the application process. This evaluation reviews an applicant's moral qualifications, along with other material criteria.

An applicant's success is determined by their ability to complete many hours of required education, pass the real estate licensing exam, pass the criminal background check, and secure the patronage of a licensed sponsor. Failure to complete any of these steps may result in the rejection of an application. Applicants may appeal the findings of a background check, and they may take the licensing exam up to three times. If an applicant fails the exam three times, they must redo their education requirements.

License Maintenance and Renewal

In the state of Texas, a licensed real estate agent must renew their real estate license every two years. Continuing education is a mandatory part of the license renewal process. Each time they renew their license, a real estate agent must complete 18 hours of continuing education courses that include legal, contract-related, and elective coursework.

In the state of Texas, business entity real estate brokers must also complete a license renewal every two years. Every business entity has a designated broker; they must be a licensed real estate broker in good standing to apply for a license renewal on behalf of a business entity. Business entity real estate brokers must submit documents that indicate their businesses' Franchise Tax Account Status, as well as Proof of Ownership documents and/or Errors and Omissions insurance. Acceptable Proof of Ownership documents vary between corporations, LLCs, and partnerships.

Depending on status and administrative conditions, some real estate agents may need to complete additional steps to renew their licenses. Real estate agents who decide to change their sponsor, as well as real estate agents who move from inactive to active status, must submit a separate Sales Agent Sponsorship form. In both instances, a real estate agent must secure a signature from their new

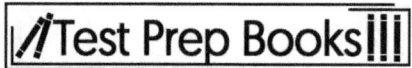

sponsor. Inactive real estate agents may not be required to complete continuing education coursework to renew their licenses. Finally, real estate agents with assumed names must ensure that the name on their government-issued IDs matches the name on their real estate license renewal application.

Standards of Conduct

The TREC holds real estate professionals to high moral and ethical standards. The commission expects all real estate professionals to be forthcoming about mistakes, mishaps, and miscalculations. Transparency goes a long way to build trust, and the TREC expects real estate professionals to disclose all pertinent information related to consumers, sales, and inspections, when applicable. The commission expects real estate agents to strive to perform their job duties at the highest level possible and take pride in their work.

The TREC offers a Fitness Determination evaluation for applicants who are unsure about their eligibility. The Fitness Determination measures an applicant's honesty, trustworthiness, and integrity by evaluating several factors related to their personal and professional background. On a Fitness Determination form, applicants list any previous criminal offenses, as well as any professional conduct violations, including unlicensed activity. Criminal activity, unlicensed activity, and violations of consumer trust are all grounds for suspension and revocation. The TREC encourages applicants to check their eligibility before applying to be a real estate professional.

As real estate professionals develop their careers, the line between ethical and unethical conduct tends to blur, especially when these professionals engage in potentially nuanced scenarios. For example, splitting fees allows two real estate professionals to split the commission from a job, but professionals must adhere to applicable rules and regulations. When a real estate professional licensed in the state of Texas operates with a foreign realtor, the two parties must ensure that the foreign broker never conducts negotiations within the physical borders of Texas. Licensed real estate agents must also tread carefully when operating with unlicensed professionals. Licensed real estate agents must not split commissions with unlicensed professionals. However, unlicensed professionals may collect a wage from licensed professionals for their work, if a license was not required to fulfil the work they completed, and if the unlicensed professional never presented themselves as a licensed professional to consumers or other parties.

Compensation for services rendered by real estate agents over the course of a professional engagement stems exclusively from the broker in charge of the engagement. Real estate agents rely on written compensation agreements to claim commission, and once these payments are made, real estate brokers provide the real estate agent with a receipt of the transaction. Only the real estate broker in charge of the engagement has the power to make these payments to real estate agents. Any other individual who worked on the project indirectly, perhaps as a salesperson or through a salesperson, must also receive payment via written consent by the supervising broker.

While the will to uphold the highest virtues of professionalism and integrity is a solid guiding principle, real estate agents should familiarize themselves with applicable rules and regulations whenever they engage in a project or sale.

Practice Quiz

1. Which two entities work together to set regulations and requirements for real estate agents who operate in the state of Texas?
    a. The Texas Real Estate Commission (TREC) and the Texas Appraisal Licensing and Certification Board (TALCB)
    b. The Texas Real Estate Committee (TREC) and the Texas Appraisal Licensing and Certification Board (TALCB)
    c. The Texas Real Estate Commission (TREC) and the Texas state government
    d. The Texas Appraisal Licensing and Certification Board (TALCB) and the Texas state government
2. To investigate complaints, investigators compile witness accounts when they complete which type of investigation?
    a. Complete investigation
    b. Headquarters investigation
    c. Witness investigation
    d. Field investigation
3. After a complaint is made, when do accusations against a real estate agent appear in a district court?
    a. After an accused real estate agent is issued a Notice of Alleged Violation
    b. After an accused real estate agent appeals a Final Order
    c. When requested by the consumer who made the complaint
    d. When an investigator discovers discrepancies between witness accounts
4. How many hours of continuing education coursework must a real estate agent complete to renew their real estate license?
    a. 15
    b. 20
    c. 18
    d. 10
5. When is it okay for real estate agents or salespeople to pay unlicensed professionals for services rendered?
    a. Once the unlicensed professional completes the work for which they were contracted
    b. Once the unlicensed professional engages team members about resources and fulfillment
    c. After the sponsoring broker provides written consent to render payment
    d. After a real estate inspector completes an evaluation of compliance and integrity

See answers on the next page.

Answer Explanations

1. A: Choice A is correct because both the Texas Real Estate Commission (TREC) and the Texas Appraisal Licensing and Certification Board (TALCB) work together to set regulations and requirements for real estate agents who operate in the state of Texas. Choice B is incorrect because TREC does not stand for the Texas Real Estate Committee. Choices C and D are incorrect because the Texas state government does not work directly with either TREC or TALCB to set regulations and requirements for real estate agents who operate in the state of Texas.

2. D: Choice D is correct because investigators compile witness accounts when they complete field investigations. Choice B is incorrect because investigators only compile and review documentation when they complete headquarters investigations. Choices A and C are incorrect because these are not names of investigations that TREC investigators complete.

3. B: Choice B is correct because accusations may be elevated to a district court after an accused real estate agent appeals a Final Order. Choice A is incorrect because a Notice of Alleged Violation is issued when a complaint is filed, and then the accused real estate agent decides how they wish to respond. Choice C is incorrect because consumers do not dictate the legal/administrative path that an investigation takes. Choice D is incorrect because it does not indicate a reason why a complaint would be elevated to a district court, though it may be relevant information at a TREC hearing.

4. C: Choice C is correct because it is the exact number of continuing education hours an agent must complete prior to having their real estate license renewed. Choices A and D are incorrect because they are less than the amount of continuing education hours required for an agent to complete prior to renewing their real estate license. Choice B is incorrect because it exceeds the amount of continuing education hours required prior to real estate license renewal.

5. C: Choice C is correct because the sponsoring broker must provide written consent for all payments rendered throughout the lifetime of a real estate project. Choice A is incorrect because payments are not necessarily made at the same time work is completed. Choice B is incorrect because payments are not necessarily made when logistics are worked out. Choice D is incorrect because payments are not dependent on an inspector's oversight.

Special Topics in Texas State Real Estate

Community Property

The state of Texas recognizes two overarching categories of marital property: community property and separate property. Most property owned by a married couple is classified as community property. A married couple jointly owns community property, and when the state of Texas interacts with community property, it perceives the married couple as a single entity.

On the other hand, separate property indicates property that is not jointly owned by the married couple. Instead, the deed or title is owned by one spouse or the other. Common examples of separate property include property retained by one spouse or the other prior to marriage, inherited property, gifted property, and property obtained via litigation. Community property and separate property are classified differently for tax purposes, and specific considerations must be given when community property factors into a divorce.

Homestead

Texas real estate law places greater protections on one's home than any other state in the United States. In many ways, the Texas homestead right acts as a safeguard between creditors and homeowners. In most instances, it prevents one's physical home, as well as the property where the home stands, from being implicated in debt collection. The only minor caveat is that a property owner must register their home or dwelling as a homestead. This is usually a very simple process. The property owner may also register personal property as part of their homestead, including heirlooms, jewelry, farming equipment, firearms, and pets.

Since either individuals or families may file for homestead rights, legal implications exist for married couples who categorize their homes as community property or separate property. A family may file for homestead rights of only one property, usually classified as community property, so spouses must handle separate property with some care.

Deceptive Trade Practices Act

The Deceptive Trade Practices Act provides broad protections against deceptive trade practices for consumers in the state of Texas. The nonspecific nature of the Deceptive Trade Practices Act often works in the favor of consumers and victims because the definition of a "deceptive trade practice" remains relatively open-ended. This allows courts to decide whether a particular practice or action constitutes an act of deception, which may benefit the consumer when a court is sympathetic to a consumer's claim.

Real estate professionals who operate in the state of Texas remain ever mindful of The Deceptive Trade Practices Act, especially when advertising. The Deceptive Trade Practices Act uses imprecise language to outlaw any action that a vendor takes to profit from a consumer's lack of knowledge. Real estate professionals in the state of Texas are expected to inform and educate consumers and clients, rather than take advantage of their ignorance. Deceptive actions place a real estate professional in legal jeopardy and compromise their fidelity.

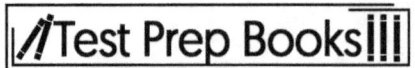

Wills and Estates

Texas' inheritance and succession laws are in many ways unique when compared with those of other states. Several years ago, the state of Texas repealed its inheritance tax, and the state of Texas does not maintain estate taxes. However, the state of Texas still requires living individuals to pay taxes on behalf of deceased individuals. These taxes include final individual federal and state income tax returns, federal estate/trust income tax returns, and federal estate tax returns. All these payments are due within a certain time from the death of the progenitor and often correspond to the size of the estate.

Wills that clearly articulate and establish a beneficiary are passed according to the will's instructions, while wills that do not clearly establish a beneficiary progress according to the state's intestate succession process. Many beneficiaries may be named in these instances. Community property, separate property, and homesteads factor into the passage of a will. Community property remains with the living spouse, while the state may intervene in the case of separate property if a will was not created.

Landlord-Tenant Issues

Rental agreements between a landlord and a tenant may be established as a verbal or written agreement, but rental agreements do not become active and defensible by law until a tenant begins to make regular rental payments to a landlord. Both a landlord and a tenant maintain certain legal rights as a condition of entering a rental agreement. A tenant maintains the right to a habitable living dwelling, while a landlord maintains the right to collect regular rental payments and extract money from tenants for significant property damages.

In the state of Texas, landlords are compelled to satisfy tenant complaints about issues impacting the livability of a rental property within three days. Factors that determine the livability of a rental property include drinking water. Landlords have a week to respond to all other tenant complaints. Tenants who fix damaged or faulty property are entitled to reimbursement from their landlords.

Consistent with the aim to maintain transparent relationships between a consumer and vendor, the state of Texas articulates certain factors that landlords must share with tenants. These mandatory disclosures include information related to the use of lead-based paint in or throughout a rental property, partners and custodial staff involved in the maintenance of rental property, and terms and conditions of setting and extracting late fees from a tenant, in the event of negligent payments.

Cities and municipalities throughout Texas maintain different levels of oversight and provide various programs designed to support tenants. For example, Dallas restricts the elevation of rent based on tenant complaints. San Antonio supports housing programs for low-income tenants.

Mechanic's and Materialman's Liens

The state of Texas recognizes a laborer's right to exert their claim on money owed from the work they contribute to a building project, directly on the property. Members of the construction industry exert this influence via a mechanic's lien. A mechanic's lien signals unpaid fees related to the construction of a property, and its presence among the records of a property may severely influence the value of a property. Its documentation on the public record encourages property owners to fulfill their financial responsibilities.

The difference between a mechanic's lien and a materialman's lien depends less on the classification of the professional who rendered services and more on the type of property upon which they worked. Different types of liens are placed on residential property than non-residential property. Nonetheless, the effect remains largely the same, and it compels property owners to fulfill outstanding payments.

Veterans' Land Board

When it was founded after World War II, the Texas Veterans' Land Board (VLB) provided significant provisions to military veterans to purchase land and property. As the passing of time coincides with the continuation of American foreign wars, the VLB continues to evolve. While the VLB started with an allocated lump sum to buy land and sell it to Texas veterans, it now has the power to offer prorated loans to veterans who aim to buy either new or existing property. Additionally, the VLB offers loans to veterans who want to improve property.

Requirements differ for veterans seeking loans for land, property, and improvement, and some stipulations limit the use of VLB loans. Veterans may only seek VLB home loans for primary residences. The VLB issues land loans only for property located entirely within the state of Texas. Regarding material, contractors, and cost, the VLB regulates home improvement loans under scrupulous guidelines.

Practice Quiz

1. Regarding which type of property does the state of Texas recognize a married couple as a single economic unit?
    a. Separate property
    b. Community property
    c. Married property
    d. Family property
2. How many pieces of property may a married couple file as a homestead?
    a. None
    b. One
    c. Two
    d. No limit
3. In the event of the death of a spouse, under what conditions will the living spouse inherit any separate property that was owned by the deceased spouse?
    a. By default, as part of the same economic entity
    b. When the separate property is in Texas
    c. If the property was purchased with a loan from the Veterans' Land Board
    d. If they are clearly stipulated as a beneficiary in the deceased spouse's will
4. Within how many days must a landlord address tenant complaints about factors that affect the livability of a rental property, including running water and heat?
    a. Seven days
    b. Ten days
    c. Three days
    d. One day
5. Which of the following is NOT a legitimate reason for receiving a loan from the Veterans' Land Board?
    a. Public building projects
    b. Home improvement
    c. Purchase of property
    d. Purchase of land

See answers on the next page.

Answer Explanations

1. B: Choice B is correct because the state of Texas recognizes married couples as a single economic entity when they claim ownership of community property. Choice A is incorrect because the state of Texas recognizes only one or the other spouse as the owner of separate property. Choices C and D are incorrect because the state of Texas does not recognize married property or family property.

2. B: Choice B is correct because the state of Texas allows a married couple to classify one piece of property, if it is a primary residence, as a homestead. Choice A is incorrect because a married couple may classify a primary residence as a homestead. Choices C and D are incorrect because a married couple may not have more than one primary residence.

3. D: Choice D is correct because the creator of a will must designate a beneficiary of separate property. Choice A is incorrect because the state of Texas only recognizes a married couple as a single economic unit when it considers community property. Choice B is incorrect because the location of the property does not determine to whom the property passes. Choice C is incorrect because interaction with the Veterans' Land Board does not influence a will.

4. C: Choice C is correct because landlords must address tenant complaints about factors that influence the livability of a dwelling within three days. Choice A is incorrect because landlords must address tenant complaints about factors that do not influence the livability of a dwelling within seven days. Choice B is incorrect because it exceeds the amount of time in which a landlord must address tenant complaints about factors that influence the livability of a dwelling. Choice D is incorrect because landlords must address tenant complaints about factors that influence the livability of a dwelling within three days, not one.

5. A: Choice A is correct because the Veterans' Land Board does not give loans for public building projects. Choices B, C, and D are incorrect because the Veterans' Land Board does give loans for home improvement, as well as the purchase of homes and land.

Practice Test #1

1. Recently a homeowner suffered damage to their heating and cooling system due to normal wear and tear through the years. What offers coverage for this type of property damage?
    a. Home insurance
    b. Home warranty
    c. Home inspection
    d. Home renovation

2. Which act can a transaction broker NOT perform?
    a. Prepare an offer
    b. Show a property
    c. Negotiate a sales price
    d. Provide MLS and tax data on a property

3. Which of the following forces has an impact on value?
    a. Economic
    b. Political
    c. Both economic and political
    d. Neither economic nor political

4. Which category of water is a stream?
    a. Groundwater
    b. Percolating water
    c. Surface water
    d. Watercourse

5. A building that is valued at $510,000 is being depreciated over 39 years. After 10 years, how much will the building have depreciated?
    a. $130,769.20
    b. $135,402.77
    c. $125,432.89
    d. $133,839.74

6. What is generally the cause of an eviction?
    a. A failure to perform under the lease agreement
    b. A modification under the lease agreement
    c. A performance of the lease agreement
    d. An extension of the lease agreement

7. A broker discovers there is a broken stove in the kitchen. Must they disclose this?
    a. No, because it is not a material defect.
    b. Yes, because it is a material defect.
    c. No, because the seller is the one who must disclose it.
    d. Yes, because the listing agreement requires it.

8. Mason and Nicole are in a lease agreement. Recently Mason excluded Nicole, the tenant, from the leased property. Which of the following words describes what occurred?
   a. Litigation
   b. Steering
   c. Expulsion
   d. Physical eviction

9. A lot has a frontage of 35' and a depth of 60'. What is the area of the lot?
   a. 2,100 sq ft
   b. 95 sq ft
   c. 1,800 sq ft
   d. 2,000 sq ft

10. Which of the following is a defense against performance, and renders an obligation discharged?
    a. Unavailability
    b. Undesirability
    c. Death
    d. Consideration

11. Evelyn and Fran are in a lease agreement; Evelyn is the tenant and Fran is the landlord. Evelyn pays a flat fee for a leased premises and pays for utilities and property taxes. What type of lease is this?
    a. Gross lease
    b. Net lease
    c. Percentage lease
    d. Index lease

12. What is a physical measurement of property boundaries?
    a. An interior inspection
    b. A covenant
    c. A survey
    d. A certificate of occupancy

13. What is NOT considered in evaluating comps in the sales comparison approach?
    a. Sales price that the current owner paid for the property
    b. Sales price of neighboring similar properties from last six months
    c. Closing costs paid to sellers in recent sales
    d. Number of bedrooms in similar properties that have recently sold

14. Which of the following best describes a contract that is made with a person under the age of majority?
    a. Void
    b. Voidable
    c. Terminated
    d. Illegal

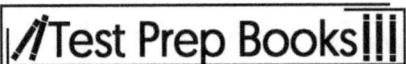

15. Some jurisdictions require joint tenancy to be created by the 4 unities of title. Which of the following is NOT one of the unities?
    a. Propriety
    b. Interest
    c. Time
    d. Title

16. Which type of agency is NOT valid in real estate transactions?
    a. Express agency
    b. Implied agency
    c. Dual agency
    d. Designated agency

17. What is the owner's equity in a property they purchased for $170,000 if there is a remaining mortgage of $50,000?
    a. $120,000
    b. $170,000
    c. $100,000
    d. $50,000

18. In which of the following forms may a warranty for fitness be part of the sales contract of a newly constructed home?
    a. In a written contract
    b. In an orally spoken
    c. In a contract implied by the circumstances
    d. All of the above

19. A buyer purchases a house for $170,000 and it measures 40' x 40'. What is the price per square foot of the house?
    a. $96.45
    b. $106.25
    c. $124.00
    d. $130.84

20. What determines the quality of materials that may be used in a building that is located within a commercially zoned area?
    a. Cumulative zoning
    b. Noncumulative zoning
    c. Building codes
    d. A special use permit

21. Clyde owns a building that has three units, and Clyde occupies one of the units. Subsequently, Clyde discriminates against a prospective tenant who is a member of a protected class. May Clyde do so?
    a. No, because discrimination is illegal in any circumstances
    b. No, because the person is a member of a protected class
    c. Yes, because the building contains four units or less and Clyde resides in one of the units
    d. Yes, because fair housing laws do not apply in renting a property

22. While giving a tour to a prospective buyer, the broker says, "You will not find a better house than this; it's the only one with a pool!" However, there are multiple properties with pools available in the neighborhood. Which term best describes the broker's statement?
    a. Puffing
    b. Misrepresentation
    c. Fraud
    d. Illusory statement

23. A potential home buyer was discriminated against based on their membership in a protected class. The home buyer was not given information about loans. What body of law was violated in this discrimination?
    a. Fair housing laws
    b. Fair lending laws
    c. Fair market laws
    d. Fair competition laws

24. A property manager has found a tenant for a new property, and this property manager collects the security deposit upon signing the lease. What does the property manager do with the money?
    a. They give half of it to the property owner and deposit half into a trust account.
    b. They deposit the entire amount into a trust account and disburse it to the owner after the tenant pays the first full month's rent.
    c. They deposit the entire amount into a trust account; then they invest that money in hopes of earning some interest before disbursing the deposit to the owner at the termination of the lease.
    d. They deposit the entire amount into a trust account to be held until termination of the lease.

25. If a buyer wanted to cancel a purchase contract because the party was unable to obtain financing, which type of clause would the buyer want in the contract?
    a. Exemption clause
    b. Contingency clause
    c. Exculpatory clause
    d. Dependent clause

26. Buyer Robert wants to pay agent Archie a retainer fee to work with him exclusively until a property is under contract. What does buyer Robert do?
    a. He writes a check made out to agent Archie's brokerage.
    b. He writes a check made out to agent Archie.
    c. He sets up a recurring payment to Archie, which will stop once a property is under contract.
    d. He writes a check made out to the closing attorney, who will give it to agent Archie at closing.

27. Mary would like to buy a house. She has a steady income and some money saved, but she has a low credit score. Which type of loan would she probably expect to qualify for?
    a. Conventional
    b. Reverse annuity mortgage
    c. Subprime
    d. Wrap-around

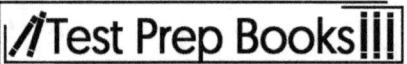

28. An agent must keep client information confidential, except in which circumstance?
    a. There is no such circumstance; client information must be preserved indefinitely
    b. When a relationship with a client is limited
    c. When the agent for the other party asks specifically
    d. If required by law

29. Adam is selling their home to Brooke. During the escrow phase, and two weeks before closing, Adam's stove breaks and a professional determines that the stove is outdated, unfixable, and in need of replacement. What kind of claim should Adam most likely pursue to get a replacement stove?
    a. Home insurance claim
    b. Home warranty claim
    c. Negligence claim
    d. Manufacturing defect claim

30. An agent who is given broad authority to conduct business on behalf of another entity is known as what?
    a. General agent
    b. Special agent
    c. Undisclosed agent
    d. Universal agent

31. Amy obtained a title commitment on a property that she just purchased. That transaction has closed. Who will NOT receive a title policy?
    a. Amy
    b. Amy's investor
    c. Amy's grantor
    d. Amy's joint tenant

32. What is a broker-in-charge NOT responsible for?
    a. Training the agents in the brokerage
    b. Renewing the licenses of the agents in the brokerage
    c. Overseeing the brokerage trust account
    d. Reviewing all contracts and agency agreements

33. Oliver owns land right next to a stream of water that passes across Oliver's vast land. However, Oliver does not use the water and just lets the water flow its natural course. Paulo is a cattle farmer that lives five miles away from the stream but travels to the stream to collect water so that Paulo may water his cattle. Under a prior appropriation jurisdiction, who has rights in the water?
    a. Oliver
    b. Paulo
    c. The state
    d. The local county

34. In a certain year, there are more homes for sale than there are people looking to purchase them. What is this is an example of?
    a. Seller's market
    b. Buyer's market
    c. Comparative market analysis
    d. Reconciliation

35. Which of the following needs to be written in a warranty deed in order to be conveyed to a grantee?
    a. Covenant against encumbrances
    b. Covenant of quiet enjoyment
    c. Covenants of warranty
    d. None of the above

36. Who determines the property tax amount?
    a. Lender
    b. Owner
    c. Abstractor
    d. Assessor

37. Zoey is buying a property. Zoey's annual income is $350,000. Subsequently, a lender determines that Zoey is able to qualify for payments that constitute 20% of Zoey's income. What is the value of the monthly payment?
    a. $5,025.00
    b. $5,833.33
    c. $6,398.40
    d. $5,393.80

38. Which scenario is considered dual agency?
    a. BIC Gary of Brokerage A represents both buyer and seller in the same transaction.
    b. BIC Gary of Brokerage A represents more than one principal.
    c. BIC Gary of Brokerage A represents a seller, and BIC Marsha of Brokerage B represents the buyer in that transaction.
    d. BIC Gary of Brokerage A represents a buyer who then uses BIC Gary to list the same house within the year.

39. What is the name of the document that shows the final allocation of amounts to each party?
    a. Mortgage
    b. Deed
    c. Abstract
    d. Settlement statement

40. Recently, Fernando passed away. Fernando's children, if any, were unable to be found and there are no known living relatives. By which process can the state take the property?
    a. Eminent domain
    b. Escheat
    c. Condemnation
    d. Inverse condemnation

41. Reagan and Tomas want to own property together, preferably on the coast, but they want to use it at different times of the year. What type of property should Reagan and Tomas purchase?
    a. Cooperative
    b. Condominium
    c. Timeshare
    d. Townhome

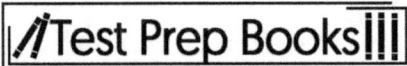

42. Evan is selling Evan's property to Fernando for $420,000. For recording purposes, what does NOT need be included on the deed?
    a. Evan's identity
    b. Execution date
    c. Party signatures
    d. Notarization

43. Buyer Brianna is buying a home for $200,000. She cannot put any money toward a down payment. What is the right loan option for her?
    a. Insured conventional loan
    b. Purchase money mortgage
    c. FHA loan
    d. VA loan

44. Listing agent Lucia has a listing that is under contract. Which word describes her relationship with selling agent Sally?
    a. Adversarial
    b. Competitive
    c. Cooperative
    d. Irrelevant

45. Diana's grandparent became deceased. Subsequently, Diana acquired the grandparent's primary residence under the probated will. What did Diana receive?
    a. Bequest
    b. Devise
    c. Adverse possession
    d. Intestate succession

46. What is another term used for a leasehold?
    a. Freehold
    b. Temporary hold
    c. Lease
    d. Hold

47. How can a borrower get the property back from the lender before a foreclosure sale happens?
    a. The borrower can pay off the interest and expenses that accrued since the last payment.
    b. The borrower can pay the loan in full without additional interest.
    c. The borrower can pay the loan in full, with interest.
    d. The borrower can buy the property at the foreclosure sale.

48. A property sold for $200,000. The selling agent earned a 3% commission and has a 60/40 split with the agent's sponsoring brokerage (with the brokerage receiving the 40%). What amount will the <u>brokerage</u> receive?
    a. $3,000
    b. $1,200
    c. $3,800
    d. $2,400

49. Which of the following is NOT a type of concurrent ownership?
    a. Tenancy by entirety
    b. Tenants in common
    c. Landlord and tenant
    d. Joint tenancy

50. Recently a buyer purchased a new home construction from a builder. The sales contract did not contain any additional warranties, and the buyers did not have an opportunity to inspect the property. Subsequently a defect in the back door was discovered. What is likely the best claim for the buyer to bring against the builder?
    a. Negligence claim
    b. Breach of contract claim
    c. Breach of warranty claim
    d. Fraud claim

51. Tristan is a holdover tenant in Victor's property. Victor recently evicted Tristan from the property. What obligation was discharged upon the eviction?
    a. Pay rent to Victor
    b. Covenant of goodwill
    c. Covenant of seisin
    d. Adverse possession

52. Which statement is an example of steering?
    a. "I think you and your family will be more comfortable on the second floor with the rest of the families."
    b. "This is the best house in the neighborhood; you will not find a better deal."
    c. "The state now owns the house next door because the neighbor is deceased."
    d. "This property has a pool in the backyard."

53. A broker secured a buyer for their client and the seller accepted. Under which of the following agreements is it possible for the client to pay the broker no commission for this sale?
    a. Net listing
    b. Open listing
    c. Exclusive listing
    d. Exclusive authorization and right to sell listing

54. Which of the following does the lender hold the borrower responsible for?
    a. Payment of taxes
    b. Maintenance of property insurance
    c. Payment of utilities
    d. Both A & B

55. A real estate licensee sold a house for $220,000. If the total commission on the transaction was 6%, what is the total commission in value?
    a. $14,000
    b. $13,200
    c. $9,800
    d. $13,900

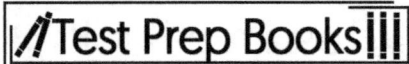

56. A property owner is looking to rent out an empty unit in their residential property. Against whom are they NOT permitted to discriminate against?
    a. A lawyer
    b. A parent
    c. A dog owner
    d. A dancer

57. When is the cost approach most commonly used?
    a. When the property produces income and is on more than ten acres of land
    b. When the property does not produce income and is on more than ten acres of land
    c. When the property produces income but has no comps available
    d. When the property does not produce income or have any comps available

58. In a listing agreement, the agent and the principal have duties to one another. Which of the following scenarios shows that the principal has respect for these duties?
    a. The seller asks the listing agent to pay for their mailbox, which was run over by a prospective buyer as they left the driveway.
    b. The seller discusses the terms of their listing with acquaintances who also happen to be real estate agents in hopes that they might get a better deal.
    c. The seller quickly accepts a last-minute showing request even though they must get their dog and two children into the car to leave the house in under 15 minutes.
    d. The seller insists that the listing agent renegotiate their commission when the accepted offer comes in just under the list price.

59. Who is NOT required to be licensed as a real estate agent?
    a. An assistant hosting an open house for a listing agent
    b. Someone reselling a personal mobile home
    c. Someone who receives compensation from the sale of land belonging to a neighbor
    d. Someone who shows a friend's house to a prospective buyer as a favor for the listing agent

60. Which of the following is considered a material matter and would require disclosure by a licensee?
    a. A broken appliance
    b. An environmental issue
    c. The seller's motivation for selling
    d. A creaky door

61. Which of the following is a statute that directly regulates the conveyance of land?
    a. Statute of frauds
    b. Statute of limitations
    c. State regulation
    d. County ordinance

62. What is an entity's brand, reputation, or notoriety called?
    a. Title
    b. Mortgage
    c. Goodwill
    d. Policy

63. With what type of institution do mortgage brokers originate loans?
    a. A single institution
    b. Private investors
    c. Credit unions
    d. Multiple institutions

64. Which statement about commissions earned by a licensee in a real estate transaction is true?
    a. These commissions are determined by agreement between the licensee and the client.
    b. These commissions should be the same no matter which brokerage the agent works with.
    c. These commissions are based on a predetermined rate schedule set by the local real estate board.
    d. These commissions must be paid by the seller client in every transaction.

65. As a disabled person, Esther is a protected under fair housing laws. Fyodor is renting an older property with an available unit on the second floor. The property has stairs that lead up to the unit. Esther is unable to use the stairs and may need an elevator, but this would be very costly to Fyodor. If Fyodor rents to Esther, would Fyodor be required to install an elevator?
    a. Yes
    b. No
    c. It depends on Esther's age
    d. It depends on local building codes

66. What is the term used to describe the conclusion of a real estate transaction?
    a. Termination
    b. Exclusion
    c. Escrow
    d. Closing

67. If the potential gross rental income from a property is $20,000, the vacancy rate is 5%, additional income from laundry and storage facilities is $700, and the operating expenses are $5,000, what is the net operating income (NOI)?
    a. $14,000
    b. $14,700
    c. $15,000
    d. $15,700

68. "From Andrew to Benjamin so long as Benjamin does not go to college." What type of present ownership was created?
    a. Life estate
    b. Fee simple absolute
    c. Defeasible fee
    d. Reversion

69. A developer recently developed land and homes to be sold on the market. In the covenants they recorded into record, they stated that the homes may only be used as single-family homes for families without children. Is this a lawful exercise of private regulation on land?
    a. Yes
    b. No
    c. If found not to violate building codes
    d. If found not to violate fair housing laws

70. Stella and Toby contract for the sale of Stella's land to Toby, but then, when Toby says they will dig up the pool in the backyard after closing, Stella decides to refuse to sell. Based on the facts provided, what is Toby's proper remedy?
    a. Damages
    b. Specific performance
    c. Liquidated damages
    d. Punitive damages

71. A physician would like to open an office in a renovated home near the town center. Which approach to value will they ask their agent to use to help them determine which property is the best investment?
    a. Income approach
    b. Commercial approach
    c. Investment approach
    d. Cost approach

72. Which of the following is another term for a gross lease?
    a. Fixed lease
    b. Net lease
    c. Percentage lease
    d. Index lease

73. Recently, Kirk rented a condo to Liam. Liam required installation of a modification to accommodate a disability, and Kirk allowed the installation for Liam's accommodation inside the unit. Additionally, Kirk required that Liam would be responsible for restoring the interior of the unit. Which of the following would Liam be responsible for restoring?
    a. Holes in the wall
    b. Torn wallpaper
    c. Faded paint
    d. Worn enamel in the sink

74. A buyer has entered a purchase agreement for the sale of a home and farmland. Which of the following will not be conveyed to the buyer?
    a. Air rights
    b. Fixtures
    c. Furniture in the home
    d. Right to exclude

75. Alexia is Brody's realtor. Brody is selling Brody's home, but Brody does not know what to sell it for. What type of report or document should Alexia conduct to help Brody determine the value of the home in the current market?
   a. Comparative market analysis
   b. Survey
   c. Inspection
   d. Assessment

76. Orville and Paul enter into an agreement to raise money for a foundation by selling other people's personal items that Orville and Paul find in said people's homes without consent. Which type of contract have Orville and Paul created?
   a. There is no contract
   b. A funding agreement
   c. A bilateral contract
   d. A service contract

77. Which statement does NOT describe a mortgage?
   a. It is the money that is lent in exchange for promise of future repayment
   b. It is in writing
   c. It can be transferred in writing to a third party
   d. It is recorded with the local government

78. Olaf is buying real property from Peter. Olaf would also like to add Peter's kitchen table to the transaction. Which of the following legal documents must be completed for the addition?
   a. Deed
   b. Note
   c. Occupancy certificate
   d. Bill of sale

79. To determine if a property has value, these four elements are considered: supply, transferability, utility, and what other element?
   a. Competition
   b. Highest and best use
   c. Demand
   d. Depreciation

80. A retirement community recently received a rental application from a 35-year-old single parent with three children. The retirement community subsequently denied the rental application because the applicant has children. Under fair housing laws, this is permissible. Why is this permissible?
   a. Because the applicant is 35 years old
   b. Because the applicant has more than two children
   c. Because the property is designated senior housing
   d. Because fair housing laws do not apply to retirement communities

Answer Explanations #1

1. B: Choice B is correct because normal wear and tear of a heating and cooling systems is covered under a home warranty. Choice A is incorrect because home insurance covers unexpected events that affect the property, such as a fire. Choice C is incorrect because a home inspection is an inspection of the property and does not provide coverage of the property in the event of damage. Choice D is incorrect because home renovation is the process of making additions or modifications to a home.

2. C: Choice C is correct because transaction brokers are allowed only to perform ministerial duties; they have customers, not clients, and cannot offer client-level services. A transaction broker does not offer advice, counsel, or expertise during the offer or negotiation phases of a deal because the agent is working on behalf of neither party exclusively; the agent is acting as a facilitator only. Choices A, B, and D are incorrect because transaction brokers may perform each of these actions while facilitating a real estate deal.

3. C: Choice C is correct because two of the forces that impact value are economic and political forces. Therefore, since both Choices A and B are correct, Choice C is the optimal choice. Choice D is incorrect because both Choices A and B are correct.

4. D: Choice D is correct because a watercourse is water that runs in a course, such as a stream. Choice A is incorrect because groundwater is water that comes from a well. Choice B is incorrect because it is another name for groundwater. Choice C is incorrect because surface water is water that has accumulated on a land surface, such as from rain or melted snow.

5. A: Choice A is correct because $\$510{,}000 \div 39 = \$13{,}076.92$. Then, $\$13{,}076.92 \times 10 = \$130{,}769.20$. Therefore, choices B, C, and D are incorrect.

6. A: Choice A is correct because a failure to perform under the lease agreement generally gives rise to an eviction. Choice B is incorrect because a modification of a lease agreement is a change in term(s) of the agreement and does generally not cause an eviction. Choice C is incorrect because a performance of a lease agreement (and its terms) would generally not give rise to an eviction. Choice D is incorrect because an extension of the lease agreement would be an extension in duration of the agreement, but it would not give rise to eviction.

7. B: Choice B is correct because a stove is affixed to the real property and is considered to be a material defect. The stove is likely to remain affixed to the property after closing and will affect the value of the property. Choice A is incorrect because the stove is a material defect. Choice C is incorrect because, although the seller would also have a duty to disclose, the seller's duty does not alter the broker's duty to disclose, which the question is about. Choice D is incorrect because the broker has a duty to disclose a material defect regardless of what the listing agreement states.

8. D: Choice D is correct because physical eviction is the process of physically excluding the tenant from a leased premises. Choice A is incorrect because litigation pertains to pursuing of a lawsuit. Choice B is incorrect because steering pertains to influencing where a potential buyer or renter should reside. Choice C is incorrect because expulsion is not the proper term to describe what occurred.

9. A: Choice A is correct because 35 feet x 60 feet = 2,100 sq ft. Choices B, C, and D are incorrect.

Answer Explanations #1

10. C: Choice *C* is correct because death is defense to performance and may discharge an obligation. Choice *A* is incorrect because unavailability is not a defense to performance, but impossibility is - as an unavailability of a specific house to sale; it is impossible to perform. Choice *B* is incorrect because it is not a defense to performance. Choice *D* is incorrect because consideration is what binds a contract for performance to rendered.

11. B: Choice *B* is correct because a tenant pays for the leased premises, utilities, and property taxes in a net lease. Choice *A* is incorrect because a tenant pays for the occupancy a leased premises, but the landlord pays for utilities, property taxes, and special assessments. Choice *C* is incorrect because a tenant pays a fee that fluctuates based on the amount of monthly revenue earned. Choice *D* is incorrect because the tenant pays a fee that fluctuates based on an index.

12. C: Choice *C* is correct because the survey is a physical measurement of property boundaries. Choice *A* is incorrect because an interior inspection is an evaluation of an improvement's interior. Choice *B* is incorrect because a covenant is a promise that runs with the land. Choice *D* is incorrect because a certificate of occupancy shows that a property may be occupied.

13. A: Choice *A* is correct because the sales price that a seller paid for the property before has no bearing on the value of the property in today's market. While it would be nice if a seller could be assured that the new sales price would be higher than what was previously paid, there is no such guarantee. Choices *B*, *C*, and *D* are all considered when doing the sales comparison approach.

14. B: Choice *B* is correct because a contract may be made with a person under the age of 18, but it is voidable at the minor's discretion. Choices *A* and *C* are different words referring to a canceled contract, but contracting with a minor does not immediately cancel the agreement. Choice *D* is incorrect because certain contracts may be legally entered into with a person under the age of 18.

15. A: Choice *A* is correct because propriety is not one of the four unities. The four unities are: (1) possession, (2) interest, (3) time, and (4) title. Therefore, choices *B*, *C*, and *D* are incorrect.

16. B: Choice *B* is the correct answer because implied agency is through action only and is not a written agreement; therefore, it is not legally recognized in real estate transactions. Choice *A* is incorrect because express agency is accomplished by establishing agency in writing. Choices *C* and *D* are incorrect because dual agency and designated agency are valid options for representing clients within a single brokerage in a real estate transaction.

17. A: Choice *A* is correct because $170,000 (purchase price) - $50,000 (liability) = $120,000 equity. Choices *B*, *C*, and *D* are incorrect.

18. D: Choice *D* is correct because a new construction warranty may be found in a written contract, may be orally spoken between the builder and the buyer, or may be implied by circumstances (and law). Choices *A*, *B*, and *C* are incorrect because all choices are permitted forms of the warranty.

19. B: Choice *B* is correct because $40' \times 40' = 1,600$ square feet, then $170,000 \div 1,600$ square feet $= \$106.25$ per square foot. Choices *A*, *C*, and *D* are incorrect.

20. C: Choice *C* is correct because building codes are used to set the standard of how a building may be constructed. Choices *A* and *B* are incorrect because, although zoning may allow a permitted use of a property, it is building codes that set the requirements of building construction. Choice *D* is incorrect

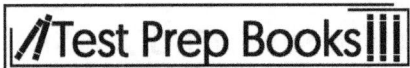

Answer Explanations #1

because a special use permit is granted by the government for particular businesses to operate, such as hospitals.

21. C: Choice *C* is correct because a person may discriminate against a member of a protected class if the building has no more than four units and the owner of the building occupies one of the units. Choice *A is* incorrect because this specific discrimination is permitted. Choice *B* is incorrect because, although generally this would be sufficient for the protections of fair housing laws, Clyde's situation is an exception to the general rule. Choice *D* is incorrect because this is a misstatement of the rule–fair housing laws do apply in renting property.

22. B: Choice *B* is correct because the broker misrepresented a factual matter about the property's pool and the pools on other properties in the area. Choice *A* is incorrect because the broker's statement involved a factual assertion about the property. Choice *C* is incorrect because the facts do not state that the broker had the required mental state for fraud. Choice *D* is incorrect because this is not an accepted term used to describe what the broker did: misrepresentation.

23. B: Choice *B* is correct because refusing to give someone information about loans is a violation of fair lending laws. Choice *A* is incorrect because the discrimination was not related to housing directly but indirectly, in relation to lending practices. Choices *C* and *D* are incorrect because these are made-up regulations.

24. D: Choice *D* is correct because a security deposit must be placed in a separate trust account and not touched until the lease is terminated. The money can then be disbursed in accordance with the lease agreement. Choice *A* is incorrect because no security deposit funds can be touched until the lease is terminated. Choice *B* is incorrect for that same reason and also because the owner may only get a small portion of it, if any, based on the stipulations in the lease agreement. The default disbursement of a security deposit is back to the tenant at the end of the lease. Choice *C* is incorrect because no security deposit funds can be disbursed until the lease has been terminated. The ability to earn interest is acceptable, and the property manager is allowed to earn and retain the interest if they have the property owner acknowledge that they are doing so.

25. B: Choice *B* is correct because a contingency clause allows a buyer to cancel on the contingency that the party is unable to secure financing. Choice *A* is incorrect because an exemption clause is used to limit or exclude liability. Choice *C* is incorrect because this clause prevents contractual liability against a party that may breach the contract. Choice *D* is incorrect because although the proceeding sale is dependent on the securing of financing, it does not best directly answer the question for the type of clause the buyer would want.

26. A: Choice *A* is correct because agents should not receive commission directly from clients, so the client should write the check to the brokerage. Choice *B* is incorrect because agents do not get paid directly from clients. Choice *C* is incorrect because a retainer fee is a non-refundable one-time fee that may or may not be applied to the brokerage fee in the event of a closed sale. Choice *D* is incorrect because attorneys do not pay agents directly.

27. C: Choice *C* is correct because borrowers with low credit scores cannot get standard conventional or government-backed loans. Choice *A* is incorrect because borrowers must have good credit to get a conventional loan. Choice *B* is incorrect because a reverse annuity mortgage converts equity in a property already owned by the borrower into periodic payments back to the borrower. Choice *D* is

Answer Explanations #1

incorrect because there would need to already be a mortgage in place for a second mortgage to be incorporated into it.

28. D: Choice *D* is correct because an agent must maintain confidentiality forever except in a few circumstances, one of which is when the agent is required by law to divulge information. It is also permissible to stop maintaining confidentiality if the client gives permission or if the agent is defending themselves against an accusation of wrongdoing in a legal setting. Choice *A* is incorrect because there are a few instances in which divulging information is allowed. Choice *B* is incorrect because a customer is not a client and so confidentiality is not required to begin with, and the question specifies the confidentiality of *client* information. Choice *C* is incorrect because client information cannot be divulged simply because someone asks for it.

29. B: Choice *B* is correct because Adam may seek a replacement stove under a home warranty for the wear and tear of using the stove. Choice *A* is incorrect because home insurance covers unexpected events, not wear and tear. Choice *C* is incorrect because nothing in the facts suggests that there was negligence on the part of the stove manufacturer. Choice *D* is incorrect because the stove was not defective; it functioned properly until recently, when it broke.

30. D: Choice *D* is correct because a universal agent is given broad authority to make decisions and purchases on behalf of a large corporation. Choices *A* and *B* are incorrect because general and special agents are not given broad authority to make decisions. Choice *C* is incorrect because there is no such thing.

31. C: Choice *C* is correct because the grantor (seller) will not receive a title policy in conjunction with the buyer. Choice *A* is incorrect because B will receive a title commitment. Choice *B* is incorrect because Amy's investor (likely a bank) will receive a lender's title policy in connection with the transaction to Amy. Choice *D* is incorrect because Amy's joint tenant is likely covered under the same policy as Amy.

32. B: Choice *B* is correct because the BIC is legally responsible for the actions of the agents in the brokerage related to real estate transactions, but the BIC does not control the licensure of individual agents. Choices *A*, *C*, and *D* are all incorrect because they are all enumerated responsibilities of the BIC.

33. B: Choice *B* is correct because Paulo made prior, beneficial use of the water for watering the cattle in Paulo's commercial business and Oliver does not use the water. Choice *A* is incorrect because Oliver does not use the water. Choices *C* and *D* are incorrect because the facts of the question do not say they made prior use of the water, nor are the state and the county persons capable of holding these rights in the water.

34. B: Choice *B* is correct because an oversupply of houses compared to the number of buyers available is called a buyer's market. Choice *A* is incorrect because a seller's market refers to the condition of too few houses for sale and too many buyers looking. Choice *C* is incorrect because a comparative market analysis is used by real estate agents as a way to quickly estimate value for a given property. Choice *D* is incorrect because reconciliation is the method appraisers use to combine the results of all approaches to estimating value for a given property.

35. D: Choice *D* is correct because the covenants do not need to be stated in a warranty deed, as they are implied by the deed type. Choices *A*, *B*, and *C*, although covenants within a warranty deed, do not need to be written in the deed to be effective.

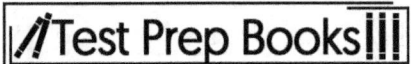

36. D: Choice D is correct because the assessor determines the property tax amount. Choice A is incorrect because a lender finances a purchase. Choice B is incorrect because the owner does not determine how much must be paid in taxes. Choice C is incorrect because an abstractor traces title.

37. B: Choice B is correct because $350,000 ÷ 12$ months $= $29,166.66$, then $29,166.66 \times 0.2 = $5,833.33$. Choices A, C, and D are incorrect.

38. A: Choice A is correct because dual agency occurs when the agent (BIC) represents both buyer and seller in the same transaction. It is true that an agent can represent more than one principal, but Choice B is incorrect because those principals might not be on opposite sides of the same transaction. Choice C is incorrect because the agents (BICs) are in different brokerages; there is no conflict of interest in this case. Choice D is incorrect because the agent is representing the client on the buyer side in one transaction and the same client on the seller side in a different transaction.

39. D: Choice D is correct because the settlement statement, or closing statement, is the final allocation of monies between parties under a purchase transaction. Choice A is incorrect because a mortgage is in interest in the land securing an obligation. Choice B is incorrect because a deed is a document that transfers title. Choice C is incorrect because an abstract is a document that shows a property's history.

40. B: Choice B is correct because escheat is the process by which the state acquires a deceased's land when there are no heirs to take it. Choice A is incorrect because eminent domain is the process by which the state takes a person's land for the benefit of the community. Choice C is incorrect because condemnation is the process of exercising eminent domain. Choice D is incorrect because inverse condemnation is the process by which a private person compels the state to exercise eminent domain.

41. C: Choice C is correct because timeshares are generally located in vacation areas and allow owners to use the property at different times within a year. Choice A is incorrect because a corporation would own the property. Choices B and D are incorrect because Reagan and Tomas would have concurrent ownership and may use it at the same time.

42. D: Choice D is correct because not all jurisdictions require signature notarization, though most do. Choices A, B, and C are incorrect because all these choices are required for recording purposes.

43. D: Choice D is correct because a VA loan is a loan for up to 100% of the purchase price with no down payment required. Choices A, B, and C are incorrect because they all require some form of down payment. The purchase money mortgage is an agreement for the seller to become the mortgage company, which means the terms could be set in such a way for no money down to be established, but it is typically a short-term arrangement, so the buyer would still need to satisfy the loan in a matter of just a few years, and a seller agreeing to no down payment in this situation would be unlikely.

44. C: Choice C is correct because agents working on opposite sides of a transaction are said to be cooperative agents. This is logical because cooperating with each other to get the job done is the best way for everyone to walk away from the transaction feeling satisfied. Choices A and B are incorrect because the agents should not be competing with one another; the transaction is about satisfying the clients. Choice D is incorrect because the relationship between the two agents is important to the outcome, not irrelevant. A bad relationship can have harmful effects on the outcome of a transaction.

45. B: Choice B is correct because a devise is a conveyance of real property under a will. Choice A is incorrect because a bequest is a transfer of personal property under the terms of a will. Choice C is

Answer Explanations #1

incorrect because adverse possession is not a probate matter. Choice D is incorrect because intestate succession describes inheritance priority when the deceased dies without a will.

46. C: Choice C is correct because lease is another term used to describe a leasehold. Choice A is incorrect because a freehold is associated with ownership. Choices B and D are incorrect because temporary hold and hold are not the proper terms.

47. C: Choice C is correct because the borrower can use redemption, an opportunity to save a property from foreclosure by paying off the loan in full with interest. Choice A is incorrect because the lender would require the loan to be paid in full, not just since the last payment missed. Choice B is incorrect because the lender would require the interest to be paid as well. Choice D is incorrect because the buyer would not be allowed to purchase the property for a reduced price at a foreclosure sale without satisfying the original loan.

48. D: Choice D is correct because $\$200,000 \times 0.03 = \$6,000$, then $\$6,000 \times 0.4 = \$2,400$. Choices A, B, and C are incorrect.

49. C: Choice C is correct because a tenant does not have ownership interest of property, it remains with the landlord. The tenant has the right to occupy and use the property. Choices A, B, and D are incorrect because these are types of concurrent ownership.

50. C: Choice C is correct because the buyer recently bought a new construction from a builder, and a new construction warranty may be implied, not expressly stated. Choice A is incorrect because there are not enough facts to show the builder was negligent. Choice B is incorrect because the defect concerns the construction of the new home and not the purchase transaction directly; however, such terms may be found in a purchase agreement. Choice D is incorrect because there are not enough facts to determine that the builder intended to commit fraud.

51. A: Choice A is correct because eviction discharges the obligation of the lessee paying rent to the lessor. Choice B is incorrect because there is no covenant of goodwill. Choice C is incorrect because this option is a covenant of ownership. Choice D is incorrect because there is no obligation of adverse possession under a lease.

52. A: Choice A is correct because it is a steering statement. Choice B is incorrect because it is a puffing statement. Choice C is incorrect because it is a statement about escheat. Choice D is incorrect because it is a factual statement about the property.

53. A: Choice A is correct because there is a scenario in a net listing where the sales price equals the predetermined amount that the seller is demanding, which would leave no additional money to be considered commission for the listing agent. Choices B, C, and D are incorrect because in all other listing agency agreements, the broker who brings the buyer is contractually owed a commission by the seller.

54. D: Choice D is correct because both Choice A and Choice B describe two of the lender-established responsibilities of the borrower, the others being protection from the loss of title and maintenance of the physical property. Choice C is incorrect because the lender does not stipulate that the borrower must pay a utility bill for the property.

55. B: Choice B is correct because $\$220,000 \times 0.06 = \$13,200$. Choices A, C, and D are incorrect.

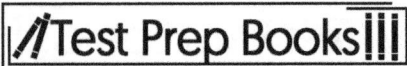

56. B: Choice *B* is correct because to discriminating against a person based on their being a parent is discrimination on the basis of familial status. Choices *A* and *D* are incorrect because members of certain occupation are not a protected class under fair housing laws. Choice *C* is incorrect because pet owners are not a protected class under fair housing laws.

57. D: Choice *D* is correct because the cost approach uses the value of the land plus the depreciated value of the building after improvements to estimate value and is best used for non-income-producing properties with no comps available. Choices *A* and *C* are incorrect because the income approach would be used for income-producing properties. Choice *B* is incorrect because if there are comps available, the sales comparison approach would be the best answer.

58. C: Choice *C* is correct because the seller has responsibilities to the agent under the agency agreement and one of those responsibilities is opportunity, meaning the seller needs to allow the agent the opportunity to have buyers see the property, as well as respecting understood social customs such as vacating the premises and removing pets during showings for an optimal showing experience. Choice *A* is incorrect because another responsibility of the seller is to provide the agent indemnity against any incidental loss that occurs during the course of the transaction. Choice *B* is incorrect because the seller owes the agent good faith in dealing with the agent and soliciting a better deal after an agency agreement has been established is not good faith. Additionally, no other ethical agent would discuss listing a property that is already listed. Choice *D* is incorrect because, while it is tempting, the seller has agreed in the agency agreement to the terms of payment to the agent, and renegotiating would be bad faith.

59. B: Choice *B* is correct because anyone can sell a personal property without having a real estate license. Choices *A*, *C*, and *D* are incorrect because it is not legal to conduct real estate business on behalf of others or receive compensation for a real estate transaction without having an active license.

60. B: Choice *B* is correct because environmental issues must be disclosed. Choice *A* is incorrect because it is unknown whether the appliance sits on a counter (like a blender) or is affixed to the property (like a stove), there is not enough information, and Choice *B* is the better choice. Choice *C* is incorrect because this would be a confidential matter, unless otherwise permitted by the seller. Choice *D* is incorrect because a creaky door would likely not be considered a material matter.

61. A: Choice *A* is correct because it requires that a conveyance of land be in a written contract. Choice *B* is incorrect because it regulates the time frame in which a person must bring a claim to recover damages or loss under a lawsuit. Choice *C* and *D* are incorrect because, although state regulations and county ordinances can apply to land conveyancing, these answer choices are not specific and do not address the question asked.

62. C: Choice *C* is correct because goodwill is an entity's intellectual property of its reputation. Choice *A* is incorrect because title is ownership. Choice *B* is incorrect because mortgage is an interest that an investor holds on a property subject to a supporting obligation. Choice *D* is incorrect because policy refers to insurance coverage.

63. D: Choice *D* is correct because mortgage brokers can shop around to get rates from multiple institutions to provide a variety of options for different borrowers. Choice *A* is incorrect because originators who are limited to a single institution are called mortgage bankers. Choice *B* is incorrect because borrowers would seek private investors independently. Choice *C* is incorrect because credit unions are available only to members.

Answer Explanations #1

64. A: Choice A is correct because the agreement between agent and client can differ from client to client; everything is negotiable. Choice B is incorrect because the Sherman Antitrust Act makes price fixing among brokerages illegal. Choice C is incorrect because it is illegal for a real estate board to establish set commission rates. Choice D is incorrect because, while the traditional method of compensation flows through the seller client and splits the commission between the two participating agents, any commission structure can be established, including having the buyer pay the commission for the selling agent.

65. B: Choice B is correct because Fyodor is required to make reasonable accommodations, but here it seems the accommodation would be unreasonable because of the substantial cost to Fyodor and the age of the property. Choice A is incorrect because the sought accommodation under these facts show that it is likely unreasonable.

66. D: Choice D is correct because closing is the conclusion of a transaction. Choice A is incorrect because this term is generally used with contract conclusions. Choice B is incorrect because this term describes excluding a party. Choice C is incorrect because escrow occurs after the purchase agreement is signed, but before closing occurs.

67. B: Choice B is correct because NOI equals potential gross rental income minus vacancy amount plus other income, all minus operating costs.

$$\$20{,}000 \text{ (Potential gross rental income)} - \$1000 \text{ (Vacancy of 5\% of \$20,000)} = \$19{,}000$$

$$\$19{,}000 + \$700 \text{ (Other income)} = \$19{,}700$$

$$\$19{,}700 - \$5{,}000 \text{ (Operating costs)} = \$14{,}700 \text{ (Net operating income)}$$

68. C: Choice C is correct because the conveyance holds a condition that Benjamin must not go to college to remain owner. Choice A is incorrect because the condition is not measured by Benjamin's (or another person's) life. Choice B is incorrect because Benjamin was not granted absolute ownership. Choice D is incorrect because reversion is a future ownership interest.

69. B: Choice B is correct because this type of discrimination is directly prohibited in selling homes to potential buyers under fair housing laws; it is discrimination based on familial status and the covenant would be invalidated. Therefore, Choices A, C, and D are all incorrect.

70. B: Choice B is correct. Toby would be entitled to specific performance because Stella is breaching the contract by refusing to sell, and money damages are generally not applicable because real estate is unique property that cannot be replaced by an exact same property. Choice A is incorrect because damages are generally not recoverable in a sale of land because a buyer could not go out and buy another same property; there is only one property, and the buyer is entitled to that property under the contract. Choice C is incorrect because the fact pattern does not mention a liquidated damages clause under the contract. Choice D is incorrect because punitive damages are not recoverable under a contract claim.

71. A: Choice A is correct because the property will be changing its use from residential to medical, which means that it will now be a commercial, income-producing property and the income approach is called for. Choices B and C are incorrect because there are no such approaches to value. Choice D is incorrect because the cost approach is for non-income-producing properties.

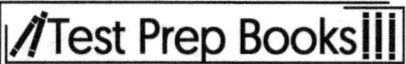

72. A: Choice A is correct because it is another term used to refer to a gross lease. Choice B is incorrect because a tenant pays for utilities and other expenses in a net lease. Choice C is incorrect because a tenant would pay a portion of revenue in a percentage lease. Choice D is incorrect because the monthly fee paid by the tenant would fluctuate based on an index.

73. A: Choice A is correct because this is damage caused by the installation of the modification by the tenant. The tenant is responsible for installation damage caused by a modification. Choices B, C, and D are examples of normal wear and tear, and a tenant would not be responsible for the repair of normal wear and tear.

74. C: Choice C is correct because furniture in a home will not be conveyed under a purchase agreement unless it is part of the listing or included in a bill of sale. Choices A, B, and D are incorrect because these are real property and they are covered under a purchase agreement.

75. A: Choice A is correct because a comparative market analysis will show what the property is worth in the current market. Choice B is incorrect because a survey determines property boundaries. Choice C is incorrect because an inspection is an evaluation of the condition of the building on the property. Choice D is incorrect because an assessment is determined by an assessor.

76. A: Choice A is correct because the facts suggest that Orville and Paul intend to take personal items from people's homes and sell the items to raise money for the charity. Taking personal items without consent is a crime: theft. Because the agreement involves performances of crimes, there is no contract—regardless of other factors or whether Orville and Paul's motive was altruistic. Therefore, Choices B, C, and D are incorrect because of the crimes that would be committed.

77. A: Choice A is correct because the money lent in exchange for the promise of payment is the loan; it is not the mortgage. Choices B, C, and D are incorrect because they are all elements of a mortgage.

78. D: Choice D is correct because a bill of sale is a document that identifies personal property that is to be sold in conjunction with a purchase agreement for real property. Choice A is incorrect because a deed transfers title. Choice B is incorrect because a note is a buyer's obligation to pay for the financing of the property purchase. Choice C is incorrect because an occupancy certificate shows that a property may be occupied by others.

79. C: Choice C is correct because demand is the missing element of value; demand is the first term in the acronym DUST. Choices A, B, and D are incorrect because they are principals of value that are fundamentally subcategories of the elements in DUST.

80. C: Choice C is correct because designated senior housing properties may discriminate based on familial status. Choice A is incorrect because the applicant's age is irrelevant for purposes of discriminating on familial status under these facts. Choice B is incorrect because this limitation would not change whether the exception applies to senior housing. Choice D is incorrect because it misstates the fair housing exception; senior housing properties may discriminate based on familial status, but all other protected classes are still protected under fair housing laws.

Practice Test #2

1. What is it called when a borrower attempts to sell a property without paying off the loan?
   a. Hypothecation
   b. Assumption
   c. Alienation
   d. Assignment

2. Vincent and Wendy are married and are buying a property. Their combined annual income is $60,000. Subsequently, a lender determines that Vincent and Wendy qualify for payments that constitute 23% of their income. What is the value of the monthly payment?
   a. $1,025.00
   b. $1,150.00
   c. $2,398.40
   d. $1,393.80

3. Global Company X wants to purchase several large tracts of adjacent properties but does not want to reveal its interest in the land until the deals are done. Global Company X contracts with an agent, Alice, to act as the principal in the transactions. In this scenario, which term best describes Alice's role?
   a. Universal agent
   b. Undisclosed principal
   c. General agent
   d. Principal agent

4. Which of the following is NOT personal property?
   a. Tangible property
   b. Chattel
   c. Fixture
   d. Intangible property

5. Russell owns land right next to a stream of water that passes across Russell's vast land. However, Russell does not use the water and just lets the water flow its natural course. Summer is a cattle farmer that lives five miles away down-stream and travels to the stream to collect water so that Summer may water her cattle. One day, Russell decides that he's going to divert the stream so that he may grow a garden. Under a riparian jurisdiction, may Russell do this?
   a. Yes
   b. No
   c. The answer depends on the size of the garden
   d. The answer depends on the size of the cattle operation

6. A building that is valued at $120,000 is being depreciated over 27.5 years. After 17 years, how much will the building have depreciated?
   a. $70,849.80
   b. $74,181.88
   c. $80,879.34
   d. $78,890.34

7. Wendy lives in a constructed home that was built ten years ago and was purchased from a builder. The written sales contract did not state any additional warranties regarding the property. Does the home have a warranty of fitness?
   a. Yes, because the home was constructed.
   b. Yes, because the builder constructed the home.
   c. No, because the home was built ten years ago.
   d. No, because the contract did not contain additional warranties.

8. Betsy is selling their grandmother's house to Christopher because Betsy's grandmother has since moved to Boca Raton. The house was built in 1963, but Betsy's grandmother did not own the property until 1982, after Betsy's grandfather was deceased. What must be given to Christopher during the escrow phase?
   a. A certificate of occupancy
   b. A special use permit
   c. EPA lead-based paint pamphlet
   d. A covenant

9. What is the one major difference between lien theory states and title theory states?
   a. The deed does not remain with the buyer in title theory states.
   b. The deed does not remain with the buyer in lien theory states.
   c. The buyer does not retain possession and ownership rights of the property in title theory states.
   d. The buyer does not retain possession and ownership rights of the property in lien theory states.

10. Which document shows the chain of title history of a property?
    a. Land survey
    b. Title commitment
    c. Abstract
    d. Deed

11. Dillon, a non-licensed professional, discovers an open source of asbestos in their commercial property. Which of the following actions should Dillon immediately take?
    a. Abatement
    b. Remediation
    c. Litigation
    d. Encapsulation

12. Which type of loan requires PMI until the borrower has 20% equity in the property?
    a. Conventional loan
    b. Insured conventional loan
    c. FHA loan
    d. VA loan

13. Recently a homeowner's house suffered damage in a grease fire. What offers coverage for this type of property damage?
    a. Home insurance
    b. Home warranty
    c. Home inspection
    d. Home improvement

Practice Test #2

14. A developer recently developed land and homes to be sold on the market. In the covenants they recorded into record, they stated that the homes may be used only as single-family homes. Is this a lawful exercise of private regulation on land?
    a. Yes
    b. No
    c. If found not to violate building codes
    d. If found not to violate fair housing laws

15. What is the term for the money that was lent to a borrower in exchange for the promise of future repayment?
    a. Mortgage
    b. Deed of trust
    c. Loan
    d. Contract for deed

16. Javier and Karina own property and have the right of survivorship. What type of ownership to Javier and Karina share?
    a. Joint tenancy
    b. Tenancy by entirety
    c. Sole propriety
    d. Estate in severality

17. What obligation is discharged when an eviction has occurred?
    a. Obligation to reside
    b. Obligation to clean
    c. Obligation to enjoy
    d. Obligation to pay

18. Briana and Caden are in a dispute on who owns a certain property. What type of lawsuit should be filed?
    a. Quiet title action
    b. Criminal action
    c. Fraud
    d. Breach of contract

19. In which approach is the value of the land calculated independently of the structure?
    a. Rural approach
    b. Cost approach
    c. Separation approach
    d. Sales comparison approach

20. Giselle holds a lease from January 13, 2002 to December 15, 2002. On September 12, 2002, what type of lease tenancy does Giselle have?
    a. Tenancy for years
    b. Periodic tenancy
    c. Tenancy at will
    d. Tenancy at sufferance

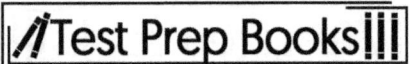

21. A seller has prepaid landscaper service fees for a 3-month duration. The prepayment amount was $900. At the end of the 1st month, the property was sold to a buyer. What is the prorated amount that will be debited to the buyer?
    a. $600
    b. $700
    c. $800
    d. $300

22. When is there a seller's market?
    a. More houses are for sale in a given month than in the previous month
    b. More houses are for sale than there are buyers to buy them
    c. Fewer houses are for sale in a given month than in the previous month
    d. Fewer houses are for sale than there are buyers to buy them

23. If the GRM of a property is 110 and the monthly potential gross income for that property is $1,400, what is the estimated value of that property?
    a. $140,110
    b. $141,000
    c. $152,727
    d. $154,000

24. Which of the following is a valid lease?
    a. Written lease
    b. Unwritten lease
    c. Short term lease
    d. All the above

25. Ian and Janet, siblings, owned a property as tenants in common. Ian and Janet did not get along with each other because of a lifelong sibling rivalry. Both refused to work together on any matter, which resulted in Ian selling their interest to Karl and Janet selling their interest to Leanne. Ian placed a deed restriction in the deed given to Karl that stated that Karl could not pull up the oak tree in the front yard. Meanwhile, Janet orally told Leanne that Leanne could not remove the oak tree from the front yard. Who may remove the oak tree?
    a. Karl only
    b. Leanne only
    c. Both Karl and Leanne
    d. Neither Karl nor Leanne

26. Anthony tells Beverly, "If you paint my house before the weekend, I'll pay you $3,000." Beverly says, "Great, you've got yourself a deal." Anthony and Beverly shake hands. Subsequently, Beverly finishes painting the house on Friday. Which type of contract did the parties create?
    a. They created a bilateral contract
    b. They created unilateral contract
    c. There is no contract
    d. It depends on whether Beverly intended to accept the offer verbally

27. Salvador is the only owner of a parcel of land without a condition. What type of ownership does Salvador have?
    a. Life estate
    b. Fee simple absolute
    c. Defeasible fee
    d. Remainder

28. Out of the following choices, who is likely to have the most goodwill?
    a. A locally known hardware store
    b. An international tech company
    c. A statewide grocery chain
    d. A nationwide toy brand

29. There are two types of involuntary alienation. One is adverse possession. What is the other?
    a. Prescriptive easement
    b. Easement right necessity
    c. Easement in gross
    d. Appurtenant easement

30. A buyer recently told their broker that they were unsure whether they could obtain financing for the current property purchase. What must the broker do?
    a. Wait to hear from the lender
    b. Disclose the matter to the selling side
    c. Wait until closing to see what happens
    d. Help the buyer secure another lender

31. A buyer named Bill is the client of a licensee named Laura, and they want to buy a house that Laura has recently listed. Which of the following statements is true?
    a. The seller and buyer must be informed of the situation and agree to limited representation.
    b. Laura cannot legally represent the buyer in this transaction.
    c. Laura should refer the buyer to a different brokerage in order to complete the sale.
    d. The buyer should represent himself in this sale since licensee Laura already works for the seller.

32. Kyle and Luke are in a lease agreement, Luke is the tenant and Kyle is the landlord. Luke is the former owner of the premises that is currently being leased from Kyle for a long-term duration. What is this?
    a. Gross lease
    b. Sale-leaseback
    c. Net lease
    d. Percentage lease

33. Under the statute of frauds, which of the following spoken, intended statements may constitute a valid contract?
    a. A sale of lands
    b. A six-month lease
    c. A marriage contract
    d. A sale of goods over $500

34. In addition to the agent-principal relationship, which of the following would be considered a fiduciary relationship?
    a. Hairdresser-client
    b. Attorney-client
    c. Teacher-student
    d. CEO-employee

35. A broker discovers there is a broken blender in the kitchen. Must they disclose this?
    a. No, because it is not a material defect.
    b. Yes, because it is a material defect.
    c. No, because the seller is the one who must disclose it.
    d. Yes, because the broker has an obligation to disclose a discovered defect.

36. The owner of a rental property in a college town wants to keep "a certain clientele" in its units to preserve "the integrity" among the property. When a rental applicant appears to not belong to this desired clientele, the landlord attempts to persuade the applicant to look elsewhere for housing. May the landlord do this?
    a. Yes
    b. No
    c. The answer depends on whether there are multiple police complaints against the property for noise violations
    d. The answer depends on whether other properties in the area are engaging in this same practice

37. Esmerelda recently became unemployed and was unable to meet some of the financial obligations arising from their property, and now the government has a lien on Esmerelda's property. What did Esmerelda not pay?
    a. HOA dues
    b. Property tax
    c. Income tax
    d. Property fee

38. What is an easement?
    a. A promise that runs with the land
    b. A right to use another's land
    c. A claim to the land to secure payment
    d. An intrusion on a neighboring property

39. Under the Civil Rights Act of 1968, as originally passed, which of the following was not a protected class?
    a. Race
    b. National origin
    c. Handicap or disability
    d. Religion

40. A real estate licensee sold a house for $180,000. If the total commission on the transaction was 6%, what is the total commission in value?
    a. $10,800
    b. $12,000
    c. $9,880
    d. $13,124

41. Donna is renting out a residential property. Whom may Donna discriminate against?
    a. A person who is blind
    b. A person with a mental impairment
    c. A person with a pet
    d. A person with a hearing impairment

42. Which document shows the transfer of money between parties at the conclusion of a transaction?
    a. Financing statement
    b. Closing statement
    c. Abstracts
    d. Commitment

43. Recently, a buyer purchased a new home construction from a neighbor, who purchased it from a builder last month. The sales contract did not contain any additional warranties, and the neighbor did not inspect the property. Subsequently, a defect was discovered. May the buyer pursue a new home construction claim against the builder?
    a. Yes
    b. No
    c. The answer depends on the jurisdiction
    d. The answer depends on the statute of limitations

44. Which entity publishes regulations and guidelines for the designated senior housing classification of properties?
    a. The state governor
    b. The landlord
    c. The local police division
    d. The Department of Housing and Urban Development

45. While giving a tour to a prospective buyer, the broker says, "You will not find a better house than this; it's the best in the neighborhood!" However, there are multiple properties available in the neighborhood. Which term best describes the broker's statement?
    a. Puffing
    b. Misrepresentation
    c. Fraud
    d. Illusory statement

46. Agent Abigail's friend Ben wants to buy a property outside of agent Abigail's service area. Agent Abigail refers Ben to a receiving agent in the desired area. What should agent Abigail do now?
    a. Continue to service her local clients but not Ben
    b. Question Ben about advice being given by the receiving agent
    c. Call the receiving agent and insist on being present for showings and inspections
    d. Call the listing agent in Ben's transaction to discuss the negotiation of repairs

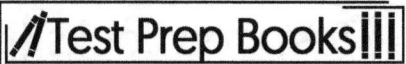

47. What is the term for the court order that allows a lender to demand that the borrower pay any outstanding balance remaining on the loan after a foreclosure sale?
    a. Deficiency judgment
    b. Right of redemption
    c. Promissory note
    d. Prepayment penalty

48. Which service would a property owner NOT expect a property manager to handle for them?
    a. Collecting rent and security deposits
    b. Marketing the property
    c. Paying the HOA fees in the property's subdivision
    d. Providing detailed financial reports

49. Meredith has a big event coming up on Friday, August 20, and they want their house painted beforehand. On Sunday, August 15, Meredith tells Neil, "If you paint my house by Wednesday, I will pay you $3,000." Neil responds, "I accept your offer, but it must be a cash payment." If there were no further contact between Meredith and Neil on that day, which kind of contract was formed between the parties on Sunday?
    a. A unilateral contract
    b. A bilateral contract
    c. A service contract
    d. There is no contract

50. Who may get a home warranty?
    a. A buyer
    b. A seller
    c. Neither a buyer nor a seller
    d. Both a buyer and a seller

51. Which of the following is implied within a lease agreement?
    a. Indefinite duration
    b. Covenant of quiet enjoyment
    c. Ownership
    d. Promise to not disturb

52. Which of the following is NOT a characteristic that makes land valuable or desirable?
    a. Uniqueness
    b. Indestructible
    c. Abundance
    d. Location

53. Karen and Lucy are entering into a contract for sale of land. Closing is to take place next month. Two weeks later, Lucy refuses to sell the land to Karen. Subsequently Karen gets a remedy from the court forcing Lucy to sell the land to Karen. What was Karen's remedy?
    a. Damages
    b. Rescission
    c. Specific performance
    d. Mutual assent

54. For the purposes of fair housing law, who is considered a child?
   a. Persons under the age of 14
   b. Persons under the age of 16
   c. Persons under the age of 18
   d. Persons under the age of 21

55. As part of the Truth in Lending Act, a loan estimate is provided within three days of a buyer applying for a loan. What does it contain information about?
   a. HOA and utility payments
   b. Estimated taxes and insurance
   c. Loan approval
   d. All of the above

56. What is the process of placing documents into public record?
   a. Notice
   b. Notarization
   c. Recording
   d. Execution

57. A lot has a depth of 90 ft and an area of 6,480 sq ft. What is the frontage of the lot?
   a. 74 ft
   b. 70 ft
   c. 72 ft
   d. 68 ft

58. Michael is the broker-in-charge of Company A and Marilyn is a licensee who works for Company A. Jerry is a licensee who works for Company B. Marilyn is representing a seller on behalf of Company A, and Jerry has just brought a buyer for this seller's house. What is Marilyn's role in this transaction, relative to Michael's role?
   a. Subagent
   b. Agent
   c. Principal
   d. Third party

59. Graham is selling his property to Helen. Both Graham and Helen have satisfied most of the requirements in the purchase agreement and all the lending ancillary requirements. Helen must vacate Helen's current residence, otherwise they will be subject to an eviction. Graham must sell the property as soon as possible, otherwise Graham will have to file for bankruptcy. Under these facts, may the parties close?
   a. No, the lender must issue a lender certification first.
   b. No, the purchasing requirements are not completed.
   c. No, escrow agent(s) have not consented to an early close.
   d. Yes, because Graham needs a new home and Helen needs money to pay off debt.

60. What law was passed to prevent lenders, real estate agents, and title companies from giving kickbacks to each other during a real estate transaction?
   a. National Consumer Protection Act
   b. Real Estate Settlement Procedures Act (RESPA)
   c. Sherman Antitrust Act
   d. Truth in Lending Act

61. Which approach to value is used in a broker price opinion (BPO)?
   a. Income approach
   b. Sales comparison approach
   c. Cost approach
   d. Capitalization approach

62. Members of which protected classes may be victims of steering?
   a. National origin
   b. Race
   c. Familial status
   d. All of the above

63. Benny, a buyer, finds a house that he is considering for a purchase. It has been updated to have four bedrooms, but it still has only one bathroom. This property will be valued lower based on which type of depreciation?
   a. Physical deterioration
   b. Material obsolescence
   c. Functional obsolescence
   d. External obsolescence

64. How large is the area of an acre?
   a. 100 feet
   b. 43,560 square feet
   c. 5,280 square feet
   d. 5,280 feet

65. Malachi and Nolan own a property together in joint tenancy. Subsequently, Nolan dies. Nolan's will states that Nolan's property interest shall pass to Oscar. Which of the following correctly states the owner(s)?
   a. Malachi and Oscar
   b. Malachi and Nolan
   c. Oscar
   d. Malachi

66. A seller is selling Ulysses' property and informs the broker in a letter that Ulysses does not want to hear any offers below $100,000. A few days letter, a prospective broker submits a $95,000 offer to the seller's broker. Is the broker required to present the offer to the seller?
   a. Yes
   b. No
   c. The answer depends on whether the buyer knew that the seller wanted at least $100,000 for the property
   d. The answer depends on whether $95,000 was a reasonable offer

67. Which of the following discharges performance under contract?
   a. Death
   b. Impracticability
   c. Impossibility
   d. All of the above

68. Which loan-to-value ratio carries the least amount of risk?
   a. 80%
   b. 50%
   c. 70%
   d. 60%

69. Zelda owns a property in a district that recently underwent a zone change, which has caused them extreme hardship in the use of the property. The property has been in Zelda's family for multiple generations, and Zelda wants to keep the property so that Zelda's heirs may use it. Which of the following may Zelda seek for the experienced hardship?
   a. A variance
   b. A nonconforming use
   c. A special use permit
   d. An eminent domain proceeding

70. Who needs to be a licensed real estate agent?
   a. The owner of an apartment building
   b. An employee of the state real estate commission
   c. A man who has been appointed trustee of an estate with a house to be sold
   d. An auctioneer who auctions farmland for local landowners

71. What is an appraiser responsible for?
   a. Estimating value
   b. Finding exact value
   c. Increasing value
   d. Notarizing value

72. The cost approach uses several factors to determine the estimated replacement cost of a property. Which factor is NOT used?
   a. Estimated value of the land
   b. Estimated cost of a reproduction
   c. Estimated material obsolescence
   d. Estimated physical deterioration

73. A property sold for $200,000. The selling agent earned a 3% commission and has a 60/40 split with the agent's sponsoring brokerage (with the brokerage receiving the 40%). What amount will the <u>agent</u> receive?
   a. $3,000
   b. $1,200
   c. $3,600
   d. $2,900

74. Under an eminent domain proceeding, what is the amount of compensation the property owner is entitled to?
    a. The future reasonable fair market value
    b. The reasonable worth to the government
    c. The current reasonable fair market value
    d. The loss that the property owner will suffer

75. Quentin and Rachel entered a contract. Subsequently, Quentin refused perform their obligation. What is the term for Quentin's conduct?
    a. Repudiation
    b. Covenant
    c. Interference of performance
    d. Revocation

76. Isaac and Jessica are in a lease agreement, Isaac is the tenant and Jessica is the landlord. Isaac pays a fee for a leased premises that fluctuates based on an index. What type of lease is this?
    a. Gross lease
    b. Net lease
    c. Percentage lease
    d. Index lease

77. Recently, Inigo rented a condo to Jackson. Jackson required installation of a modification to accommodate a disability, and Inigo allowed the installation for Jackson's accommodation. Where may a modification NOT be made?
    a. Inside the unit
    b. Outside the building
    c. In the laundry room
    d. In the building's lobby

78. A buyer wants to purchase a seller's property but can only get a loan for half the sales price. The seller agrees to carry a mortgage for the balance of the sales price. Which type of seller financing is this?
    a. Contract for deed
    b. Purchase money mortgage
    c. Junior (subordinate) mortgage
    d. Assumable mortgage

79. Who needs to sign a dual agency contract, and when do they need to sign it?
    a. The buyer and seller at closing
    b. The seller at the time of listing
    c. The buyer before an offer is presented and by the seller before acceptance
    d. The agent at the time of listing

80. What type of property may qualify for a §1031 exchange?
    a. Primary residence
    b. Commercial property
    c. Investment property
    d. Industrial property

Answer Explanations #2

1. C: Choice C is correct because alienation occurs when the borrower tries to sell the property without paying off the loan. Choice A is incorrect because hypothecation is the act of pledging a property as collateral while retaining the right of ownership and possession. Choice B is incorrect because assumption is the process of a buyer taking the seller's place on a mortgage. Choice D is incorrect because assignment refers to the ability of the borrower to transfer in writing the loan obligation to a third party.

2. B: Choice B is correct because $60,000 ÷ 12$ months $= \$5,000.00$, then $\$5,000.00 \times 0.23 = \$1,150.00$. Choices A, C, and D are incorrect.

3. B: Choice B is correct because agent Alice is representing herself as the principal (buyer) in order to shield the identity of her client from the seller. In any contract dispute, the liability rests with her. Choice A is incorrect because a universal agent has broad authority to conduct business for a large entity, but that entity is still the named principal in any real estate transaction. Choice C is incorrect because a general agent is typically the licensee/subagent who works on behalf of the agent (BIC) for a particular client. Choice D is incorrect because there is no such thing as a principal agent.

4. C: Choice C is correct because the fixture is considered real property. Choice A is incorrect because personal property may be tangible. Choice B is incorrect because chattel is another word for personal property. Choice D is incorrect because personal property may be intangible property.

5. B: Choice B is correct because, under a riparian jurisdiction, a riparian owner may make reasonable use of a watercourse but not to the extent it interferes with another riparian owner's use. Here, Russell's diverting the stream would affect Summer's use downstream and would be unreasonable; there would be no water downstream for Summer to use if the stream were diverted. Choice A is incorrect for the preceding reason. Choices C and D are irrelevant to the determination of Russell's unreasonable use of the stream that will affect Summer's use downstream.

6. B: Choice B is correct because $\$120,000 ÷ 27.5 = \$4,363.64$. Then, $\$4,363.64 \times 17 = \$74,181.88$. Therefore, choices A, C, and D are incorrect.

7. C: Choice C is correct because an implied warranty of fitness applies to new construction, but here the property is ten years old. The property at one time would have had such a warranty because it was a newly constructed home built by a builder and the warranty did not need to be expressed in a written contract. However, due to the age of the property, it has expired. Choices A, B, and D are incorrect because of the preceding reasons.

8. C: Choice C is correct because a seller must give a copy of an EPA pamphlet about lead to a buyer if the home was built prior to January 1, 1978. Choice A is incorrect because a certificate of occupancy permits a property to be occupied, and here the house is already occupied. Choice B is incorrect because a special use permit is obtained for a particular business to operate, such as a hospital. Choice D is incorrect because Betsy is not required by law to give Christopher a covenant.

9. A: Choice A is correct because in title theory states, the title is given to the buyer, who then issues a deed of trust to a trustee to hold. The lender is the beneficiary of this deed of trust until the loan is satisfied. Choice B is incorrect because the title (deed) goes to the buyer at closing in lien theory states.

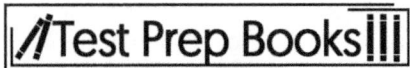

Choices C and D are incorrect because the buyer always retains possession and ownership rights of the property after closing.

10. C: Choice C is correct because the abstract shows a property's history, including the chain of title history. Choice A is incorrect because a land survey shows a property's boundaries. Choice B is incorrect because a title commitment shows a commitment to title insurance after closing. Choice D is incorrect because a deed is a document that transfers title.

11. D: Choice D is correct because Dillon should immediately encapsulate and seal the open source; later, a licensed professional can handle the matter. Choice A is incorrect because abatement is the process of removing the asbestos but should only be handled by a professional, not by Dillon. Choice B is incorrect because remediation is the process of removing mold. Choice C is incorrect because litigation is the pursuit of a legal suit; it does not directly solve the issue of which action Dillon should take immediately upon discovering the open source.

12. B: Choice B is correct because in an insured conventional loan, PMI is required until the buyer achieves 20% equity in the property. At that point, the PMI can be removed. Choice A is incorrect because in a conventional loan, the borrower has contributed a large enough down payment that 20% or more equity is already in place and no PMI is necessary. Choice C is incorrect because mortgage insurance in an FHA loan is financed into the loan and can never be removed. Choice D is incorrect because no PMI is required in a VA loan.

13. A: Choice A is correct because home insurance covers damage from an unexpected event, such as a fire. Choice B is incorrect because a home warranty covers normal wear and tear to particular portions of the property, such as a heating and cooling system. Choice C is incorrect because a home inspection is an inspection of the property and does not offer coverage in the event of damage. Choice D is incorrect because home improvement is the process of adding improvements to a home.

14. A: Choice A is correct because a single-single family home is a type of residential building and would not violate fair housing laws. Choice B is incorrect for the reason stated in the explanation of Choice A. Choice C is incorrect because nothing in the facts suggests that there is any questionable matter regarding *how* the homes are built. Choice D is incorrect because, as stated in the explanation of Choice A, there is not a violation of fair housing laws.

15. C: Choice C is correct because a loan is money that is lent to a borrower in exchange for a promise of future repayment. Choice A is incorrect because the mortgage is the lien attached to the property for which the loan was secured. Choice B is incorrect because a deed of trust is similar to a mortgage but has a trustee, instead of the borrower, holding the title to the property until the loan is satisfied. Choice D is incorrect because a contract for deed is a type of seller financing in which the seller allows the buyer to move onto the property and make installment payments directly to the seller.

16. A: Choice A is correct because joint tenants have the right of survivorship. Choice B is incorrect because tenancy by entirety is shared by spouses and the facts do not state that Javier and Karina are married. Choice C is incorrect because sole propriety ownership is held by one person, or artificial person. Choice D is incorrect because it is another term for sole propriety.

17. D: Choice D is correct because an eviction discharges the tenant's obligation to pay for the leased premises. Choice A is incorrect because there is no obligation to reside. Choice B is incorrect because

Answer Explanations #2

there is no obligation to clean, unless otherwise stated. Choice *C* is incorrect because there is no obligation to enjoy.

18. A: Choice *A* is correct because a quiet title action determines who owns a property. Choice *B* is incorrect because criminal proceedings are initiated by the state, not private persons. Choice *C* is incorrect because facts do not show fraudulent conduct. Choice *D* is incorrect because the facts do not show that a contract is involved in this dispute.

19. B: Choice *B* is correct because estimating the value of the land is necessary as one of the factors in the cost approach. Choices *A* and *C* are incorrect because there are no such approaches as these. Choice *D* is incorrect because the sales comparison approach does not separate the land from the structure.

20. A: Choice *A* is correct because a tenancy for years lease shows a predetermined expiration date. Choice *B* is incorrect because nothing in the facts state that this lease is renewable, such as a month-to-month duration. Choice *C* is incorrect because tenancy at will has an infinite duration, but here the expiration date is December 15, 2002. Choice *D* is incorrect because B is still within the lease duration and has not stayed on the property past the expiration date.

21. A: Choice *B* is correct because $1,200 ÷ 6$ months $= \$200$, then $200 \times 2 = \$400.00$ proration. Choices *A*, *C*, and *D* are incorrect.

22. D: Choice *D* is correct because a seller's market occurs when the number of available properties is less than the number of buyers. Choices *A* and *C* are incorrect because numbers moving up or down from one month to the next do not, in and of themselves, signify a larger market trend. Choice *B* is incorrect because more listings available than buyers signifies a buyer's market.

23. D: Choice *D* is correct because estimated market value equals GRM times monthly potential gross income.

$110 \text{ (GRM)} \times \$1400 \text{ (Monthly income)} = \$154,000 \text{ (Estimated market value)}$

24. D: Choice *D* is correct because a lease may be in writing or spoken, and short-term or long-term in duration. Therefore, Choices *A*, *B*, and *C* are incorrect.

25. B: Choice *B* is correct because Janet made a nonbinding request of Leanna, which Leanne has the choice to obey or not obey; Leanne can remove the tree or not remove the tree. Choice *A* is incorrect because Ian put a deed restriction in the deed to Karl, and it is binding on Karl. Choices *C* and *D* are incorrect for the preceding reasons.

26. B: Choice *B* is correct because Anthony created a unilateral contract that could be accepted only by Beverly's performance: painting the house before the weekend. Choice *A* is incorrect because there was no offer for a bilateral contract, Beverly could only accept Anthony's offer by performing. Even though Beverly said "Great, you've got yourself a deal," that means nothing in forming a contract. There was no contract until Beverly started and finished painting the house before the weekend. Choice *C* is incorrect because as discussed, there was a contract formed. Choice *D* is incorrect because it is irrelevant; whether Beverly wanted to accept verbally, the offer could only be accepted by performance.

27. B: Choice *B* is correct because B is the only owner of this parcel of land, which is fee simple absolute. Choice *A* is incorrect because if Salvador only had a life estate, there would be another owner who would hold the future interest. Choice *C* is incorrect because there is no stated condition that Salvador must follow to remain the owner of the property. Choice D is incorrect because Salvador is the only owner and therefore holds the present and future interest of the property.

28. B: Choice B is correct because an international tech company is likely to be more well-known and reach a larger market than the other options. Therefore, choices A, C, and D are incorrect.

29. A: Choice A is correct because a prescriptive easement may be required under similar circumstances as adverse possession. Choice B is incorrect because easement by necessity occurs when an owner is unable to reach owned land because it is land locked. Choice C is incorrect because an easement in gross is an easement held by a particular person to use the land for that person's benefit. Choice D is incorrect because an appurtenant easement is an easement of a land (servient estate) that allows another's land (dominant estate) to use and benefit the other's land.

30. B: Choice B is correct because the broker has a duty to disclose a material matter, such as a buyer not being able to obtain financing, to the selling side of the transaction. Choice A is incorrect because that is not the duty imposed on the broker and the question asks what the broker *must* do. Choice C is incorrect because based on the facts provided, there may not be a closing because of failure of obtaining financing. Choice D is incorrect because the broker does not have a duty to secure another lender for the buyer.

31. A: Choice A is correct because both buyer and seller must agree to dual agency before acceptance of an offer in which the agent represents both clients. The clients are acknowledging that a conflict of interest may arise and that some elements of their representation may be limited during the transaction. Choice B is incorrect because licensee Laura has the legal right through dual agency to represent buyer and seller in the same transaction. Choice C is incorrect because there is no need to refer the client to another brokerage if the clients are both willing to accept dual agency. Another option is designated agency, in which the client (buyer) is referred to another agent within the same brokerage. Choice D is incorrect because the buyer has already established interest in having agent representation for the real estate deal; instead of handling the purchase alone, the buyer can simply request another agent within that brokerage to complete the transaction using designated agency.

32. B: Choice B is correct because a landowner that sells property to another and then leases the property on a long-term duration is a sale-leaseback. Choices A, C, and D are incorrect because generally the tenant is not the former landowner of the premises and the lease is not for long-term duration; a sale-leaseback is used when the tenant is a former owner (of the premises) that leases the premises with the intent to remain for a long-term duration.

33. B: Choice B is correct because a verbal agreement for a six-month lease is sufficient for a contract. Choices A, C, and D are incorrect because these are all agreements that need to be in a written contract to be a valid contract; spoken words are insufficient to form a contract in these instances.

34. B: Choice B is correct because an attorney has the same fiduciary responsibilities that an agent has toward their client. Choice A is incorrect because the hairdresser is not legally required to keep any client communications confidential. Choice C is incorrect because there is no legal contract signed; it is a social agreement between a respected elder and an impressionable student. Choice D is incorrect because the CEO has no legal responsibility to keep communications confidential, nor do they have contractual loyalty to their employees.

Answer Explanations #2

35. A: Choice *A* is correct because a broken blender would not be considered a material defect. The seller is likely to take the blender with them after closing, and it will not affect the purchase transaction. Choice *B* is incorrect because the broken blender is not a material defect. Choice *C* is correct because the seller does not have a duty to disclose a defect regarding the seller's personal property. Choice *D* is incorrect because a broker has a duty to disclose material defects, not all defects.

36. B: Choice *B* is correct because it is an example of steering, and under fair housing laws steering is prohibited. Choice *A* is incorrect because, as discussed in the explanation of Choice *B*, this is steering. Choices *C* and *D* are incorrect because these considerations are irrelevant when engaging in the prohibited practice of steering.

37. B: Choice *B* is correct because the tax must be paid to the government, or it may result in a lien on the property. Choice *A* is incorrect because HOAs are generally private entities and missing HOA dues would not place a government lien on the property. Choice *C* is incorrect because income tax is directly associated with a person's income, but not with their property—here the amount of money owed was for the property. Choice *D* is incorrect because the amount is called a "property tax," not a property fee.

38. B: Choice *B* is correct because this is the definition of an easement. Choice *A* is incorrect because this is the definition of a covenant. Choice *C* is incorrect because this is the definition of lien. Choice *D* is incorrect because this is the definition of encroachment.

39. C: Choice *C* is correct because handicap or disability was not a protected class until the amending act followed in the 1980s. Choice *A*, *B*, and *D* are incorrect because these are protected classes under the Civil Rights Act of 1968.

40. A: Choice *A* is correct because $\$180{,}000 \times 0.06 = \$10{,}800$. Choices *B*, *C*, and *D* are incorrect.

41. C: Choice *C* is correct because Donna may discriminate against a person who has a pet when renting a residential property. Choices *A*, *B*, and *D* are incorrect because these are examples of a person with a handicap/disability and are a protected class under fair housing laws.

42. B: Choice *B* is correct because a closing statement shows the transfer of money between parties at the conclusion of a transaction. Choice *A* is incorrect because a financing statement is the transfer of money between the buyer and the investor. Choice *C* is incorrect because an abstract is a document that shows a property's history. Choice *D* is incorrect because a commitment shows that title insurance may be extended to a property at the conclusion of a transaction.

43. C: Choice *C* is correct because jurisdictions are not uniform in whether a secondary title holder of a new construction may pursue a breach of new construction warranty against the builder. In some jurisdictions, only the initial purchaser may bring the breach of new construction warranty claim. Choices *A* and *B* are incorrect because there is no uniformity on this matter among jurisdictions. Choice *D* is incorrect because the buyer purchased the property from the neighbor after the neighbor had owned it for a month; the new construction is a little over a month old. Statute of limitation restrictions generally give two or three years to bring a claim; after just one month, there is likely plenty of time to bring a claim under an applicable statute of limitations.

44. D: Choice *D* is correct because the Department of Housing and Urban Development publishes regulations and guidelines regarding senior housing classification of properties. Choices *A* and *B* are incorrect because the state governor and a landlord are not the legal authority to publish regulations

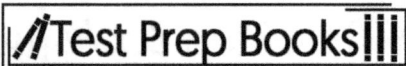

and guidelines regarding senior housing classification. Choice C is incorrect because the local police division may enforce the regulation and guidelines, but it does not publish the regulations and guidelines for designated senior housing classification.

45. A: Choice A is correct because it is a statement that cannot be determined to be factual (or nonfactual); it is an embellished marketing statement. Choices B and C are incorrect because the broker did not make a factually incorrect statement about the property; the statement may be true or untrue. Choice D is incorrect because this is not an accepted term used to describe what the broker did: puffing.

46. A: Choice A is correct because a referring agent should not participate in the referred transaction once it has been handed off. Choices B, C, and D are incorrect because the referring agent should not interfere in the transaction in any way.

47. A: Choice A is correct because a deficiency judgment allows a lender to demand the balance of payment on a loan after foreclosure proceedings. Choice B is incorrect because that refers to the ability of a borrower to pay the balance of a loan, plus interest and expenses, in order to keep a property that has gone into foreclosure. Choice C is incorrect because a promissory note is the promise that outlines the details of how a borrower will pay the loan back to the lender. Choice D is incorrect because the prepayment penalty refers to the practice of lenders penalizing borrowers for paying a loan off faster than originally contracted, in an attempt to avoid paying some of the interest.

48. C: Choice C is correct because the task of paying HOA dues falls to a property owner, not the property manager. Choices A, B, and D are incorrect because they represent specific contractual obligations that the property manager has to the property owner.

49. D: Choice D is correct because Meredith presented a unilateral contract that could be accepted by painting the house by Wednesday, but Neil rejected the offer by presenting a counteroffer that required a cash payment and the facts do not state that Meredith accepted it. Choice A is incorrect because Neil rejected Meredith's offer. Choice B is incorrect because the facts do not state that Meredith accepted Neil's counteroffer. Choice C is incorrect because, as discussed, there is no contract.

50. D: Choice D is correct because a buyer or seller may get a home warranty. Choices A, B, and C are incorrect because both a buyer and seller may get a home warranty.

51. B: Choice B is correct because the covenant of quiet enjoyment is implied within a lease agreement; a tenant may use and enjoy the leased premises as desired. Choice A is incorrect because a lease is stated for a definite duration, therefore it is unable to be indefinite in duration. Choice C is incorrect because a lease (or leasehold) is distinct from ownership and only allows the right to possess. Choice D is incorrect because the correct term is "covenant of quiet enjoyment."

52. C: Choice C is correct because there is not an abundance of land. There is a determined amount of land, which creates scarcity. Choice A is incorrect because land is valuable because it is unique. Choice B is incorrect because land is valuable because it is indestructible. Choice C is incorrect because land is valuable and desirable because of a parcel's location.

53. C: Choice C is correct because specific performance is a court order forcing a party to perform a specific act. Choice A is incorrect because, in this context, "damages" is another term used for money. Ordering Lucy to pay money would not be the same thing as ordering them to sell their land. Choice B is incorrect because this term describes canceling a contract; therefore, Karen would not get land under

Answer Explanations #2

this choice. Choice D is incorrect because mutual assent is the meeting of the minds, also known as acceptance of an offer.

54. C: Choice C is correct because, for the purposes of fair housing, a child is considered a person that is under the age of 18. Choices A, B, and D are incorrect because these are not the threshold age required for child classification under fair housing laws.

55. B: Choice B is correct because a loan estimate provides estimates of the interest rate, monthly payment, taxes, insurance, prepayment penalties, and closing costs. Choice A is incorrect because HOA fees and utility costs are not included on the loan estimate. Choice C is incorrect because the loan estimate is not a determination of whether a loan is approved. Choice D is incorrect because all three items are not part of a loan estimate.

56. C: Choice C is correct because recording is a process of entering documents into public record. Choice A is incorrect because although recording is generally used to give notice to others regarding certain subject matters, the process is referred to as recording. Choice B is incorrect because notarization regards certifying that a signature is genuine and not made under duress on a document. Choice D is incorrect because execution refers to the completion of a legal document.

57. C: Choice C is correct because $\frac{6,480 \text{ sq ft}}{90 \text{ ft}} = 72$ ft. Choices A, B, and D are incorrect.

58. A: Choice A is correct because Marilyn is the subagent for Company A in the agency agreement that Company A has with the seller. Choice B is incorrect because Michael is the agent (BIC) in the agency agreement with the seller. Choice C is incorrect because the seller is the principal in the agency agreement with Company A. Choice D is incorrect because the third parties who are not involved in the Company A agency agreement are Jerry and their buyer.

59. B: Choice B is correct because, under the facts provided, closing may not occur until the purchase agreement terms are completed. Choice A is incorrect because the lender may issue a certification that lending requirements are completed, but it is not required. Choice C is incorrect because, *if* escrow agents were involved, they could not consent to an early closing because *not all* the requirements have been completed under the terms under the contract. Choice D is incorrect because, while the parties may face severe detriment from a later close, they cannot close because the requirements have not been satisfied.

60. B: Choice B is correct because RESPA addresses real estate transaction cost inflation and promotes competition among service providers. Choices A and D are incorrect because the National Consumer Protection Act and the Truth in Lending Act are two names for the same law, which addresses the disclosure of all costs involved in the loan process. Choice C is incorrect because the Sherman Antitrust Act ensures "healthy and free market competition" related to the practice of real estate, establishing commission rates, etc.

61. B: Choice B is correct because the BPO uses only the sales comparison approach; a BPO is a less formal version of an appraisal. Choice A is incorrect because the BPO is not used for income-producing properties. Choice C is incorrect because typically only appraisers use their expertise to calculate an estimated value by using this method. Choice D is incorrect because capitalization approach is used to value commercial and investment properties but is not part of a BPO.

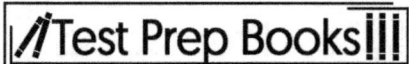

Answer Explanations #2

62. D: Choice *D* is correct because members of all these classes may be victims of steering. Choices *A*, *B*, and *C* are incorrect because these are not the only classes that may be victims of steering.

63. C: Choice *C* is correct because the property is showing functional obsolescence by still having only one bathroom even though the number of bedrooms has increased; consumers would expect more in today's market. Choice *A* is incorrect because nothing was said about the house being physically in bad shape. Choice *B* is incorrect because there is no such thing. Choice *D* is incorrect because external obsolescence refers to outside influences that affect the desirability of the property.

64. B: Choice *B* is correct. Choices *A* and *D* are incorrect because an acre is a measurement of area, not distance. *C* is incorrect and significantly smaller than an acre.

65. D: Choice *D* is correct because Malachi and Nolan shared joint tenancy, which has the right of survivorship. When a joint tenant dies the remainder of joint tenants acquire the deceased's property interest. Choices *A* and *C* are incorrect because Oscar is unable to acquire ownership interest because Nolan had no interest to give, regardless of what Nolan's will states. Choice *B* is incorrect because B is deceased, and the deceased may not own property.

66. B: Choice *B* is correct because the broker was provided with a writing from the seller stating the preference of offers (the letter). Choice *A* is incorrect because the broker does not have a duty to present the offer. Choices *C* and *D* are incorrect because the choices are irrelevant in determining whether the broker has a duty to present an offer to the seller and Ulysses, based on the $100,000 limitation Ulysses' seller provided in writing to the broker.

67. D: Choice *D* is correct because all choices are a valid legal defense is to performance and can discharge an obligation to perform. Therefore, Choices *A*, *B*, and *C* are incorrect because *all* choices discharge a contractual performance under a contract because they are valid legal defenses.

68. B: Choice *B* is correct because lower ration shows lower risk, and 50% is the lowest option. Choices *A*, *C*, and *D* are incorrect.

69. A: Choice *A* is correct because a variance may be sought because of the hardship that Zelda is experiencing. Choice *B* is incorrect because a nonconforming use describes a use that differs from that specified in a later ordinance, and there is no mention of a pre-existing use here. Choice *C* is incorrect because a special use permit is obtained for particular businesses to operate, such as hospitals. Choice *D* is incorrect because a government would institute an eminent domain proceeding, not a private person.

70. D: Choice *D* is correct because the auctioneer is selling real estate on behalf of others; therefore, the auctioneer needs an active license. Choice *A* is incorrect because no license is needed to own an apartment building. Choice *B* is incorrect because the state commission is a government entity and not participating in or benefiting from individual transactions; therefore, no license is needed to work there. Choice *C* is incorrect because the trustee has legal permission to act as the seller representative to sell the house.

71. A: Choice *A* is correct because an appraiser's job is to estimate value. Choice *B* is incorrect because appraisers do not present a singular, definitive answer to a property's value; they simply estimate the value at that moment in time based on the three methods they have available to them. Choice *C* is incorrect because it is not an appraiser's job to increase value, merely to honestly estimate value. Choice *D* is incorrect because notarizing value does not exist.

Answer Explanations #2

72. C: Choice C is correct because there is no such thing as estimated material obsolescence. Choices A, B, and D are all factors used in the cost approach of estimating value.

73. C: Choice C is correct because $200,000 \times 0.03 = \$6,000$, then $\$6,000 \times 0.6 = \$3,600$. Choices A, B, and D are incorrect.

74. C: Choice C is correct because it is how the value of the property is determined when calculating "just compensation." Choices A, B, and D are incorrect because those matters are not evaluated when determining "just compensation."

75. D: Choice A is correct because a repudiation is conduct that expresses an intention to not complete a required contractual obligation. Choice B is incorrect because a covenant is a promise that runs with the land. Choice C is incorrect. It would be interference of performance only if Quentin attempted to interfere with someone else's performance, not Quentin's own performance. Choice D is incorrect because revocation is the cancelling of a contract, but for revocation to occur, Rachel would need to consent to the cancellation, and that did not occur here.

76. D: Choice D is correct because the tenant pays a fee that fluctuates based on an index. Choice A is incorrect because a tenant pays a flat fee for a leased premises in a gross lease. Choice B is incorrect because a tenant pays a flat fee in addition to utilities and property taxes in a net lease. Choice C is incorrect because a tenant pays a fee that fluctuates based on the amount of monthly revenue earned.

77. B: Choice B is correct because an accommodating modification may not be made on the outside of a building. Choices A, B, and D are incorrect because an accommodating modification may be made inside of a unit or in common areas, such as a laundry room or lobby.

78. C: Choice C is correct because in a junior mortgage, the seller agrees to carry a mortgage on the balance of the purchase price that the borrower can't get a loan for. Choice A is incorrect because contract for deed is a type of seller financing in which the seller allows the buyer to move onto the property and make installment payments directly to the seller. Choice B is incorrect because a purchase money mortgage is an agreement for the seller to become the mortgage company, but only for a very short loan term. Choice D is incorrect because an assumable mortgage has the buyer taking the seller's place on a mortgage; additionally, the buyer will need to bring the balance in cash or get another loan to cover the balance of the sales price.

79. C: Choice C is correct because both parties must agree to dual agency before a contract can be accepted. Choice A is incorrect because the dual agency must be agreed to prior to acceptance of the contract; at closing is too late and could affect the successful completion of the sale. Choices B and D are incorrect because they represent both parties to the listing agreement, and there is no buyer in the equation yet. The option of dual agency can be discussed at this point to prepare the seller if this situation arises.

80. C: Choice C is correct because investment property may qualify for a §1031 exchange. Choices A, B, and D are incorrect because these types of properties cannot qualify for a §1031 exchange tax deferral transaction.

Practice Test #3

1. Which of the seller financing options is most similar to "rent-to-own"?
   a. Assumable mortgage
   b. Junior mortgage
   c. Purchase money mortgage
   d. Contract for deed

2. Concerning real estate, what is the purpose of police power?
   a. To take property away from citizens
   b. To tax citizens for their property
   c. To regulate how property should be used
   d. To regulate how property should be sold

3. In the context of real estate, what is steering?
   a. Influencing a potential home buyer or residential renter to purchase or rent a certain property based on the buyer or renter's status
   b. Influencing homeowners to sell property cheaply because of the fear of people of another class moving into the neighborhood
   c. Using police power to regulate how land may be used in a particular area
   d. Making a factually incorrect statement about a property

4. Owen and Paige are in a lease agreement. The leased premises only has one bathroom and it recently quit functioning. Paige, the tenant, contacted Owen and requested that Owen service the bathroom so that Paige may be able to use it. However, Owen refused because Owen does not want to service the bathroom. Which of the following words describes what occurred?
   a. Discrimination
   b. Constructive eviction
   c. Physical eviction
   d. Zoning

5. Under a unilateral contract, who is the obligor?
   a. The person who has an obligation for performance
   b. The person who has an obligation to receive performance
   c. The person who benefits from performance
   d. The person who has a forbearance of performance

6. Rhys is buying real property from Talia. Talia's listing states that Talia's kitchen table is part of the listing and Rhys would like to purchase the table in conjunction with the purchase of real property. Which of the following legal documents must be completed for the addition?
   a. Deed
   b. Bill of sale
   c. Mortgage
   d. No additional document is needed

7. A building that is valued at $120,000 is being depreciated over 27.5 years. After 8 years, how much will the building have depreciated?
    a. $31,487.21
    b. $33,638.73
    c. $34,909.12
    d. $32,000.00

8. How many days of non-payment by the mortgagor must the mortgagee allow before initiating the foreclosure process?
    a. 60
    b. 90
    c. 120
    d. 180

9. The essential elements of a listing agreement are a written, express agreement, a negotiable commission, a specified price and terms, and one other element. What is that element?
    a. A record of repairs and improvements made to the property in the last ten years
    b. A list of suggested potential buyers
    c. A specific termination date
    d. A retainer fee, as stipulated by the brokerage

10. What is the name of the judicial proceeding that compiles a deceased person's assets and liabilities?
    a. Probate
    b. Quiet title
    c. Will
    d. Boundary dispute

11. Who is generally permitted sell a company's goodwill?
    a. A salesperson
    b. A broker
    c. A lender
    d. An abstractor

12. Greg is selling their home to Hilda. Hilda does not like that there is a pool in the backyard and is thinking of removing it. Greg does not want this to happen because ducks from the nearby pond sometimes swim in the pool. What could Greg do to preclude Hilda from removing the pool?
    a. Put a restriction in the deed
    b. Record a lien on the property
    c. Record an easement on the property
    d. Record an installment contract on the land

13. In a finance transaction, who does not determine the conditions of closing?
    a. The buyer
    b. The investor
    c. A prior seller
    d. Buyer's title attorney

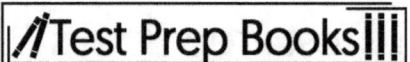

14. Which of the following would be a valid reason for the seller to terminate a listing?
    a. The subagent's license was revoked
    b. The seller got married
    c. The BIC's license was revoked
    d. The basement of the house flooded

15. If the sales price for a property is $100,000 and the monthly gross rental income for this property is $1250, what is the gross rent multiplier (GRM)?
    a. 80
    b. 0.8
    c. 9
    d. 90

16. What do you call a person who does not represent anyone in a transaction but simply provides ministerial services to facilitate the deal?
    a. Principal
    b. Transaction broker
    c. Third-party broker
    d. Power of attorney

17. A group of investors seeks to establish a hospital in a newly expanded commercial area of the city. Which of the following must be obtained for a property to be available for its intended use?
    a. A variance
    b. A special use permit
    c. A nonconforming use
    d. A city easement

18. What must a licensee who does not have a broker-in-charge license do?
    a. Use an assistant for all transactions
    b. Get a broker-in-charge license within three years of initial licensure
    c. Hang their license under a broker-in-charge before conducting real estate business
    d. Get the broker-in-charge's permission before listing a property

19. Lilly owns stock in a corporation and leases her residential unit from this corporation. What kind of property does Lilly live in?
    a. A condominium
    b. A cooperative
    c. A timeshare
    d. An industrial property

20. Recently, Gabriela rented a property to Hailey. Hailey required installation of a structural modification to accommodate a disability, and Gabriela allowed the installation for Hailey's accommodation. Who has the direct obligation of covering the installation cost?
    a. Gabriela
    b. Hailey
    c. The State
    d. Department of Housing and Urban Development

21. In the contractual relationship between a property owner and a property manager, which type of agent does the property manager agree to be?
   a. Special agent
   b. Universal agent
   c. Undisclosed agent
   d. General agent

22. In an agreement, a buyer pledges a property as collateral without giving up ownership or possession, but the agreement also says that the buyer allows the lender to sell the property if the buyer defaults on the loan. What is this agreement called?
   a. Subordination
   b. Hypothecation
   c. Assignment
   d. Assumption

23. A rental property company attempts to place a certain class of persons in a certain part of the renting community because they believe that type of renter will be more comfortable there. What is the renting company doing?
   a. Blockbusting
   b. Steering
   c. Puffing
   d. Zoning

24. What does amortization refer to?
   a. The act of paying off a loan in full
   b. The act of paying only the interest on a loan
   c. The act of reducing the balance on a loan by paying installments over a set period of time
   d. The act of incorporating one loan into the balance of a second loan

25. In the income approach, what does the appraiser use?
   a. Reproduction cost
   b. Depreciation schedules
   c. Capitalization rate
   d. Replacement cost

26. What is the purpose of a home warranty?
   a. To allow coverage protection to help reduce the stress and cost of broken systems of a home during escrow
   b. To allow coverage in the event that the transaction fails
   c. To allow coverage in the event of unexpected events
   d. To allow coverage in the event recording documents are not executed properly

27. What is the more common term for a partially amortized loan?
   a. Straight term mortgage
   b. Adjustable rate mortgage
   c. Balloon mortgage
   d. Subprime mortgage

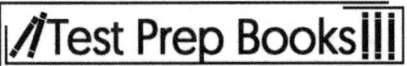

28. If a licensee is on inactive status, this means
    a. They must receive compensation for referrals.
    b. They must not conduct any real estate business.
    c. They may work as an assistant to show houses.
    d. They may conduct an open house for a listing agent.

29. What is required for a government to exercise its eminent domain power?
    a. Condemnation
    b. Abatement
    c. Remediation
    d. Inverse condemnation

30. Which of the following must be bargained for in a contract?
    a. Performance
    b. Consideration
    c. Acceptance
    d. Offer

31. Rebecca and Shelby are in a lease agreement, and recently the garbage disposal quit functioning (through no fault of Shelby). Shelby, the tenant, contacted Rebecca and requested that Rebecca service the garbage disposal so that Shelby may be able to use it. However, Rebecca refused because he does not want to service the garbage disposal. Which of the following phrases describes what occurred?
    a. Physical eviction
    b. Constructive eviction
    c. Breach of quiet enjoyment
    d. No eviction or breach

32. Recently, a buyer purchased a new office construction from a reputable builder. The sales contract did not contain any additional warranties, and the buyer did not inspect the property. Subsequently, a defect was discovered. May the buyer pursue a new construction claim against the builder?
    a. Yes
    b. No
    c. The answer depends on the jurisdiction
    d. The answer depends on the statute of limitations

33. "From Claire to Diego for the life of Erin and remainder to Frank". Who are the owners?
    a. Claire and Diego
    b. Diego and Frank
    c. Diego, Erin, and Frank
    d. Claire, Diego, and Frank

34. Ideally, where should a licensee look for comps when conducting a comparative market analysis?
    a. The same street
    b. The same school district
    c. The same state
    d. The national average

35. What is shown on a title commitment?
    a. History of the property
    b. Clouds of title
    c. Terms of financing
    d. Loan agreement

36. Hope allowed Ivy to come onto Hope's land for the day so that Ivy may mow Hope's grass. What did Hope give Ivy?
    a. An easement
    b. An encroachment
    c. A lis pendens
    d. A license

37. What is the financial gain realized from the sale of a capital asset?
    a. Income
    b. Capital gain
    c. Expense
    d. Deduction

38. Which of the following is an odorless toxic substance and a byproduct of combustion?
    a. Radon
    b. Carbon monoxide
    c. Mold
    d. Asbestos

39. How does buyer agent Brian receive payment for a closed transaction?
    a. Directly from their buyer client
    b. Directly from the seller
    c. From the attorney at closing
    d. From their brokerage after closing

40. Recently Mary rented a property to Noel. However, Noel required accommodations for a disability. Assuming the accommodation is reasonable, which of the following may Noel request?
    a. A common area modification
    b. A policy modification
    c. A reserved parking spaced closer to the building
    d. All of the above

41. A lot has a frontage of 40' and an area of 2,800 sq ft. What is the depth of the lot?
    a. 2,760 ft
    b. 95 ft
    c. 70 ft
    d. 1,500 ft

42. Mickey owns land right next to a stream of water that passes across Mickey's vast land. However, Mickey does not use the water and just lets the water flow its natural course. Naomi is a cattle farmer that lives five miles away from the stream but travels to the stream to collect water so that Naomi may water her cattle. Under a riparian doctrine jurisdiction, who has rights in the water?
    a. Mickey only
    b. Naomi only
    c. Both Mickey and Naomi
    d. Neither Mickey nor Naomi

43. Alejandro recently constructed a new commercial property in a new and upcoming entertainment district. Alejandro intends to open a restaurant so that they finally achieve their dream of becoming a chef. Which of the following must Alejandro obtain before the restaurant can be opened?
    a. Special use permit
    b. Certificate of compliancy
    c. Certificate of occupancy
    d. Commercial business easement

44. What shows the potential value of property based on similar properties being sold in the area?
    a. Abstract
    b. Comparative market analysis
    c. Lender points
    d. Clouds on title

45. To what standard must a new construction conform for purposes of a new construction warranty?
    a. A workmanlike manner
    b. A professional manner
    c. A building expert's manner
    d. An excellent manner

46. Which of the following would show a property owner where the property's boundaries are located?
    a. A legal description
    b. An address
    c. An easement
    d. A section

47. Umberto missed a payment to the lender and is afraid that the lender will now foreclose on Umberto's home. Umberto had promised the lender that timely payments would be made every month. The note defines default as three missed payments. The jurisdiction states that, unless otherwise agreed, foreclosure proceedings occur after five missed payments. May the lender foreclose on the home?
    a. Yes, because Umberto originally promised to make timely payments.
    b. Yes, because Umberto did not provide a reason why they had a late payment.
    c. No, because default is defined as three missed payments.
    d. No, because the jurisdiction allows five missed payments.

48. Which of the following represents an agent's fiduciary obligations to a client?
    a. Obedience, transportation, accounting, transcription, disclosure, loyalty
    b. Obedience, accounting, transcription, disclosure, loyalty, confidentiality
    c. Obedience, loyalty, accounting, reasonable care, confidentiality, disclosure
    d. Obedience, loyalty, accounting, transcription, disclosure, reasonable care

49. A leasing agent is renting out an apartment on behalf of their employer, the apartment company. While giving a tour to a lone potential renter, the leasing agent takes the potential renter's application, and subsequently the potential renter's application is denied. After the denial of the application, the potential renter says that they were discriminated against because they have children. Assuming there is no information on the application regarding the potential renter's familial status, was the potential renter discriminated against based on familial status?
    a. No
    b. Yes
    c. The answer depends on whether the potential renter has bad credit
    d. The answer depends on whether the potential renter has an eviction on public record

50. What is the main distinction between adverse possession and prescriptive easement?
    a. Duration
    b. Exclusion
    c. Openness
    d. Continuous conduct

51. Preston and Quinn own property together without the right of survivorship. What type of ownership do Preston and Quinn share?
    a. Tenancy by entirety
    b. Tenants in common
    c. Landlord and tenant
    d. Joint tenancy

52. The neighborhood that buyer Barry wants to move to has an HOA. This is an example of which principle of value?
    a. Contribution
    b. Conformity
    c. Competition
    d. Change

53. Under fair lending laws, who may the lender NOT discriminate against?
    a. A doctor
    b. A foreign resident
    c. An indigent
    d. A lawyer

54. Buyer Brad is buying seller Sara's property, but Sara would like to remain on the property for a year after the purchase. What is this arrangement called?
    a. Contract for deed
    b. Wrap-around mortgage
    c. Right of redemption
    d. Sale and lease back

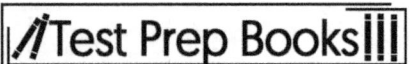

55. A seller has prepaid HOA fees for a 6-month duration. The prepayment amount was $1,200. At the end of the 4th month, the property was sold to a buyer. What is the prorated amount that will be debited to the buyer?
    a. $200
    b. $400
    c. $300
    d. $100

56. Under the Fair Housing Amendment Act, members of which classes of persons were given protection?
    a. National origin and sex
    b. Handicap or disability and familial status
    c. Familial status and sex
    d. Nation origin and handicap or disability

57. What is a benefit of using an FHA loan rather than a conventional loan?
    a. There is no down payment required
    b. There is no mortgage insurance required
    c. There is no minimum credit score requirement
    d. The required down payment is smaller

58. What is one element that an appraiser considers when using the income approach to value?
    a. Rationalization
    b. Stabilization
    c. Capitalization
    d. Multiplication

59. Michael is the broker-in-charge of Company A, and Marilyn is a licensee who works for Company A. Jerry is a licensee who works for Company B. Marilyn is representing a seller on behalf of Company A, and Jerry has just brought a buyer for this seller's house. What is Jerry's role in this transaction, relative to Michael's role?
    a. Subagent
    b. Agent
    c. Principal
    d. Third party

60. There is an earned a commission amount of $9,000 on a $180,000 property sold. What is the commission rate?
    a. 3%
    b. 10%
    c. 5%
    d. 6%

61. Iago and Jose have contracted for the sale of Jose's land to Iago. The written contract states that Jose promises to sell the land to Iago and Iago promises to buy the land from Jose. Which type of contract have Iago and Jose entered?
   a. Unilateral
   b. Bilateral
   c. Service contract
   d. Implied contract

62. Cassidy and Damian are in a lease agreement; Cassidy is the tenant and Damian is the landlord. Cassidy pays a flat fee for a leased premises, but Damian covers the utilities and property taxes. What type of lease is this?
   a. Gross lease
   b. Net lease
   c. Percentage lease
   d. Index lease

63. From a financial evaluation, what is goodwill considered to a business?
   a. An identity
   b. An asset
   c. A fund
   d. A legal document

64. What is the process of excluding a tenant from a leased premises so that a landlord may regain possession of the premises?
   a. Condemnation
   b. Abatement
   c. Eviction
   d. Escheat

65. What would a home warranty cover?
   a. Heating and cooling system
   b. Title defects
   c. Lending defects
   d. Unexpected events

66. Victor has made a contract to purchase a property from Wendy, with closing to occur in six weeks. However, Victor recently became unemployed and does not think they can take on the financial obligation. What may Victor seek?
   a. Voider
   b. Cancellation
   c. Rescission
   d. Modification

67. A broker currently has a property listed for sale. Five years ago, a murder occurred at this property. Is the broker required to disclose the murder?
   a. Yes
   b. No
   c. The answer depends on the jurisdiction
   d. The answer depends on whether the seller was involved

68. Which type of depreciation describes the normal wear-and-tear that a property incurs?
   a. External obsolescence
   b. Physical deterioration
   c. Functional obsolescence
   d. Objective deterioration

69. Xavier purchased Yvette's home, and subsequently Xavier discovered that there were material defects that were not disclosed and fixing them would be very costly. What source of law would be most relevant to when Xavier may pursue litigation against Yvette?
   a. The mortgage
   b. Statute of limitations
   c. The deed
   d. The note terms

70. A seller is selling Tara's property and informs the broker over the phone that Tara does not want to hear any offers below $100,000. A few days letter, a prospective broker submits a $95,000 offer to the seller's broker. Is the broker required to present the offer to the seller?
   a. Yes
   b. No
   c. The answer depends on whether the buyer knew that the seller wanted at least $100,000 for the property
   d. The answer depends on whether $95,000 was a reasonable offer

71. Which of the following would be a monetary amount that would not need to be prorated?
   a. Rent
   b. Pre-paid landscaping services
   c. Security deposit
   d. Taxes to be paid in arrears

72. A property sold for $200,000. There is a 50/50 split of a 6% commission between the listing and selling agent. What is the amount each agent will receive?
   a. $6,300
   b. $7,200
   c. $5,700
   d. $6,000

73. A prospective buyer was touring a seller's house, and the prospective buyer asked the broker whether the seller would accept an offer of $100,000. The broker knew the seller wanted a reasonable price for property, and a recent comparative market analysis had showed that the property was worth $130,000. The broker responded, "The seller is not accepting offers less than $120,000." Did the broker violate a duty?
   a. Yes, they broke a duty owed to the seller.
   b. Yes, they broke a duty owed to the prospective buyer.
   c. No, because the broker did not think it was a reasonable offer.
   d. No, because the broker knew the seller would not like the offer.

74. If an assessor has determined that a property has an actual value of $370,000, it is subject to an assessment rate of 28%, and the tax rate is 93 mills, what is the annual tax?
   a. $10,342.80
   b. $10,328.79
   c. $8,328.79
   d. $9,634.80

75. What is market price?
   a. The most probable price that a property would sell for in an open and competitive market
   b. The unbiased, estimated value of a property
   c. The cost of creating an exact replica of a property
   d. What a willing and able buyer will pay for a property and what a seller will accept

76. Connie and Doug have entered a contract for the purchase of Doug's property. Connie is nervous about buying a home for the first time. Connie wants to make sure that Doug has actual interest in the property that is being sold. What would Connie most want to examine?
   a. Doug's criminal history
   b. Court records
   c. The property's title
   d. The property's deed

77. Grace and Hunter are in a lease agreement, Grace is the tenant and Hunter is the landlord. Grace pays a fee for a leased premises that fluctuates based on the amount of revenue earned monthly. What type of lease is this?
   a. Gross lease
   b. Net lease
   c. Percentage lease
   d. Index lease

78. Which approach to value is used most by residential real estate agents?
   a. Sales comparison approach
   b. Cost approach
   c. Income approach
   d. Comparable investment approach

79. Which of the following is prohibited under the Sherman Antitrust Act?
   a. Blockbusting
   b. Redlining
   c. Market allocation
   d. Steering

80. What does a lease give a tenant?
   a. Ownership
   b. Present possession
   c. Future interest
   d. Police power

Answer Explanations #3

1. D: Choice D is correct because contract for deed is a type of seller financing in which the seller allows the buyer to move onto the property and make installment payments directly to the seller. Choice A is incorrect because in an assumable mortgage, the buyer takes the seller's place on a mortgage; additionally, the buyer needs to bring the balance in cash or get another loan to cover the balance of the sales price. Choice B is incorrect because in a junior mortgage, the seller agrees to carry a mortgage on the balance of the purchase price that the borrower can't get a loan for. Choice C is incorrect because a purchase money mortgage is an agreement for the seller to become the mortgage company, but only for a very short loan term.

2. C: Choice C is correct because police power regulates the property within its jurisdiction. Choices A, B, and C may be examples of exercising authority over property, but none are the broad, overarching reason for police power in relation to real property.

3. A: Choice A is correct because it is the definition of steering. Choice B is incorrect because it is the definition of blockbusting. Choice C is incorrect because it is the definition of zoning. Choice D is incorrect because it is the definition of misrepresentation.

4. B: Choice B is correct because the refusal of Owen to fix the bathroom interferes with Paige's right to use and enjoy the leased premises (including the bathroom) as Paige desires. Choice A is incorrect because discrimination is treating another differently based on a classification. Choice C is incorrect because Owen did not physically exclude Paige from the premises. Choice D is incorrect because zoning is an exercise of the government's police power.

5. A: Choice A is correct because an obligor is the person with the obligation to perform. Choice B is incorrect because the obligee has the obligation to receive performance. Choice C is incorrect because this could describe the obligee. Choice D is incorrect because it is a contradictory statement regarding a non-performance of a performance.

6. D: Choice D is correct because the personal property is part of the listing and therefore is covered by the purchase agreement. Choice A is incorrect because a deed transfers title. Choice B is incorrect because a bill of sale is not required because the kitchen table is part of the listing. Choice C is incorrect because a mortgage is an interest in land, not a legal document.

7. C: Choice C is correct because $120,000 \div 27.5 = \$4,363.64$. Then, $\$4,363.64 \times 8 = \$34,909.12$. Therefore, choices A, B, and D are incorrect.

8. C: Choice C is correct because the foreclosure process officially begins after 120 days of non-payment. Choices A and B are incorrect because a property is considered to be in pre-foreclosure status if non-payment occurs for less than 120 days. Choice D is incorrect because the process does not have to wait 180 days.

9. C: Choice C is correct because a listing agreement requires a specific termination date. Choice A is incorrect because the listing agreement does not itself address repairs and improvements; the property disclosure is the appropriate place for a seller to disclose this type of information to potential buyers. Choice B is incorrect because the seller is hiring the listing agent to do the work of finding buyers for the property. If the seller had a list of potential buyers, they might not need the listing agent. Choice D is incorrect because listing agreements do not require a retainer fee to be paid. The agreement does, however, address the method of payment for the listing agent, and this might include a retainer fee in some cases.

10. A: Choice A is correct because probate is the judicial process of compiling a deceased person's assets and liabilities. Choice B is incorrect because quiet title is a judicial process to determine ownership of a property. Choice C is incorrect because a will is not a judicial proceeding. Choice D is incorrect because a boundary dispute is a proceeding to determine who owns a portion of land.

11. B: Choice B is correct because a broker license is generally required to sell goodwill on behalf of another. Choice A is incorrect because the salesperson does not meet the licensing requirements to sell a company's goodwill. Choice C is incorrect because a lender does not have the proper licensing. Choice D is incorrect because an abstractor researches title.

12. A: Choice A is correct because Greg may restrict the property against Hilda's potential use through a deed restriction. Choice B is incorrect because a lien would give Greg an interest in the property, not preclude Hilda from removing the pool. Choice C is incorrect because an easement is used to give land rights to another person, not to ducks. Choice D is incorrect because an installment contract is a type of sales contract that requires regular installment payments until the debt is satisfied; it has nothing to with restricting use of the land.

13. C: Choice C is correct because a prior seller has no interest in the property, and therefore would have no say. Choice A is incorrect because the buyer may add conditions during escrow. Choice B in incorrect because the investor may require additional requirements during escrow. Choice D is incorrect because the title attorney shows what conditions must be completed to discharge pre-existing obligations on the property.

14. C: Choice C is correct because if the BIC loses their license, they can no longer legally represent clients in real estate transactions or supervise licensees in the practice of real estate. Choice A is incorrect because the agency agreement is between the agent (BIC) and the principal. The subagent is working on behalf of the agent. If one subagent loses their license, another can be assigned to complete the transaction. Choice B is incorrect because marriage does not affect the contractual relationship between agent and principal. Choice D is incorrect because the flooding of a basement does not reflect complete destruction of the property and therefore does not invalidate the agreement.

15. A: Choice A is correct because GRM equals sales price divided monthly potential gross income.

$$\$100{,}000 \text{ (Sales price)} \div \$1{,}250 \text{ (Monthly income)} = \$80 \text{ (GRM)}$$

16. B: Choice B is correct because a transaction broker simply provides ministerial services and remains neutral during the course of a transaction. Choice A is incorrect because the principal is a client who has enlisted an agent to assist them (through the creation of an agency agreement). Choice C is incorrect because a third-party broker technically doesn't exist. A third party in a real estate transaction is anyone who is outside of the agency agreement between a principal and an agent on one side of a transaction. Choice D is incorrect because a power of attorney is a written document bestowing legal authority, not a person.

17. B: Choice B is correct because a special use permit is granted for certain businesses to operate, such as hospitals. Choice A is incorrect because a variance is granted when a use does not conform to a

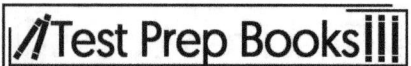

Answer Explanations #3

zoning, but here there is a conforming use because a hospital is a commercial entity in the commercial district. Choice C is incorrect because, as stated for Choice B, the use conforms to the zoning. Choice D is incorrect because an easement is used to establish a permitted use in the land by a non-owner (here, the city); it would not be useful for what the group is attempting to accomplish.

18. C: Choice C is correct because licensees must have a BIC license to work independently of a brokerage. Choice A is incorrect because having an assistant does not remove the need for an agent to hang their license under a broker-in-charge. Choice B is incorrect because no agent ever needs to get a BIC license unless starting a brokerage of their own or accepting that role in an existing brokerage. Choice D is incorrect because, even though the BIC signs all buyer and seller agency agreements, permission is not necessary. The BIC's signature indicates that the paperwork has been completed thoroughly and properly within the bounds of real estate law.

19. B: Choice B is correct because the unit is owned by the corporation and Lilly, a shareholder, leases the unit from the corporation. Choice A is incorrect because the corporation owns the unit, not Lilly. Choice C is incorrect because Lilly does not have an ownership interest in the unit itself. Choice D is incorrect because the unit is residential property and industrial property is a type of commercial property.

20. B: Choice B is correct because Hailey is a tenant seeking a structural modification and the tenant has the obligation of covering the installation costs. Choice A is incorrect because Gabriela is the landlord, and the landlord does not have the obligation of covering installation costs of a structural modification for a requesting tenant. Choice C is incorrect because the state does not have the obligation of covering the installation costs of a structural modification for a private lease. Choice D is incorrect because the Department of Housing and Urban Development does not have the obligation of covering installation costs of a structural modification for a private lease.

21. D: Choice D is correct because a property manager is a general agent. Choice A is incorrect because the property manager is not necessarily the special agent (management company), but is authorized to work on behalf of the management company on behalf of the property owner. Choice B is incorrect because a property manager is not authorized to make large decisions on behalf of the property owner. Choice C is incorrect because there is no such thing as an undisclosed agent.

22. B: Choice B is correct because hypothecation is the act of pledging a property as collateral while retaining the right of ownership and possession. Choice A is incorrect because the subordination clause stipulates that the primary mortgage will always be satisfied first. Choice C is incorrect because assignment refers to the ability of the borrower to transfer in writing the loan obligation to a third party. Choice D is incorrect because assumption is the process of a buyer taking the seller's place on a mortgage.

23. B: Choice B is correct because this is an example of steering. Choice A is incorrect because blockbusting means influencing homeowners to sell property cheaply because they fear that people of another class may move into the neighborhood. Choice C is incorrect because puffing means giving an embellishing statement about a property. Choice D is incorrect because zoning is an exercise of police power over how land may be used.

24. C: Choice C is correct because amortization is the reduction of the balance of a loan over time. Choice A is incorrect because paying a loan in full is called satisfaction (also defeasance). Choice B is

Answer Explanations #3

incorrect because an interest-only loan is called a straight term loan. Choice D is incorrect because absorbing one loan into another is a wrap-around loan.

25. C: Choice C is correct because the capitalization rate is part of the formula for estimating value of income-producing properties. Choices A, B, and D are incorrect because they are all used in the cost approach to estimating value.

26. A: Choice A is correct because this is the purpose of a home warranty. Choice B is incorrect because this is not the purpose of a home warranty. Choice C is incorrect because this is the purpose of home insurance coverage. Choice D is incorrect because this is the purpose of title insurance.

27. C: Choice C is correct because a partially amortized loan is frequently called a balloon mortgage; in such a mortgage, a short-term series of periodic payments is followed by one large payment to satisfy the loan. Choice A is incorrect because a straight term loan is an interest-only loan. Choice B is incorrect because an adjustable rate mortgage uses an economic index to determine the interest rate, which is adjusted from time to time as the index rises and falls. Choice D is incorrect because a subprime mortgage is given when low credit scores make the borrower ineligible for lower-interest loan options.

28. B: Choice B is correct because no real estate business can be conducted on behalf of other people if the agent does not have an active license. Choices A, C, and D are incorrect for the same reason.

29. A: Choice A is correct because it is the process the state must go through to exercise its eminent domain power. Choice B is incorrect because abatement is the process for removing a contaminant, such as asbestos. Choice C is incorrect because remediation is the process of removing the underlying cause for a problem, as when a property owner minimizes dampness or improves ventilation to stop mold from growing. Choice D is incorrect because an inverse condemnation is instituted by a private person, not the government.

30. B: Choice B is correct because consideration is the "bargained-for exchange" that enforces a contract. Choice A is incorrect because performance may be a portion of consideration (or related to consideration), but performance alone is not sufficient to form a contract. Choices C and D are incorrect because offer and acceptance stages occur before there is a bargained-for exchange under contract formation. Bargaining and determining what the offer and acceptance should be are instances of negotiation.

31. D: Choice D is correct because Rebecca did not physically exclude Shelby from the premises, Rebecca did not breach the covenant of quiet enjoyment to Shelby, and a non-functioning garbage disposal does not rise to the level of substantial interference of a right to enjoy and use a leased premises to the same extent that a non-functioning bathroom would. Therefore, Choices A, B, and C are incorrect.

32. B: Choice B is correct because new construction warranties are implied in residential properties, not in commercial properties such as an office building. Choice A is incorrect because an office building is not a residential property. Choice C is incorrect because, although jurisdictions may allow such a claim, it would need to be implemented by a statute, and here there is no mention of such a statute. Choice D is incorrect because the statute of limitations period would not answer the question of whether the buyer has a right to a new construction warranty claim against a commercial property builder.

33. B: Choice B is correct because Diego was granted a life estate pur autre vie measured by Erin's life, and Frank is the future owner after Erin's death. Choice A is incorrect because Claire no longer holds an

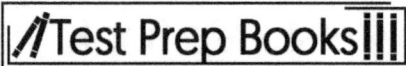

interest in the land after this conveyance. Choice *C* is incorrect because Erin was not granted an ownership interest; her life is the measuring life of Diego's ownership. Choice *D* is incorrect because Claire is not an owner.

34. B: Choice *B* is correct because it is the most approximate geographical location to the subject property being evaluated. Choices *A, C,* and *D* are incorrect because the comparable properties may not be within an immediate area of the subject property and may be subject to different influences of price due to location.

35. B: Choice *B* is correct because a title commitment shows clouds of title. Choice *A* is incorrect because a commitment will not show the history of the property. Choices *C* and *D* are incorrect because a commitment will not show the financing terms of the property purchase.

36. D: Choice *D* is correct because Ivy was granted permission to enter Hope's land for the use of Ivy mowing the land. Choice *A* is incorrect because this was a single grant of permission and not a conveyed right to use the land whenever Ivy desires. Choice *B* is incorrect because an encroachment is an unauthorized intrusion by a neighboring property. Choice *C* is incorrect because a lis pendens is legal notice that there is a pending lawsuit regarding a real property's title.

37. B: Choice *B* is correct because capital gain is gain realized from the sale of a capital asset. Choice *A* is incorrect because income is earned through a person, not through the sale of a capital asset. Choice *C* is incorrect because an expense is a debit of money for particular purpose. Choice *D* is incorrect because a deduction is a reduction in the value of a capital asset.

38. B: Choice *B* is correct because carbon monoxide is a toxic substance and is a byproduct of combustion. Choice *A* is incorrect because it is not a byproduct of combustion. Choice *C* is incorrect because mold occurs when there is a moisture accumulation. Choice *D* is incorrect because asbestos is a mineral found in building materials.

39. D: Choice *D* is correct because all real estate commissions are funneled through the brokerage. Choices *A* and *B* are incorrect because the agents should not receive commission directly from clients. Choice *C* is incorrect because attorneys should disburse commissions to the brokerage, not the individual agents.

40. D: Choice *D* is correct because a reasonable accommodation for a disability may take the form of a common area modification, a policy change, or a parking space closer to the building. Choices *A, B,* and *C* are incorrect because all choices are examples of permitted accommodations for a disability.

41. C: Choice *C* is correct because $\frac{2{,}800 \text{ sq ft}}{40 \text{ ft}} = 70$ ft. Choices *A, B,* and *D* are incorrect.

42. A: Choice *A* is the correct answer because, under a riparian jurisdiction, the land-owner whose land borders the watercourse (stream) has rights in the water. Choice *B* is incorrect because Naomi is trespassing and does not have rights in the stream under a riparian jurisdiction because their land is located five miles away from the stream. Choices *C* and *D* are incorrect because, as discussed above, Mickey has rights in the watercourse and Naomi does not.

43. C: Choice *C* is correct because a certificate of occupancy must be granted before people may occupy a property. Choice *A* is incorrect because a special use permit is granted by the government for particular businesses to operate, such as hospitals. Choice *B* is incorrect because the name of the

Answer Explanations #3

certificate being sought is a certificate of occupancy. Choice D is incorrect because an easement is not required for a business to operate here.

44. B: Choice B is correct because a comparative market analysis will show a property's potential value based on similar properties being sold. Choice A is incorrect because an abstract is a property's history in a document format. Choice C is incorrect because these regard payment amounts in a finance transaction. Choice D is incorrect because clouds on title are outstanding obligations on a property.

45. A: Choice A is correct because the new construction must be built in a "workmanlike manner"; this is the legal threshold of the requirement for a new construction warranty. Choices B, C, and D are incorrect because they are made-up standards.

46. A: Choice A is correct because a legal description will state the boundaries (and location) of a property. Choice B is incorrect because an address will not state a property's boundaries, but it will show where it is located. Choice C is incorrect because an easement is a right to use land. Choice D is incorrect because a section is a form of measurement and alone (under a government survey system) is not sufficient to describe a property's boundaries.

47. C: Choice C is correct because the parties defined default as three missed payments, and the lender cannot foreclose on a property until the borrower is in default. Choice A is incorrect because the parties agreed that default occurs after three missed payments. Choice B is incorrect because it is irrelevant to determining when default occurs under the lending terms. Choice D is incorrect because the statutes state that default is five missed payments unless the parties agree to a different term. Here, the parties agreed that three missed payments was default.

48. C: Choice C is correct because the fiduciary duties are represented by the acronym OLD CAR. Choices A, B, and D are incorrect because they include transportation and transcription, which are not fiduciary.

49. A: Choice A is correct because there was no information about familial status on the application given to the leasing agent. Therefore, by inference, the denial of the application was not based on familial status. Choice B is incorrect because the information regarding familial status was not made known to the leasing agent before the denial of the application. Choices C and D are incorrect because these are legitimate reasons why a rental application would be denied, however here this may have been one of the actual reasons why the potential renter was denied—not based on familial status.

50. B: Choice B is correct because adverse possession requires exclusive possession of the property, but prescriptive easement does not. Choice A is incorrect because both require some duration of statutory compliance before the interest may be granted to the non-owner. Choice C is incorrect because both require openness in use. Choice D is incorrect because both require continuous conduct.

51. B: Choice B is correct because it is concurrent ownership of unmarried persons, and Preston and Quinn do not have the right of survivorship. Choice A is incorrect because the facts do not state that Preston and Quinn are married. Choice C is incorrect because this is not a form of concurrent ownership. Choice D is incorrect because this type of concurrent ownership has the right of survivorship.

52. B: Choice B is correct because conformity refers to the strengthened value of a property when similarity exists and is enforced, as in the established HOA rules and restrictions. Choice A is incorrect because contribution refers to the cost one part of a property will have upon the value of the whole. Marble floors or an in-ground pool do not necessarily add dollar-for-dollar value to the property. Choice

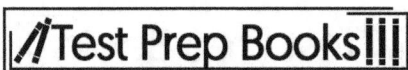

C is incorrect because competition refers to the effect on value of the saturation of the market for the property being sold. Too many available and it is a buyer's market; too few, and it's a seller's market. Choice D is incorrect because change refers to the natural evolution of a neighborhood through growth, stability, decline, and revitalization.

53. B: Choice B is correct because a person of national origin may not be the basis for a fair lending discrimination. Choice A and D are incorrect because a person may be discriminated against based on occupation. Choice C is incorrect because a person may be discriminated against based on wealth.

54. D: Choice D is correct because in a sale and lease back arrangement, the seller leases it back from the buyer immediately after the purchase. Choice A is incorrect because contract for deed is a type of seller financing in which the seller allows the buyer to move onto the property and make installment payments directly to the seller. Choice B is incorrect because in a wrap-around mortgage, a second mortgage is incorporated into an existing one. Choice C is incorrect because the right of redemption allows a borrower to rescue a property from foreclosure by paying to the lender the balance in full, plus interest and expenses.

55. B: Choice B is correct because $\$1{,}200 \div 6$ months $= \$200$, then $200 \times 2 = \$400.00$ proration. Choices A, C, and D are incorrect.

56. B: Choice B is correct because the Fair Housing Amendment Act (FHAA) added both handicap or disability and familial status as protected classes under fair housing laws. Choice A is incorrect because national origin and sex were not added as protected classes under FHAA. Choice C is incorrect because familial status was added under FHAA, but sex was not. Choice D is incorrect because national origin was not added as a protected class under FHAA, but handicap or disability was.

57. D: Choice D is correct because conventional loans are not government-backed, and they typically require a larger down payment. Choices A, B, and C are incorrect because both FHA and conventional loans have specific requirements for down payments, mortgage insurance, and minimum credit scores.

58. C: Choice C is correct because an appraiser using the income approach will factor in the capitalization rate as part of the calculation of the estimated value of an income-producing property. Choices A, B, and D are incorrect because they are not part of any method of estimating value.

59. D: Choice D is correct because a third party is anyone who is not a party to the agency agreement signed between agent and principal. Jerry presumably has an agency agreement of his own through Company B with his buyer. Choices A, B, and C are incorrect because they represent the roles played by the parties in the agency agreement through Company A.

60. C: Choice C is correct because $\$9{,}000 \div \$180{,}000 = 0.05$, then covert 0.05 to 5% by moving decimal over two spaces. Choices A, B, and D are incorrect.

61. B: Choice B is correct because Jose has promised to sell their land to Iago in exchange for Iago's promise to buy Jose's land, creating a bilateral contract. Choice A is incorrect because both Iago and Jose have exchanged promises in exchange for performance. Choice C is incorrect because Iago and Jose entered a contract for the sale of lands, not a service. Choice D is incorrect because the fact pattern states that the parties entered a written contract (necessary because it was of sale of land), and therefore it was not implied.

Answer Explanations #3

62. A: Choice *A* is correct because in a gross lease, a tenant pays for the occupancy of a leased premises, but the landlord pays for utilities, property taxes, and special assessments. Choice *B* is incorrect because a tenant pays for utilities and property taxes in a net lease. Choice *C* is incorrect because a tenant pays a fee that fluctuates based on the amount of monthly revenue earned. Choice *D* is incorrect because the tenant pays a fee that fluctuates based on an index.

63. B: Choice *B* is correct; goodwill is an asset of an entity. Choice *A* is incorrect because goodwill is not an alternative name or identity of the company. Choice *C* is incorrect because goodwill is not a fund. Choice *D* is incorrect because goodwill is an asset, not a legal document.

64. C: Choice *C* is correct because this is the definition of eviction. Choice *A* is incorrect because condemnation is the procedure that the state must go through to exercise its eminent domain power and take property. Choice *B* is incorrect because abatement is the removal process of asbestos from a building. Choice *D* is incorrect because escheat is the process by which the state acquires a decedent's real property.

65. A: Choice *A* is correct because a home warranty would cover a heating and cooling system. Choice *B* is incorrect because title insurance would cover title defects. Choice *C* is incorrect because a home warranty would not cover lending defects. Choice *D* is incorrect because an unexpected event would be covered under home insurance, not a home warranty.

66. C: Choice *C* is correct because this would allow Victor and Wendy to rescind the contract and put Victor and Wendy in a position that Victor and Wendy were in before entering a contract. Choices *A* and *B* are incorrect because these terms are not legal options; they have no legal definition in this context. Choice *D* is incorrect because modification implies that the contract will proceed to closing, but here it is clear that Victor does not want to proceed to closing.

67. C: Choice *C* is correct because jurisdictions vary on whether a murder must be disclosed and there is no uniform duty or no duty to this matter. Choices *A* and *B* are incorrect because jurisdictions are not uniform on whether a murder must be disclosed. Choice *D* is incorrect because, although this may be true in jurisdictions that allow non-disclosure, it does not address jurisdictions that require disclosure (regardless of who was involved).

68. B: Choice *B* is correct because normal wear and tear is physical deterioration. Choices *A* is incorrect because external obsolescence refers to outside influences that affect the desirability of the property. Choice *C* is incorrect because functional obsolescence refers to outdated design elements, like having only one bathroom in a large house or a wood-burning stove for heat. Choice *D* is incorrect because neither is a term used in real estate appraisal.

69. B: Choice *B* is correct because the statute of limitations determines how long a party has to bring a lawsuit against another. Choice *A* is incorrect because a mortgage is an interest in land, not a source of law. Choice *C* is incorrect because a deed conveys land ownership interest; it is not a source of law. Choice *D* is incorrect because the note or promissory note determines the lending agreement between the buyer and lender.

70. A: Choice *A* is correct because a broker is required to present all offers unless a seller notifies the broker *in writing* otherwise. Choice *B* is incorrect because it would have been correct if Tara had provided the broker with a writing stating their preference, but Tara told the broker orally over the

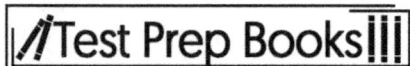

phone. Choices C and D are incorrect because the choices are irrelevant in determining whether the broker has a duty to present an offer to a seller.

71. C: Choice C is correct because a security deposit is not prorated. Choices A, B, and D are incorrect because a property and services would be used by different owners at different times.

72. D: Choice D is correct because $200,000 \times 0.06 = \$12,000$, then $\$12,000 \times 0.5 = 6,000$. Choices A, B, and C are incorrect.

73. B: Choice B is correct because the broker owes a duty of honesty to everyone, and nothing in the facts states that the seller told the broker that the seller was not accepting offers less than $120,000. Choice A is incorrect because the duty violated was specifically directed to the prospective buyer, not the seller. Choices C and B are incorrect because the broker did violate a duty of honesty owed to the prospective buyer.

74. D: Choice D is correct because $370,000 \times 0.28 = \$103,600$ assessed value, then $\$103,600 \times 0.093 = \$9,634.80$ annual tax rate. Choices A, B, and C are incorrect.

75. D: Choice D is correct because market price is what a willing and able buyer will pay and what a seller will accept. Choice A is incorrect because it describes market value, not price. Choice B is incorrect because an appraisal is the estimated value of a property. Choice C is incorrect because the cost of a replica is simply part of the calculation for estimated value using the cost approach.

76. C: Choice C is correct because title determines who holds legal or equitable interest in a property. Choice A is incorrect because Doug's criminal history will not show whether Doug owns the property. Choice B is incorrect because examining the title may require looking at court records to determine title (and claims to the property), but court records are not the only thing evaluated in a title examination. Choice D is incorrect because examining the title may require reviewing a deed, but it is not the only matter that is evaluated in a title examination.

77. C: Choice C is correct because a tenant pays a fee that fluctuates based on the amount of monthly revenue earned. Choice A is incorrect because a tenant pays a flat fee for a leased premises in a gross lease. Choice B is incorrect because a tenant pays a flat fee in addition to utilities and property taxes in a net lease. Choice D is incorrect because the tenant pays a fee that fluctuates based on an index.

78. A: Choice A is correct because the sales comparison approach is used for existing residential homes, comparing recent sales data for similar neighboring properties. Choice B is incorrect because the cost approach is used primarily by appraisers for properties with no comps available. Choice C is incorrect because the income approach would be used for income-producing properties. Choice D is incorrect because there is no such approach to value.

79. C: Choice C is correct because dividing customers using certain geographic or other metrics is specifically prohibited under the Sherman Antitrust Act. Choices A, B, and D are incorrect because they are all prohibited under the Fair Housing Act, not the Sherman Antitrust Act.

80. B: Choice B is correct because a lease conveys present possession of a leased premises to a tenant. Choice A is incorrect because the landlord retains ownership of the leased premises, while the tenant receives present possession of it. Choice C is incorrect because a lease does not convey a future interest. Choice D is incorrect because police power is the state's authority to regulate.

Index

Abstract, 69, 121, 132, 138, 150, 153, 164, 174
Acceleration Clause, 38, 42, 43
Accounting, 40, 44, 45, 165
Acre, 16, 146, 156
Actual Eviction, 63
Adjustable-Rate Mortgage (ARM), 34
Adverse Possession, 72, 122, 123, 133, 141, 152, 165, 175
Agency, 21, 22, 44, 45, 46, 47, 48, 49, 50, 51, 76, 81, 82, 83, 118, 120, 121, 129, 132, 133, 134, 148, 152, 155, 157, 171, 172, 176
Agency Relationship, 44, 45, 46, 47, 48, 50, 51
Agent, 22, 29, 32, 34, 44, 45, 46, 47, 48, 49, 51, 52, 58, 69, 70, 71, 80, 81, 82, 83, 84, 85, 93, 94, 119, 120, 122, 124, 125, 126, 128, 131, 132, 133, 134, 135, 137, 142, 143, 145, 147, 148, 149, 152, 154, 155, 161, 162, 163, 165, 166, 168, 170, 171, 172, 173, 175, 176
Air Rights, 10, 18, 126
Alienation, 39, 137, 149
Anticipation of Value, 28
Appurtenances, 10, 18, 19
Appurtenant Easement, 14, 141, 152
Assignment, 38, 62, 137, 149, 161, 172
Assumable Mortgage, 37, 148, 157, 158, 170
Attached Artificial Property, 10
Attached Natural Property, 10
Attorney-In-Fact, 45
Bankruptcy, 49, 145
Base Flood, 22
Bequest, 72, 122, 132
Bilateral Contract, 61, 64, 127, 140, 144, 151, 176
Bill of Sale, 11, 19, 72, 136, 170
Breach of Contract, 39, 62
Broker, 29, 42, 44, 45, 46, 49, 50, 51, 52, 53, 58, 59, 70, 77, 80, 81, 82, 83, 85, 99, 116, 119, 120, 123, 128, 130, 133, 141, 142, 143, 145, 146, 152, 153, 154, 156, 159, 160, 166, 167, 168, 171, 172, 177, 178
Broker Price Opinion (BPO), 29, 146
Brokerage Fee, 82, 130
Broker-In-Charge (BIC), 45, 81
Building Codes, 20, 21, 118, 125, 126, 129, 139

Buyer Qualification Ratios, 91
Buyer Representation Agreement, 44, 48, 50
Capital Gain, 71, 163, 174
Capitalization, 30, 95, 146, 155, 161, 166, 173, 176
Capitalization Approach, 30, 146, 155
Capitalization Rate Formula, 30
Change, 21, 27, 28, 41, 56, 62, 94, 128, 136, 147, 165, 174, 175
Chattel, 11, 137, 149
Closing, 29, 30, 36, 39, 40, 42, 43, 47, 52, 53, 54, 58, 63, 64, 69, 70, 71, 82, 92, 117, 119, 120, 125, 126, 128, 132, 135, 141, 143, 144, 148, 149, 150, 152, 153, 155, 157, 159, 163, 167, 177
Closing Costs, 30, 36, 40, 70, 117, 155
Closing Disclosure (CD), 40
Closing Statement, 70, 71, 132, 143, 153
Coastal Plains, 22
Commercial Banks, 36
Commission Splits, 93
Common Interest Ownership Properties, 15
Comparative Market Analysis (CMA), 29
Comparison With Subject, 29
Competition, 28, 40, 83, 119, 127, 155, 165, 175
Completion, 44, 45, 49, 82, 155, 157
Concurrent Ownership, 14, 123, 132, 133, 175
Condominiums, 15
Confidentiality, 44, 131, 165
Conformity, 28, 165, 175
Consideration, 60, 61, 64, 65, 80, 117, 129, 162, 173
Construction Loan, 35
Constructive Eviction, 63, 158, 162
Contingency Clause, 64, 119, 130
Contract for Deed, 37, 42, 43, 139, 148, 150, 157, 158, 165, 170, 176
Contract of Sale, 64
Contribution, 14, 28, 165, 175
Conventional Loan, 29, 34, 35, 36, 122, 130, 138, 150, 166, 176
Conventional Loans, 29, 35, 36, 176
Cooperating Agent, 46
Cooperatives, 15

Index

Cost Approach, 29, 30, 31, 32, 124, 126, 134, 135, 139, 146, 147, 151, 156, 169, 173, 178
Counteroffer, 60, 154
Credit Unions, 36, 37, 125, 134
Cumulative Ordinances, 21
Customer, 45, 50, 51, 131
Debt-to-Income, 64, 91
Decimals, 87
Declaration of Covenants, Conditions, and Restrictions, 23
Deed, 15, 23, 37, 39, 64, 69, 70, 71, 74, 75, 121, 122, 127, 131, 132, 136, 138, 139, 140, 149, 150, 151, 158, 159, 168, 169, 170, 171, 177, 178
Deed of Trust, 39, 149, 150
Default, 39, 62, 73, 130, 164, 175
Defeasance, 38, 39, 42, 43, 172
Defeasible Fees, 12, 13
Demand, 27, 28, 33, 38, 42, 43, 127, 136, 144, 154
Depreciation, 28, 31, 72, 94, 127, 146, 161, 168
Designated, 20, 45, 49, 62, 79, 81, 118, 127, 129, 136, 143, 152, 154
Destruction, 49, 171
Devise, 72, 122, 132
Disclosed Principal, 46
Disclosure, 22, 23, 40, 44, 45, 47, 52, 53, 58, 59, 81, 124, 155, 165, 170, 177
Doctrine of Ad Coelum, 10
Down Payment Assistance (DPA), 35
Dual, 45, 118, 121, 129, 132, 148, 152, 157
DUST, 27, 33, 56, 136
Easement, 13, 14, 72, 74, 75, 141, 142, 152, 153, 159, 160, 163, 164, 171, 172, 174, 175
Easement by Necessity, 14, 152
Easement In Gross, 14, 141, 152
Economic Forces, 27
Emblements, 11, 18, 19
Eminent Domain, 20, 25, 26, 121, 132, 147, 148, 156, 162, 173, 177
Encroachment, 13, 14, 153, 163, 174
Encumbrance, 13
Environmental Impact Report, 20, 21
Equal Credit Opportunity Act (ECOA), 40
Equity, 32, 34, 35, 73, 90, 118, 129, 130, 138, 150

Escheat, 20, 25, 26, 85, 86, 121, 132, 133, 167, 177
Escrow, 54, 58, 59, 62, 63, 64, 70, 71, 76, 91, 120, 125, 135, 138, 145, 155, 161, 171
Escrow Agent, 70, 145, 155
Estate In Severality, 14, 139
Estimate the Accrued Depreciation, 31
Estimate the Building's Reproduction or Replacement Cost, 31
Estimate the Value of the Land, 31
Eviction, 63, 73, 116, 117, 123, 128, 133, 139, 145, 150, 158, 162, 165, 167, 177
Exclusive Agency, 47, 48
Exclusive Buyer Agreement, 48
Exclusive Listing, 47, 123
Exclusive Right to Purchase, 48
Exclusive Right to Sell, 47
Expiration, 13, 44, 49, 54, 63, 92, 151
Express Agency, 44, 118, 129
Express Contracts, 44
Expressed Contracts, 60
External Obsolescence, 31, 32, 33, 146, 156, 168, 177
Fair Housing Amendments Act (FHAA), 78
Fee Simple Absolute, 12, 125, 141, 151
FHA-Insured Loan, 35
Fiduciary Relationship, 44, 142
Fixed Lease, 65, 126
Fixture, 10, 11, 18, 19, 137, 149
Floodplain, 22
Force Majeure, 49
Fraction, 87, 89, 92, 96
Freehold Estates, 12
Fully Amortized Loan, 34
Functional Obsolescence, 31, 33, 146, 156, 168, 177
General Agent, 46, 49, 120, 137, 149, 161, 172
Goodwill, 99, 123, 124, 133, 134, 141, 159, 167, 171, 177
Government Survey System, 16, 175
Grantee, 12, 13, 23, 60, 64, 67, 68, 69, 70, 74, 75, 121
Grantor, 12, 13, 23, 60, 64, 67, 68, 69, 70, 74, 75, 120, 131
Gross Lease, 65, 117, 126, 136, 141, 148, 157, 167, 169, 176, 178
Gross Rent Multiplier (GRM), 31, 95, 160

Index

Group Boycotting, 83
Highest and Best Use, 28, 127
Holdover Tenant, 13, 123
Home Warranty, 54, 116, 120, 128, 131, 138, 144, 150, 154, 161, 167, 173, 177
Housing Expense, 91
Implied Agency, 44, 118, 129
Implied Contracts, 60
Improvement, 10, 11, 14, 18, 19, 129, 138, 150
Improvements, 10, 11, 15, 16, 19, 23, 28, 31, 33, 134, 150, 159, 170
Income Approach, 29, 30, 32, 33, 95, 126, 134, 135, 146, 161, 166, 169, 176, 178
Index Lease, 65, 117, 126, 148, 167, 169
Installment Land Contract, 37
Insured Conventional Loans, 35
Intangible, 11, 18, 98, 137, 149
Intestate, 72, 122, 133
Involuntary Alienation, 72, 141
Joint Tenancy, 14, 118, 123, 139, 146, 156, 165
Joint Tenants, 14, 72, 150, 156
Junior (Subordinate) Mortgage, 37, 148
Latent Defects, 52, 59
Lease, 13, 15, 61, 63, 64, 65, 66, 67, 68, 79, 116, 117, 119, 122, 128, 130, 133, 139, 140, 141, 144, 148, 151, 152, 154, 158, 162, 165, 167, 169, 172, 178
Lease Purchase, 64, 67
Leasehold, 12, 13, 65, 122, 133, 154
Leasehold Estates, 12
Legal Description, 15, 16, 69, 74, 75, 164, 175
License, 13, 14, 80, 81, 83, 99, 134, 156, 160, 163, 171, 172, 173
Lien, 13, 14, 20, 38, 39, 42, 43, 90, 138, 142, 149, 150, 153, 159, 171
Life Estate, 12, 13, 125, 141, 151, 173
Life Estate Pur Autre Vie, 13, 173
Life Insurance Companies, 36
Listing, 11, 19, 44, 46, 47, 48, 49, 50, 52, 53, 76, 78, 81, 82, 93, 116, 122, 123, 124, 128, 133, 134, 136, 143, 148, 157, 158, 159, 160, 162, 168, 170
Listing Agreement, 44, 46, 47, 48, 49, 50, 82, 116, 124, 128, 157, 159, 170
Loan Estimate, 40, 145, 155
Loan Factor Charts, 90
Loan Interest, 90, 91
Loan Payment Chart, 90
Loan-to-Value (LTV) Ratio, 89
Location, 14, 15, 30, 33, 55, 56, 75, 100, 102, 144, 154, 174, 175
Loss of Authority, 49
Loss of Title, 38, 49, 133
Lot, 10, 17, 27, 29, 30, 46, 52, 88, 96, 117, 145, 163
Loyalty, 44, 45, 152, 165
Market Allocation, 84, 169
Market Price, 27, 169, 178
Market Value, 20, 27, 29, 31, 94, 148, 151, 178
Master Plan, 21
Material Defects, 52, 153, 168
Material Facts, 44, 52, 53, 55, 56
Merger, 14
Metes and Bounds, 16
Mill, 92
Mineral Rights, 10, 18
Monthly Installment, 91
Mortgage, 14, 34, 35, 36, 37, 38, 39, 40, 41, 42, 43, 63, 64, 69, 72, 73, 77, 78, 89, 90, 91, 118, 119, 121, 124, 125, 127, 130, 132, 134, 136, 139, 148, 149, 150, 157, 158, 161, 166, 168, 170, 172, 173, 176, 177
Mortgage Bankers, 36, 37, 134
Mortgage Brokers, 36, 37, 125, 134
Mortgage Servicing Disclosure, 40
Mortgagee, 38, 39, 42, 159
Mortgagor, 38, 39, 42, 159
Multi-Family Rental, 98
Mutual Agreement, 49, 60, 61, 62
National Consumer Protection Act, 40, 146, 155
Negative Amortization, 34
Net Lease, 65, 117, 126, 129, 136, 141, 148, 157, 167, 169, 176, 178
Net Listing, 47, 123, 133
NOI Formula, 30
Nonconforming Use, 21, 25, 147, 156, 160
Noncumulative Zoning Ordinance, 21
Novation, 62
Obedience, 44, 45, 165
Obligee, 61, 62, 64, 170
Obligor, 61, 62, 64, 158, 170
Office Space, 98, 100, 102
OLD CAR, 44, 175
Open Buyer Representation Agreement, 48

Open Listing, 47, 123
Option Contract, 64, 67, 68
Parcel, 10, 14, 15, 16, 27, 84, 88, 141, 151, 154
Partially Amortized Loan, 34, 161, 173
Partially Disclosed Principal, 46
Party, 13, 23, 38, 39, 42, 44, 45, 49, 52, 53, 60, 61, 62, 65, 66, 68, 69, 70, 71, 76, 83, 92, 93, 94, 119, 120, 121, 122, 127, 128, 130, 135, 145, 149, 154, 160, 166, 171, 172, 176, 177
Percentage, 15, 37, 43, 65, 76, 82, 87, 89, 91, 92, 93, 96, 97, 117, 126, 136, 141, 148, 167, 169
Percentage Lease, 65, 117, 126, 136, 141, 148, 167, 169
Performance, 49, 61, 62, 64, 67, 77, 90, 116, 117, 126, 128, 129, 135, 144, 147, 148, 151, 154, 156, 157, 158, 162, 170, 173, 176
Periodic Tenancy, 13, 139
Personal Property, 10, 11, 18, 19, 72, 100, 102, 132, 134, 136, 137, 149, 153, 170
Physical Characteristics, 15, 30
Physical Deterioration, 31, 146, 147, 168, 177
Physical Forces, 27
Plottage, 29
Police Power, 20, 26, 86, 158, 169, 170, 172, 178
Political Forces, 27, 128
Power of Attorney (POA), 45
Prepayment Penalty, 36, 38, 42, 43, 144, 154
Prescriptive Easement, 72, 141, 152, 165, 175
Price Fixing, 83, 135
Primary Mortgage Markets, 38
Principal, 30, 34, 36, 38, 39, 42, 44, 45, 46, 49, 50, 51, 72, 82, 90, 91, 121, 124, 132, 137, 142, 145, 149, 155, 160, 166, 171, 176
Private Money Lenders, 37
Procuring Cause, 82
Progression, 28
Promissory Note, 39, 62, 64, 74, 75, 144, 154, 177
Property, 10, 11, 12, 13, 14, 15, 16, 18, 19, 20, 21, 22, 23, 25, 26, 27, 28, 29, 30, 31, 32, 33, 34, 35, 37, 38, 39, 41, 42, 43, 44, 45, 46, 47, 48, 49, 50, 51, 52, 53, 54, 55, 56, 57, 58, 59, 60, 62, 63, 64, 65, 67, 68, 69, 70, 71, 72, 73, 75, 76, 77, 78, 79, 80, 81, 82, 84, 85, 88, 89, 90, 91, 92, 93, 94, 95, 98, 100, 102, 116, 117, 118, 119, 120, 121, 122, 123, 124, 125, 126, 127, 128, 129, 130, 131, 132, 133, 134, 135, 136, 137, 138, 139, 140, 141, 142, 143, 144, 145, 146, 147, 148, 149, 150, 151, 152, 153, 154, 156, 157, 158, 159, 160, 161, 162, 163, 164, 165, 166, 167, 168, 169, 170, 171, 172, 173, 174, 175, 176, 177, 178
Property Management Services, 49
Protection Clause, 82
Puffing, 80, 85, 119, 133, 143, 154, 161, 172
Purchase Agreement, 10, 11, 18, 19, 59, 63, 64, 70, 126, 133, 135, 136, 145, 155, 170
Purchase Money Mortgage, 37, 122, 132, 148, 157, 158, 170
Quitclaim Deed, 70, 74, 75
Real Estate Agent, 29, 34, 40, 44, 46, 54, 55, 56, 57, 80, 81, 83, 124, 131, 146, 147, 169
Real Estate Settlement Procedures Act (RESPA), 40, 146
Real Property, 10, 11, 12, 14, 18, 19, 67, 68, 69, 71, 72, 86, 100, 102, 127, 128, 132, 136, 149, 158, 170, 174, 177
Reasonable Accommodation, 78, 79, 135, 174
Reasonable Care, 44, 45, 165
Recent Sales Data, 29, 178
Recorded Plat, 16
Recording, 23, 63, 70, 71, 122, 132, 145, 155, 161
Rectangular Description, 16
Referral Fee, 48, 82
Regression, 28
Regulation Z, 40
Remainder, 12, 13, 74, 75, 82, 141, 156, 162
Renunciation, 49
Retail Property, 98
Retainer Fee, 82, 119, 130, 159, 170
Reverse Annuity Mortgage (RAM), 35
Reversion, 12, 13, 74, 75, 125, 135
Revocation, 49, 148, 157
Right of First Refusal, 65
Sale and Lease Back, 35, 176
Sale-Leaseback, 65, 141, 152
Sales Comparison Approach, 29, 117, 129, 134, 139, 146, 151, 155, 169, 178
Sales Concessions, 30
Satisfaction, 38, 39, 73, 90, 172
Savings and Loans Associations (S&Ls), 36

Index

Secondary Mortgage Market, 38
Section, 16, 30, 94, 164, 175
Seller Financing, 37, 43, 148, 150, 157, 158, 170, 176
Selling, 40, 46, 64, 76, 77, 82, 89, 93, 94, 95, 98, 99, 120, 122, 124, 127, 135, 138, 140, 141, 145, 146, 147, 152, 156, 159, 168
Selling Agent, 46, 82, 93, 94, 122, 135, 147, 168
Service Fee, 82, 140
Sherman Antitrust Act, 83, 135, 146, 155, 169, 178
Skill, 44, 45
Social Forces, 27
Sole Propriety, 14, 139, 150
Special Agent, 46, 120, 131, 161, 172
Special Use Permit, 21, 25, 26, 118, 130, 138, 147, 149, 156, 160, 164, 171, 174
Special Warranty Deed, 70
Statute of Frauds (SOF), 60
Statute of Limitations, 66, 143, 153, 162, 173, 177
Steering, 80, 117, 123, 128, 133, 146, 153, 155, 158, 161, 169, 170, 172
Straight Term Loan, 34, 172, 173
Subagent, 45, 46, 145, 149, 155, 160, 166, 171
Subprime Loan, 35
Substitution, 28
Supply, 27, 28, 33, 87, 127
Supply and Demand, 27, 28
Surface Rights, 10, 18
Survey, 14, 16, 32, 117, 127, 129, 136, 138, 150
Tangible, 11, 18, 60, 137, 149
Taxation, 20
Tenancy at Sufferance, 13, 139
Tenancy at Will, 13, 139, 151
Tenancy by Entirety, 14, 15, 123, 139, 150, 165
Tenancy for Years, 13, 139, 151
Testate, 72
Third, 12, 13, 38, 39, 45, 46, 70, 76, 83, 127, 145, 149, 155, 160, 166, 171, 172, 176
Tie-In, 84
Time of Sale, 29
Title Insurance, 14, 63, 69, 70, 150, 153, 173, 177
Townhomes, 15
Township, 16
Trade Fixtures, 11, 18, 19
Transaction, 11, 27, 40, 44, 45, 46, 47, 48, 49, 52, 54, 61, 63, 64, 65, 67, 69, 70, 71, 81, 82, 84, 93, 94, 95, 99, 116, 120, 121, 123, 125, 127, 128, 129, 131, 132, 133, 134, 135, 141, 143, 145, 146, 149, 152, 153, 154, 155, 157, 159, 160, 161, 163, 166, 171, 175
Transferability, 27, 28, 32, 33, 127
Truth In Lending, 40, 145, 146, 155
Undisclosed Principal, 46, 137
Unilateral Contract, 61, 140, 144, 151, 154, 158
Universal Agent, 46, 120, 131, 137, 149, 161
USDA Loan, 36
Utility, 15, 20, 27, 28, 29, 31, 32, 33, 52, 55, 92, 127, 133, 145, 155
VA-Guaranteed Loan, 36
Variance, 21, 25, 26, 147, 156, 160, 171
Verification of Data, 29
Visible Defects, 52, 59
Warranty Deed, 70, 74, 75, 121, 131
Wetlands, 22
Wrap-Around Mortgage, 165, 176
Zoning, 16, 20, 21, 25, 26, 28, 30, 56, 57, 85, 118, 129, 158, 161, 170, 171, 172

Dear PSI Real Estate Test Taker,

Thank you for purchasing this study guide for your PSI Real Estate exam. We hope that we exceeded your expectations.

Our goal in creating this study guide was to cover all of the topics that you will see on the test. We also strove to make our practice questions as similar as possible to what you will encounter on test day. With that being said, if you found something that you feel was not up to your standards, please send us an email and let us know.

We have study guides in a wide variety of fields. If you're interested in one, try searching for it on Amazon or send us an email.

Thanks Again and Happy Testing!
Product Development Team
support@testprepbooks.com

Online Resources & Audiobook

Included with your purchase are multiple online resources. This includes the practice tests in an interactive format and this book in audiobook format. There is also a convenient study timer to help you manage your time.

Scan the QR code or go to this link to access this content:

testprepbooks.com/online387/texas-real-estate

The first time you access the page, you will need to register as a "new user" and verify your email address.

If you have any issues, please email support@testprepbooks.com.

Thank you for letting us be a part of your studying journey!

www.ingramcontent.com/pod-product-compliance
Lightning Source LLC
Chambersburg PA
CBHW080410300426
44113CB00015B/2471